Effective Operations and Controls for the Small Privately Held Business

Effective
Operations
and Controls
for the Small
Privately Held
Business

Rob Reider,
PhD, MBA, CPA

BICENTENNIAL
1807
WILEY
2007
BICENTENNIAL

John Wiley & Sons, Inc.

Library of Congress Cataloging-in-Publication Data:

Reider, Rob, 1940–
   Effective operations and controls for the small privately held business / Rob Reider.
     p. cm.
   ISBN 978-0-470-22276-8 (cloth)
  1. Small business—Management. 2. Private companies—Management. I. Title.
  HD62.7.R45 2008
  658.02'2—dc22   2007026262

OTHER BOOKS BY ROB REIDER

WILEY PROFESSIONAL MANAGEMENT BOOKS

Benchmarking Strategies: A Tool For Profit Improvement

Improving the Economy, Efficiency, and Effectiveness of Not-For-Profits

Managing Cash Flow: An Operational Focus (with Peter B. Heyler)

Operational Review: Maximum Results at Efficient Costs

Operational Review: Workbook (Case studies, forms, and exercises)

FICTION

Road to Oblivion: The Footpath Back Home

A novel of discovery

Contents

Preface

Ownership of one's own small business—known as the *American Dream*—is an overwhelming, driving passion for millions of workers. Many workers feel the need to escape the nine (or earlier) to five (or later) syndrome, the nonidentity or lack of recognition in the workplace, and the stagnation and suffocation of organizational bureaucracy. While many feel these pangs, fewer act on them to take the risk of starting and building a small business.

Millions of small businesses change hands every year, and hundreds of thousands of new small businesses start up—each owner hoping that he or she has the answer to quick success. Businesses in operation in this country cover a wide spectrum—from the small, Mom-and-Pop corner store to the large national and multinational corporation. These businesses offer many products and services as well as opportunities for success to their owners. However, statistics claim over 80 percent small business casualties (i.e., small business folding up) within the first two years of operations—what makes you think you can beat those odds?

The most important thing to understand in starting and building a successful small business is how to start the business right and continue to operate it right—that is, doing the right thing, the right way, at the right time. This means knowing the right questions to ask (and some of the answers) about overall business operations, not just concerning the technical aspects but also about how to daily operate a successful small business. This encompasses things such as financing, planning, managing, purchasing, customer service, operations, cash management, sales and marketing, financial and accounting considerations, and organizing—not only for the present but for the future as well.

This *how-to* book will help you to know which questions to ask, how to avoid mistakes and pitfalls, and how to evaluate your own personal assets and skills objectively. The time spent preplanning for your small business in the area of the feasibility of operation for a potential venture, or in planning for growth of an existing business, will help ensure greater success and the avoidance of unnecessary mistakes.

The early bird may get the worm, but the second mouse gets the cheese.

The innovator may not always get the spoils; sometimes it is the follower.

Areas to be covered in this book include:

- How the small business operates and the barriers to implementing effective operating systems and procedures
- Implementing value-added operating procedures to help the small business become more economical, efficient, and effective in its operations
- Using operating best practices and techniques to decrease costs and increase revenues, resulting in maximizing real profits
- Transforming non–value-added functional costs (e.g., accounting, personnel, management) to real profit contribution through the use of effective small business management
- Strengthening operational performance throughout the business through a strategic focus perspective
- Identifying the operating procedures that are necessary to each and every function and activity

Half of all small businesses are below average.

This book focuses mainly on private, closely held, nonregulated small businesses, often family owned and operated, with the need for developing and implementing effective operating procedures just as critical (maybe more so) as with larger corporations. As a yardstick, the small business is defined as those privately held businesses with less than $100 million in revenues and less than 500 employees that do not require an audit. This includes over 80 percent of all businesses in this country.

The focus of this book is to assist those starting (or wishing to start) a business or desiring to improve an existing business by providing guidance for the business owners and managers as to operating efficiently and effectively within a control environment that provides for growth and profitability. This book provides basic good business sense for implementing operating procedures and controls where their cost is negligible compared to the value provided to the business. For the small business to operate most efficiently and profitably—moving toward growth and prosperity—proper guidance and direction needs to encompass every operating facet of the business.

The uniqueness of this book is in the emphasis on the small business, with its inherent operating constraints, and on the use of effective practices that enhance rather than hamper efficient operations. These are operating practices that small business owners will want to implement rather than ignore to their detriment. This book should be a "must have" for all small business owners and managers, as well as external business advisors, who desire to improve their business operations and profitability. It is intended to be a how-to book as well as a handy reference to effectively implementing best practice operating procedures and controls to assist the small business to operate economically, efficiently, and effectively in a controlled environment—encompassing every operating facet of the business.

In a Sarbanes-Oxley world that combats some of the practices that created financial and operational abuses in a number of major corporations, the small business, both public and private, due to its unregulated nature, may be even more susceptible to such financial and operational abuses. However, without effective accounting/financial and operating practices and controls, many of these abuses go undetected. And sometimes it is the small business owners (and their family members) who are the very culprits exercising such abuses. This book outlines the development of effective operational practices and control systems for the nonregulated small business that are cost effective and enhance operations and resultant profitability. With all the fuss about Sarbanes-Oxley and the large, publicly held entity, the small business and its need for effective operations and controls has been neglected.

Let us start by envisioning your business. What is it? Can you describe it? What makes it unique? Why would customers come to your business rather than others already in existence? Does it excite you, and create a *wow* factor for you and others? Take a moment to think about your business venture. Use the following seven-point checklist to help you in your thinking.

CHECKLIST FOR STARTING, DEVELOPING, MAINTAINING, AND IMPROVING YOUR SMALL BUSINESS

1. The Grand Idea
- [ ] What is your idea?
- [ ] Uniqueness—what makes it different?
- [ ] Business model—how does it work?
- [ ] WOW factor!—how does it sparkle?
- [ ] Why will it be successful?
- [ ] Are there other similar businesses?

2. Type of Organization
- [ ] Sole proprietorship (Schedule C)
- [ ] Partnership (Form 1065)
- [ ] Corporation: regular, S corporation, limited liability (Forms 1120, 1120S)
- [ ] On-site versus absentee ownership

3. Financing
- [ ] Your money
- [ ] Other people's money (OPM)
- [ ] Friends and relatives
- [ ] Investors
- [ ] Financial institutions
- [ ] Buffer cash and working capital
- [ ] Payback restrictions

4. **Planning**
- ☐ Businesses you're in
- ☐ Strategic thrusts
- ☐ Competitive advantages
- ☐ Products/services to offer
- ☐ Customer base
- ☐ Methods of sales
- ☐ Type of business: wholesale, retail, internet, service

5. **Facilities and Equipment**
- ☐ Location and type of facility
- ☐ Furniture and equipment
- ☐ IT computer needs: hardware and software
- ☐ General controls
- ☐ Application controls
- ☐ Single user, multi-user, network (LAN and/or WAN)

6. **Operating Systems**
- ☐ Planning systems
- ☐ Customer service
- ☐ Cash management
- ☐ Sales and marketing
- ☐ Cost systems
- ☐ Accounting/financial
- ☐ Reporting systems
- ☐ Management systems
- ☐ Personnel and staffing
- ☐ Operating systems and procedures

7. **Organizational Concerns**
- ☐ Policies and procedures
- ☐ Management and supervision
- ☐ Operating staff
- ☐ Support staff and services
- ☐ Outsourcing services (i.e., payroll, bookkeeping, temporary help)
- ☐ Professional support (i.e., legal and accounting)
- ☐ Responsibility and authority

Acknowledgments

This book couldn't have been written without the input of the various small business clients, colleagues, seminar participants, and small business people that I have encountered throughout the years. Knowingly or not they have provided insights and material for this book—the good, the bad, and the ugly. I couldn't have written such an encompassing book without them. There are too many to name but I appreciate each and every one of them. The data gathering is a team effort; the writing is a lonely effort.

I am also grateful to my wife Barbara who has patiently stood by while I plugged along each day to put this book together. Without her willingness to stand by while I talked to myself—sometimes in joy, other times in frustration—this project may not have been completed.

I also want to thank the people at John Wiley & Sons who made this book happen. First of all, Sheck Cho, the Executive Editor on this project (and all of my other Wiley books from the beginning) who has "mothered" the project through from the concept to the final product. Also, many thanks to Lisa Vuoncino, Production Editor, who kept me on target to meet all of the schedule deadlines and provided technical support throughout the entire project. A special thanks to the Wiley behind the scenes technical support personnel—editors, typesetters, reviewers, and so forth.

CHAPTER 1

Understanding the Small Business Environment

In today's many-faceted and multidisciplined economic environment, small privately owned business management must place greater emphasis on increasing results with fewer resources. Small businesses do this by evaluating the economy, efficiency, and effectiveness of organizational operations. In recent years, public business leaders from all sizes of organizations have discovered that by broadening their focus to include all operating activities, not just the sales function, they have an added valuable tool in achieving their business goals. However, many times, the small business owner sees these other activities as a cost center rather than a profit center. The small business owner needs to view operations in a new mindset—not as costly retardants that get in the way of efficient operations. If this is not possible due to the owner's resistance, then the possibility of success may diminish.

Keep in mind that before you can aid your nonregulated small business with the advice provided in this book, it is important to understand the landscape of the small business, and specifically the privately held small business being addressed here. Let us start by understanding the small businesses that can be best improved through implementing effective operating procedures.

UNDERSTANDING THE SMALL BUSINESS

The typical privately held small business differs from a larger publicly held business in a number of ways that affect the use of best practice systems to enhance operations. These differences cover everything from government and regulatory compliance issues to the goals and motivations of the owners.

Closely held and/or family owned and operated businesses have different obligations to stakeholders than do publicly owned larger businesses, which are required to report to stockholders and the Securities and Exchange Commission (SEC). The owners of a privately owned small business have the right to operate their business in whatever (hopefully legal) manner they desire. However, the small business owner must guide and direct the small business to operate the business in a proper environment so that the business grows in the desired direction. Unfortunately, the desires of the owners (e.g., to maximize nontaxable cash in their pockets) may be in conflict with the exercise of proper business practices.

For instance, owners' desires may be to:

- Maximize sales, whether reported or not, at whatever price they can get.
- Spend whatever is necessary, with minimal regard to cost accounting, to operate the business.
- Maximize the amount of cash from the business.
- Charge off the greatest amount of expenses, business and personal, to the business as business expenses.
- Minimize the amount of net income reported as taxable (a loss, if possible).
- Minimize the amount of federal and state taxes paid.
- Recast the results of operations to add back questionable business expenses when the owners decide to sell the business.

I expect my business always to be here—and so far, so good.

Conversely, the quest for proper operations and controls may include:

- Proper recording of all sales, whether paid for in cash or billed
- Determination that each sale produces a contribution to the bottom line

- Control of necessary operating costs to manage the business properly
- Guidance and direction for the business to grow and prosper
- Internal accounting and operating controls that ensure proper operating and data recording controls
- Financial and operating reporting that reflect accurate information
- Preparation of tax returns that accurately reflect the results of operations

In a small business, the owner/operator's desires, plans, and monetary resources, and not corporate plans, provide guidance and direction for business decisions. The owners, regardless of their business acumen and expertise, reserve the right to operate their business any way they want. With all of the urgings of others, and because of their lack of obligation to public reporting, small business owners may ignore outside advice and guidance and continue to operate their business in an uncontrolled environment.

The optimist is one who doubles the same efforts after failing— expecting different results.

The small business owner is typically focused on day-to-day operations in a crisis-management-type approach rather than on a big-picture, long-term-planning approach. Many times the small business owner assumes that if the business brings in sufficient sales, then the business is doing well and growing, even though increased sales often brings even greater costs and fewer real profits. It is the focus of this book to ensure that the small business operates most effectively in a controlled environment in the most economical, efficient, and effective manner. One can more clearly assist the small business owner in understanding that the business does not necessarily grow through additional sales but through profitable sales with realistic cost structures that provide real cash profits to the bottom line. Helping the small business to operate more profitably via the big picture of operating a growing business also helps to dispel the notion that the small business cannot afford to implement outside advice.

Moving fast is not necessarily the same as making progress.

Resources and capabilities within the small business are much more limited than in a large publicly held organization, particularly in the accounting/financial and information technology (IT) areas. In many small businesses the owners are involved in almost every aspect of operations as there may not be sufficient resources to hire the necessary competent non-value-added-type personnel such as in the accounting and IT areas. The owners may control those transactions to be entered into the accounting system, such as holding out certain cash sales, rather than having all business-related transactions flowing properly within a controlled environment. Almost all small businesses today use a microcomputer-based system or network with purchased packaged accounting software to process their accounting transactions. However, in most cases, neither the owners nor the computer operators have sufficient accounting and IT expertise to ensure that all accounting transactions are entered properly into the accounting system in a controlled environment and that no transactions are entered that should not be entered. Often, the computer operator may be anyone who is available, like a relative, a friend, a part-time person, or the owner's teenage child. It is the owner's responsibility to ensure that the computerized accounting system operates within a well-defined control environment that ensures the validity of all transactions entered and reports produced.

The sooner you are behind, the greater the time to catch up.

SMALL BUSINESS MANAGEMENT

The complexities of operating a successful small business enterprise have grown considerably over the years. No longer can the individual responsible for the small business's accounting functions be merely a data entry clerk who enters transactions as provided by the owner or other managers into a computer system using purchased packaged software. As with larger organizations, the small business needs not only someone to post accounting transactions, but also someone who can be responsible for such diverse areas of the business as:

- Organizational planning
- Operational management and controls
- Budgeting, either formal or informal
- Basic financially related business decisions
- Computerization and its related controls
- Management, operations, and administration
- Personnel, hiring, orientation, training, evaluation, salary increases, promotions, firings, and the assignment of job responsibilities and expectations

Recent trends for the successful small business owner include a decision-making, internal operations, managerial, and problem-solving point of view. In a small business, where one individual possessing expertise in some of these areas but not in all assumes the role of owner or manager and may not have adequate expertise, the business is in itself operating in an ineffective operating environment. In some instances, an outsider is asked to perform the primary role of operations and/or financial manager. An effective small business manager must have a hand in every aspect of the business—financial and operational—and must know more about the company's operations than anyone else. The business manager becomes the internal business advisor to the small business owner.

SMALL BUSINESS COMPUTERIZATION

Computerization has given even the smallest of businesses access to many new operational and financial management techniques. These techniques include:

- **Planning and budgeting systems**. Define the desired direction, develop plans as to how to get there, and monitor progress toward goals and objectives.

- **Capital investment analysis**. Determine whether the business needs to expand with additional investment, use present resources more effectively, or retrench certain operations by disposing of resources—or using them differently.

- **Operations research**. Apply mathematical models to solving business problems such as levels of inventory to maintain, how to distribute products, and cost-versus-benefit analysis.

- **Variance analysis**. Control plus-and-minus variances from expected results and take corrective action.

- **Breakeven analysis**. Determine the specific level of desired sales where all direct, indirect, and fixed costs are covered through the sale of an individual product, enabling management to improve their cost-to-pricing and related profit decisions.

- **Cost accounting systems**. These encompass collecting accurate data as to direct costs (material and labor), indirect costs (such as quality control, and machine maintenance), functional costs (such as purchasing, accounting, IT, and personnel), and customer costs (sales and marketing, servicing, complaints, phone calls, and after-delivery service).

- **Return on investment**. Ensure that management is using company resources effectively so that they provide a bottom-line real return that exceeds the cost of the investment and related operations.

- **Reporting systems**. Design them so that management can properly control all aspects of the business in a controlled environment ensuring that the business operates most economically, efficiently, and effectively.

All of these needs have combined to produce a more complex business environment and an increased set of responsibilities for small business owners—many of which far exceed their capabilities. The small business owner and manager of today must be involved in all aspects of the business's operations, and these days this includes IT electronic operations. The use of computers is how people do business today, even in the smallest of businesses. Computerization, while helping to manage businesses more effectively, has also introduced some operating problems such as poor integration, outdated databases, data security, and a general lack of IT knowledge by the business owner. Most small business owners are not the best people to be left to deal with IT issues. If the small business cannot afford its own IT staff, the external IT advisor can help advise or outside IT consultants can be used to help maintain the necessary strong IT arm of the business. For most small businesses, this can be accomplished only by working with outside experts.

You do not have the experience until after you need it.

OPERATIONAL MANAGEMENT FUNCTION

Somebody, internal and/or external, connected to every small business— regardless of his or her title—must plan and pull together, review, analyze, interpret, and make decisions as to courses of action relative to the financial and operational requirements and consequences of company operations. In even the smallest of businesses, there is almost no aspect of its operations that does not have both financial and operational requirements and related consequences.

Depending on the nature of the small business and how it operates, the operational management function could include such activities as:

- Determining the financial resources necessary to meet desired plans and allocate resources to operating programs and activities
- Forecasting as to the extent that these requirements can be met through internal generation of funds, and how much needs to be obtained outside the company
- Developing the best plans for using internally generated funds and obtaining external funding that will provide a desired return on investment
- Establishing and maintaining a system of financial controls relative to the effective allocation and uses of funds
- Formulating programs to provide the most effective profit-volume-cost relationships, and to provide effective monitoring of such programs

- Analyzing financial results of all operations, reporting the facts to top management, and making recommendations concerning future operations

The operational manager must be familiar not only with financial and accounting concerns but also with activities and policies in such operational areas as manufacturing and/or service delivery, marketing, purchasing, sales, personnel relations, and general management. These functions encompass planning, directing, and measuring the results of the small business's monetary operations.

> You can't fix the financial without fixing the operational.

THE FAMILY BUSINESS

Many small businesses are closely held businesses owned and controlled by family members. A *family business* can be defined as a small business enterprise where two or more family members (e.g., husband and wife, parent and child, brothers and/or sisters) own and/or manage the business. These types of businesses are also known as *mom-and-pop* businesses. They can range in size from over $100 million in annual sales to less than $100,000 and from 500 employees to 2 employees, and by type such as manufacturing, service, professional practice, retail, and so on.

The family business, which is normally privately owned, has many advantages for its owners, which include:

- **Power and control**. Family owners make any decisions they desire and set the rules for nonfamily employees.
- **Different strokes**. Family owners/members take special privileges such as working hours, benefits, use of company assets, and access to inventory.
- **Accountability**. Different criteria from those of hired management: As part of the family, whatever you do is right.

- **Job security**. Family members do not normally get fired, but they may get promoted.

- **Company policies**. These do not apply to family members, as infractions will be forgiven.

- **Flextime**. Ownership has its privileges; family members come and go as they please. Family members can come in late, and even if they do, they can still leave early.

- **Compensation**. For family members, this is whatever the business will bear, regardless of their contribution (sometimes not even on-site—so-called phantom employees).

- **Business write-offs**. Charge whatever expenses you can to the business for the owners and other family members, including legitimate business expenses, questionable business expenses, and outright personal expenses.

- **Family inheritance**. The business may be the owner's principal asset that is seen as a living trust for the children.

- **Retirement-in-place**. Even after the time that owners can no longer contribute effectively to the business, they still may be compensated from the business as a form of early retirement or semiretirement.

Note that many of these advantages to the family business owner and family members may become major constraints to effective small business operations. However, you need to understand and take them into account, for many times the family business owner will balk at sound internal operating practice recommendations, even when they are in their own best interests, if they get in the way of one or more of the items listed above.

The case study in Exhibit 1.1 depicts the advantage of a family business to the father but the disadvantage to his sons.

Owning and operating a family business also has some potential drawbacks to which many a family business owner or manager has fallen victim, including:

- **Workaholism**. The business becomes your life. In the past, and presently, with many downsized or let-go employees deciding to operate their own business rather than go back into the employment

EXHIBIT 1.1   Cashing In?

Joe Pep owns a small chain of three pizzerias, which his three sons operate. When Joe comes to visit, he always empties the cash register. His so-called cash disbursement is never recorded on the books. The sons have no idea as to the amount of cash that leaves the business through Joe's cash withdrawals. Joe sees this practice as an advantage to being a small business owner. The extent of the sons doing the same form of cash disbursement is not known, nor are the cash registers reconciled to daily sales. Each son, responsible for one of the stores, is paid a small salary plus half the profits of the store.

What changes to operating practices would you suggest implementing in this situation considering Joe and his sons' needs?

Suggested Response

As Joe is the owner of the business, it might be difficult to convince him that this practice of nonrecorded cash withdrawals is not best for him—it is a ready source of nontaxable cash that goes directly into his pocket. All of this cash is never recorded, so that these unrecorded sales never get on the books and reduce the amount of each store's sales and profits, resulting in reducing the sons' share of half the profits. Joe's practice may encourage the sons to do the same. There is no way to know what the real sales and profits are—only relying on those actually recorded on the books.

1. Convince Joe and his three sons that this practice is counter to building the business and that all sales must be recorded to properly control the business.
2. Establish daily cash register reconciliation and settlement procedures to ensure that all sales posted on the cash register reconcile to the cash-in in the register.
3. Establish a cost accounting and inventory control system to determine that material costs have a reasonable comparison to the amount of sales.
4. Develop effective reporting by store that shows the real volume of sales, actual material costs, and effective net profit margins by product and net profit per store—for one-half distribution to each son.
5. The reported data provided to the business and each son should assist them in effectively building the business on sound business principles.
6. Show Joe and his three sons that by conducting the business based on sound business practices, each of them will wind up with greater compensation even with paying more (but the right amount of) taxes.

---

ranks, many small business owners have totally enmeshed themselves in the business. They are willing (and sometimes forced) to work long hours in their attempt to make the business successful, or they have no choice due to lack of success. In this situation, it becomes more difficult to convince such an owner to use more effective and proper business practices to operate the business in a more controlled environment.

- **Poor crisis management**. There may be an inability to properly manage and control (even though when one owns a small business one has the right to operate the business any way one desires). Normally this creates a crisis management situation. It could be the owner doing more than she should and getting into areas of the business she should not be in—reluctant to hire additional personnel, as it is money coming out of her pocket. Running from one crisis to another prevents the owner from focusing on proper management and control techniques. It also keeps the owner involved in all aspects of the business except proper management.

- **Lack of business acumen**. Think in terms of on-the-job training versus professional management skills. There are many people who have always wanted to operate their own small business or who have left a job to be on their own, but there is no guarantee that these individuals have adequate business acumen to effectively operate the business they have gone into. However, as the years go by and these owners remain in business, some even successfully, there is a tendency for them to convince themselves that they know all about operating their business. Who needs outside help—why pay for it?

- **Success in spite of yourself**. Maybe it is the business niche and/or good employees. Some small business owners get lucky and the business is successful in terms of net profit. However, such success must be analyzed as to the root cause. Many times it is not due the owner's magical management skills but rather that they fell into a niche market presently in demand (i.e., popular coffee shop, fast-food franchise, quick-oil-change garage) or that they somehow hired good employees who operate the business from an excellent customer service standpoint in spite of the owner. When such an owner says to me, "You can't argue with success," I respond by asking, "Would you like to be *more* successful?" Sometimes this translates into getting the owner less involved in the business so that the others can be more effective.

- **Minimal rewards**. There can be long hours with minimal compensation. The small business owner may have shoveled himself into a hole, with the business making him a slave to long hours and hard work but producing minimal monetary rewards. He is in a stuck position requiring some outside assistance to help him make the business more successful. However, he is also in a position where he cannot afford to pay for it.

- **Inability to get out**. Too many resources tied up—what can they do? Many times small business owners have the bulk, if not all, of their resources tied up in the business. In addition, they may have been operating this business for many years. It might be extremely difficult for them personally to sell or get out of the business to enter the employment market. Their only solution seems to be to work to make the business more successful. However, they may be flogging a dead horse.

- **Family incompetence**. This relates to owners, spouse, children, relatives, and so on. With all best intentions, the owners and their relatives working in the business may be outright incompetent to run the business that they have decided to operate. For example, someone with a caustic personality might not be best suited to operate a retail store that requires close customer contact for success. In some instances, it may be that the owners have placed specific family members in positions in which they are ill qualified to perform adequately (for example, a playboy son assigned the role of plant manager over serious working machinists). How can one deal not only with business issues but also with family dynamics and personnel issues?

- **Business demands**. Business comes first, and family and friends second. The owners may be so immersed in the details and crises of their business that they have no time for family and friends, or to simply focus on managing the business rather than having the business managing them. This makes it extremely difficult for one to get their attention and convince them that there are better ways to manage their business with less stress and greater results.

- **Business consumes the owners' assets**. There could be an all-encompassing drain on financial assets. The owners may have been fortunate to have some capital (or borrowed some—usually from friends and relatives) to start up their business. However, now that the business is off the ground, the owners' wonderful and revolutionary idea has not been as successful as they had fantasized. Month after month, the owners have had to put additional capital into the business, operating on a negative cash flow, while being unable to take much out of the business for themselves. They have become like the gambler who keeps hoping that the next poker hand will get all of their lost money back. It is probably not going to happen unless something unforeseen and fortunate occurs; it may be time for the owners to cut their losses and get out of the business.

Again, these issues need to be taken into account when assisting the small business to grow and prosper. Many times the small business (owners, family, and others) needs a family therapist and analyst as well as a business advisor. As you help to implement value-added effective operating practices and controls, you must also educate the family business owners as to the proper procedures for operating a business—making them more successful in spite of themselves. This is an ongoing process, of which one must be continually aware.

I am still looking for the functional family business.

Family Dynamics

In providing consultative services for a closely held family business, it is often difficult to separate business issues from family concerns. In many cases, family dynamics from home tend to carry over into the family business, creating issues that may affect the business such as:

- Conflict resolution: sibling battles, parental favors, spousal-control battles, in-law issues, and so on
- Family-versus-business interests; sons'/daughters' marital status (e.g., single parent with preschool children); high-versus-low lifestyles (e.g., matching compensation to lifestyle), and so on
- Haloing and discounting family members; favorite/nonfavorite children; unwanted in-laws; likable son-/daughter-in-law
- Family role carryover: nurturing spouse, loved/unloved child, envied relative, over/underachiever, and so on

- Exploitation or taking advantage: child to parent, sibling to sibling (e.g., brother taking care of a sister), taking care of elderly founder, and so on

- Sibling rivalry or interfamily competition: older versus younger, brother/sister versus brother/sister, two sides of family (e.g., siblings of two different family founders)

- Compensation struggles: Who should get more money? Is it based on need or based on value of family member to the business?

- Contribution issues: Are family members being objectively evaluated based on contribution and compensated accordingly, or evaluated based on family position?

- Management concerns as to how to run the business: older owner versus younger, better-educated child; more than one family owner; expertise issues, and so on

- Succession issues: Who takes over or inherits the business—the family member who has contributed the most to the business, or a more logical inheritor who might not be part of the business or who might not even be a family member?

You must be prepared to deal with the business operational issues as well as some of the family dynamics issues as stated above. Many times you become more of a family counselor than a business counselor, as shown in the case study in Exhibit 1.2.

EXHIBIT 1.2   Case Study: Family Business

Dad is an orthopedic surgeon, age 62, getting ready to retire in a few years. Mom has worked with him in the practice as Office Manager since he started on his own over 30 years ago. He is the principal shareholder in a group practice connected to the largest of 3 hospitals in a town of approximately 300,000 in population.

He has two nonfamily member associates who have been with the practice almost from the beginning. Each of them expects to take over the practice when Dad retires. One of these associates also has a daughter in the practice, whom he expects to succeed him.

Within the past ten years, Dad's two sons and a daughter have joined the practice. In addition, the daughter in-law married to the oldest son is employed as the laboratory supervisor. The oldest son is conservative like his father and is content to let his Dad run the practice the way he always has. The younger son, however, has recently joined the practice and is full of new ideas to increase the practice and each of their compensation—such as branch locations, increased laboratory services, advertising and marketing, and so on.

The older son's wife (the laboratory supervisor) and Mom agree with him. As a result, the two sons have stopped talking to each other. The daughter refuses to take sides, but is considering joining another practice.

Dad is beside himself as to what to do at this point and fears for his impending retirement. Mom just wants the family back—wants her sons and daughter and their families to all come to dinner at the same time.

From the scenario above, provide advice as to the major areas of concern and make recommendations as to what they should do:

1. What issues are involved in this situation?
2. What steps would you recommend to take to deal with these issues?

Suggested Response

What issues are involved in this situation?
- Strategic, long term, short term, and detailed planning
- What businesses the practice should be in; medical practice, laboratory services, surgery, branches and so on
- Operations; how to best run the practice.
- Organizational structure; how to manage and operate the practice
- Family versus nonfamily participation; management and operations
- Family dynamics; sibling rivalries, family role carryover, conflict resolution, management concerns, and so on
- Succession issues; who takes over the business from Dad, family versus nonfamily, continuity concerns, and so on.

What steps would you recommend to deal with these issues in providing advice and/or consultation to this client?
- Separate family issues from business issues.
- Develop plans—strategic, long term, short term, and detail—with all concerned that can be agreed to by all.
- Deal objectively with succession issues on a fair basis with both family and nonfamily members.
- Develop management and operating systems and procedures so that the business can continue successfully—whether Dad is there or not.
- Develop authority and responsibility relationships for all members of the practice with an objective relationship to the levels of compensation.
- Develop a system for valuing each practice principal's contribution to the business and an agreed-on objective basis for valuing their basis in the practice for future retirements or severances.

Basic Operating Formula

Many small business owners have some measure of success or survival through their knowledge and skills in a technical area (such as sales, retailing, engineering, auto mechanics), but may possess minimal knowledge relative to basic good operating practices. I have found in working with certain small business clients that it is helpful to share some accounting basics that may have been studied back in Accounting 101 but that they have never learned or comprehended. The formula shown in Exhibit 1.3 exemplifies the basic relationship between sales or revenues, costs or expenditures, and the resultant profit (or loss).

EXHIBIT I.3   **Small Business Success Formula 1**

$$R - E = P$$

R = Revenues (or sales)

E = Expenditures (or costs)

P = Profit (or the bottom line)

By including an additional dollar of sales to the business, the top line increases (gross sales), but unless expenditures are less than the amount of the sale, the contribution to the profit line will be zero or less (i.e., a negative or loss). However, by reducing expenditures by a dollar (all other things being equal), the reduction will fall directly to the bottom line and increase profits on a dollar-by-dollar basis. Accordingly, small business success is dependent on the small business owner acquiring only quality sales from quality customers (i.e., those sales that contribute a desired profit to the bottom line) and maintaining costs at a minimum. Of course, the small business owner must be aware of the costs and related pricing structure for each of the company's products and services and customers.

Why the Small Business Is in Existence

Before one even thinks about implementing effective small business operating practices and controls, it is necessary to determine why the seriously operated small business is in existence. When small business owners are asked this question, invariably the answer is "to make money." Although this is true and certainly important to survival and growth, there are really only two reasons for a small business to exist:

1. **Customer service business**. To provide goods and services to satisfy desired customers so that they will continue to use the business's goods and services and refer it to others.

2. **Cash conversion business**. To create desired goods and services so that the investment in the small business is converted to cash as quickly as possible with the resultant cash-in exceeding the cash-out (net profits or positive return on investment).

This means that the small business is in business to stay for the long term—to serve its customers and grow and prosper. If it can operate under the above two concepts, the possibilities for success increase and the business is more likely to expand in the right directions. Typically, reporting controls emphasize sales, costs, and calculated profits. It is equally important to control the level of customer service to ensure ongoing growth, as well as properly controlling the cash conversion cycle. The small business operates on cash, not recorded profits. Proper operating practices encompassing these concepts help to ensure that the small business maintains its focus and operates in the most effective manner—doing the right thing, the right way, at the right time.

Businesses the Small Business Is Not In

Once short-term thinking is eliminated, small business owners realize they are not in the following businesses and decision making becomes simpler:

- **Sales business**. Making sales that cannot be collected profitably (sales are not profits until the cash is received and the total cost of the sale is less than the amount collected) creates only numerical growth. Unless small business owners understand this concept, they may continue to believe that increased sales create positive growth for their business. The focus is to make quality sales to quality customers. Proper operating controls over each sale, as to its real profitability, looking at sales price less related costs such as direct product costs, functional costs (such as purchasing, billing, and collections), customer-related costs, and the cost of money, should enable the small business to recognize such opportunities.

- **Customer order backlog business**. Logging customer orders is a paperwork process to impress the owners and internal management.

Unless this backlog can be converted into a timely sale and profitable collection, there is only a future promise, which may never materialize. The small business owner cannot really afford the luxury of customer backlog where every customer and every order must be handled as the only one. Once a customer order is received, the small business must process and fill it (and collect) in the shortest time possible. Controls need to be implemented that ensure each customer order is entered into the production system upon receipt and handled in the desired times until completion.

- **Accounts receivable business**. Get the cash as quickly as possible, not the promise to pay. But, remember, customers are the company's business; keeping them in business is keeping the company in business. Normally, cash is already out to vendors and/or into inventory, complicating the cash conversion process. As many small businesses, such as retailers, are already in the cash business, accounts receivable are not their problem; control of cash is the problem. For those small businesses that offer billing terms, consideration should be given to establish a cash-only policy over small sales, where the amount of the sale is less than the cost of billing and collections, and for sales under a certain amount, say $500. For instance, the small business may establish controls to ensure cash collectibility either in advance or at the time of delivery. All sales resulting in accounts receivable would be reported as exceptions for follow-up.

- **Inventory business**. Inventory does not equal sales. Keep inventories to a minimum—zero, if possible—by procuring raw materials from vendors only as needed, producing for real customer orders based on agreed-on delivery dates, maximizing work-in-process throughput, and shipping directly from production when the customer needs the product. If inventory is the business, such as with a wholesaler, retailer, or distributor, then once again the small business wants to ensure that inventories are kept to a minimum within the constraints of fully serving customers. However, the owners must be in touch with costs and selling prices and knowing what items are in demand by the customer base. Making buying mistakes that result in selling off inventory at markdown prices is not the course to take for making the business successful. Such markdown practices usually only result in absorbing losses, setting bad precedent for customer expectations, and ignoring the root of your problems—lack of knowledge of the business and/or its customers.

- **Employment business**. The trick here is to get by with the least number of employees possible. Never hire an additional employee unless absolutely necessary; rely on cross-training and transferring good employees. Not only do people cost ongoing salaries and fringe benefits, but they also need to be paid attention to—which results in organization building. This is extremely important to the small business, as it cannot afford to solve its problems (as large corporations do) by hiring or downsizing. The small business must solve similar problems with fewer employees, but be more flexible. Controls over the area of personnel include hiring statistics, effective use of personnel, productivity reporting, and results produced per employee.

> The pessimistic small business owner is the one who winds up in the markdown business hoping to recover through volume.

If the small business does both of these successfully—that is, pay attention to its business, and stay out of the businesses it should not be in, it will more than likely (outside economic factors notwithstanding) grow and prosper through well-satisfied customers and keep itself in the positive cash conversion business—in spite of itself. The small business owner must decide which of the above factors (i.e., businesses to be in and not to be in) it wishes to embrace as its business criteria, which ones it does not wish to include as criteria, and which additional criteria to include. These criteria become the overriding conditions on which the business conducts its operations and against which it is measured. It is these agreed-on criteria that define the operating practices that need to be established.

Embracing the correct criteria is one issue; enforcing the application of the criteria is another issue. As previously mentioned, often small business family issues come to bear that create violations of good business principles, as shown in the case study in Exhibit 1.4.

EXHIBIT 1.4 Slacking

Lou is the president of a small business that manufactures men's leisure slacks. Every Friday after work, Horace, the receiver/shipper, and also Lou's brother-in-law, loads his SUV with bundles of slacks. You happened to notice this routine. Upon investigation, you found no paperwork for the transaction, which was never posted to the books. Horace had a booth at the local in-door flea market, where he sold the slacks as irregulars at much less than retail. There was no indication of any returns. When you brought it to Lou's attention, Lou told you "What can I do. He's my wife's brother. Until I'm ready to divorce her, I've got Horace.

What operating deficiencies do you identify and how would you present them to the owner? What would you suggest to correct this situation from a control and business practices standpoint?

Suggested Response

Control Deficiencies

- *Inventory and production control*: Taking product out of stock without proper recording results in inaccurate inventory levels and records where there may be an expectation that such inventory is still on-hand. In addition, to make up for the lost items, assuming there is customer demand, requires additional unnecessary production orders placed into manufacturing.
- *Customer orders*: If these items were produced to fill customer orders, not only will the company be unable to fill such orders, but the company will have to enter additional manufacturing orders requiring the customer to wait—a violation of good customer service.
- *Cost accounting*: As these products are taken out of inventory without a corresponding sale, the result is an increase in cost for all other sales, making the overall cost data on which to base operating decisions inaccurate. While the owner does not know the extent of what is going out the door, the cost of such items, whether known or not, is passed on to his other customers or comes out of his pocket.

Corrective Measures

- *Inventory and production control*: If the owner insists that Horace continue running his side business out of inventory, handle such inventory issues as such and Horace's demands as part of customer production requirements. Also, record any returned merchandise by Horace. Such inventory issues should be billed out to Horace at a price that at least covers costs.
- *Customer orders*: Harold should be treated as another customer, even if sold at wholesale or preferred prices. He should be cautioned that no merchandise leaves the plant facility without proper recording. While it is all right to help a family member, proper business practices must be maintained to allow the owner to manage properly.
- *Cost accounting*: All costs need to be properly recorded into the business's records so that proper business decisions can be made, such as costing and pricing decisions by product line, product, and customer.

Helpful Systems

In many small businesses today, the owners are grasping for ways to become competitive and maintain market position—or merely to survive. The owners and management have sensed that many of their systems are detrimental to growth and have held them back. These are the very systems that are supposed to be helpful; for example:

- Planning systems, long and short term, that resulted in formal or informal plans but not in actual results

- Budget systems that became costly in terms of allocating resources effectively and controlling costs in relation to results

- Organizational structures that created unwieldy hierarchies or gaps in responsibilities, which produced systems of unnecessary policing and control

- Cost accounting structures (usually lack thereof) that obscured true product costs and resulted in pricing that constrained competitiveness or ignored profitability

- Computerized accounting systems that produced elaborate reporting without enhancing the effectiveness of operations

- Sales functions and forecasts that resulted in selling those products that maximized sales commissions but may not have been the products to sell and produce for effective growth

- Operating practices that perpetuated outmoded systems ("we've always done it that way") rather than promoted best practices

Effective operating practices that ensure that these systems are operating most effectively, together with other techniques, are tools to make these systems helpful as intended and direct the organization toward its goals. With the passage of time, good intentions and initially helpful systems tend to deteriorate. Operational reviews are then necessary to help get the small business back on track by pinpointing operational deficiencies, developing practical recommendations, and implementing positive changes.

Management Responsibility

Small business owners and managers at all levels should be held accountable for using the scarce resources entrusted to them to achieve maximum results at the least possible costs. Although management should embrace best practice operating concepts and apply them as they proceed, in the typical small business this is rarely the case.

More normally, small business owners and management need to be sold on the value of differential systems. In selling the benefits of implementing such operating practices, it is important to stress that unlike other techniques that cost time and money for uncertain results, best operating practices can pay for themselves. In effect, the operations and control environment becomes a profit center instead of a cost center.

With the success of best practice operating practices, management quickly realizes that the more effective the operating practices in place and the more recommended economies and efficiencies are implemented, the greater the savings and results. In addition, the residual capability for implementing and performing best practice operating procedures remains in each operating area, so that operations personnel can continue to apply these concepts on an ongoing basis.

Keep in mind that the intent of implementing best practice operating practices is not to be critical of present operations, but to review operations and develop a program of best practices and continuous positive operational improvements by working with management and staff personnel. The concept of best practices should be sold as an internal program of review directed toward improved economies and efficiencies that will produce increased operational results.

> The successful small business owner is the one who listens and tries alternative approaches looking for the path to success.

OPERATING AREAS TO BE ADDRESSED

While typically the small business owner's major concern is daily operations, to be most effective one must include any and all organizational functions and activities that hinder or help the effort to maintain the business in the most economical, efficient, and effective manner possible. In this regard, you must be aware of basic business principles that help to enhance the organization's success as well as those that the company should avoid. With these principles in mind, you can analyze the small business's operations to identify areas for improvement in which best practices can be implemented that maximize the chances of success and minimize the risk of failure. Although the primary focus in identifying and establishing these operating practices is on the manner in which scarce resources are used, considering the sources and uses of resources and the policies and procedures used to deal with over- and underoperational conditions, there are specific areas that need to be addressed.

The first step in the successful identification and implementation of effective small business operating practices is to define the company's desired criteria for results as related to its reason for existence and basic business principles. These organizational criteria typically encompass the company as an entity as well as its major functions. Such criteria then become the basis for establishing controls to monitor progress toward these criteria. An example of such an organization-wide criteria structure is as follows:

- Operate all activities in the most economical, efficient, and effective manner as possible.
- Provide the highest-quality products to customers at the least possible cost.
- Satisfy customers so that they continue to use the company's products and refer the company to others.
- Convert the cash invested in the business as quickly as possible so that the resultant cash in exceeds the cash out to the greatest extent possible.
- Achieve desired results using the most efficient methods so that the company can optimize the use of limited resources.
- Maximize net profits without sacrificing quality of operations, customer service, or cash requirements.
- Based on established organization-wide criteria as stated earlier, you can then assist the small business in establishing related criteria for its major areas of operations such as:
  - Sales function
  - Direct cost
  - Functional activities

Sales Function

In the best of circumstances, the criteria for the most effective and efficient sales operation involve making sales to the right customers who provide a profit source to the small business. A strong sales function creates realistic sales forecasts that result in a present or future real customer order. Sales orders and corresponding compensation systems should reinforce the goals of the company—that is, what items to sell, how much of each item to sell, at what price, and to whom. And finally, customer sales should be integrated with other functions of the company, such as manufacturing, engineering, accounting, purchasing, and so on.

- Are sales made to quality customers with the right products at the right time?
- Does each sale make a contribution to profits?
- Are all costs compared to the sale, such as product costs (direct material and labor), assignment of product-related activity costs (e.g., manufacturing processes, quality control, shipping, and receiving), functional costs (e.g., purchasing, accounts payable, billing, and accounts receivable), and customer costs (e.g., marketing, selling, support services, and customer service)?
- Do sales relate to an agreed-on sales forecast? Is the company selling the right products to the right customers?
- Do sales integrate with an effective production scheduling/control system?
- Are sales being made to the right customers—can they be collected profitably?
- Do realistic sales forecasts result in a present or future real customer order?
- Are sales for those products, as determined by management, to the right customers, at the right time, and in the right quantities?
- Do actual customer sales correlate directly with management's long- and short-term plans?
- Do sales efforts, and corresponding compensation systems, reinforce the goals of the company?

- Are customer sales integrated with other functions of the company, such as manufacturing, engineering, accounting, purchasing and buying, and so on?

Direct Cost

The small business wants to operate in the most efficient manner with the most economical cost in the timeliest manner, considering processes such as customer order entry, production and service delivery throughput, and customer delivery. The small business should integrate manufacturing and service delivery processes with sales efforts and customer requirements, and increase productivity of manufacturing and service delivery operations on an ongoing basis. Direct cost control goals should include eliminating, reducing, or improving all facets of the business's operations including activities such as receiving, inventory control, production control, storeroom operations, quality control, supervision and management, packing and shipping, and maintenance. The small business owner should also be concerned with minimizing the amount of resources, such as personnel, facilities, and equipment, that are allocated to the manufacturing or service-delivery process.

- Are sales orders entered into an effective production control system, which ensures that all sales orders are entered into production in a timely manner to ensure on-time, quality deliveries?
- Is work-in-process kept to a minimum so that only real customer orders are being worked on rather than building up finished-goods inventory?
- Are the most efficient and economical production methods used to ensure that the cost of the product is kept to its realizable minimum?
- Are direct materials and labor used most efficiently so that waste, reworks, and rejects are kept to a minimum?
- Are non-direct labor (and material) costs such as quality control, supervision and management, repairs and maintenance, material handling, and so on kept to a minimum?
- Are all operations conducted in the most efficient manner with the most economical costs?

- Are manufacturing and service delivery processes integrated with sales efforts and customer requirements?

- Are manufacturing and service delivery operations conducted in the timeliest manner considering processes such as customer order entry, timely throughput, and customer delivery?

- Is there a system in effect to increase productivity in all operations on an ongoing basis?

- Are controls in effect to eliminate, reduce, or improve all facets of business operations?

- Do procedures exist to eliminate, reduce, or improve all facets of manufacturing and service-delivery operations?

- Are resources minimized, such as personnel, facilities, and equipment, that are allocated to the manufacturing or service-delivery process?

- Are raw material and finished-goods inventories kept to a minimum?

- Are raw materials delivered into production on a just-in-time basis?

- Are finished goods completed in production just in time for customer delivery?

- Is the business working toward getting out of the inventory business?

Functional Activities

While the emphasis for many small business owners is to continually increase sales, it is the responsibility of the owner to obtain profitable sales from quality customers, convert a sale into cash as quickly as possible, and add real profits to the bottom line—more important components in operating a successful small business. Many times the small business cannot control the acquisition of customer sales when needed, sometimes resulting in making a sale for less than a desired profit margin (possibly at a loss). However, the small business can initiate efforts to control and reduce its internal functional costs, resulting in increasing its profit margins and creating greater flexibility in its pricing policies. Remember, a dollar of cost saved is a dollar that goes directly to the bottom line. Some of the areas of concern for typical functional costs are:

Accounting Functions—General

- What is the purpose and necessity of each of the accounting functions and related activities, such as accounts receivable, accounts payable, payroll, budgeting, and general ledger?
- Is each of the accounting functions operated in the most economical and efficient manner?
- Are effective procedures in place that result in the accounting functions becoming more analytical than mechanical?
- Are computerized procedures developed that integrate accounting purposes with operating requirements?
- Do reporting systems exist that provide management with the necessary operating data and indicators that can be generated from accounting data?
- Is there a process that identifies, eliminates, or reduces all unnecessary accounting operations?

Billing, Accounts Receivable, and Collections

- Are bills sent out in a timely manner—at the time of shipment or before?
- Are accounts receivable processing procedures the most efficient and economical?
- Is the cost of billing, accounts receivable processing, and collection efforts more than the amount of the receivable or the net profit on the sale?
- Is the number and amount of accounts receivable continually analyzed for minimization?
- Are any customers paying directly or through electronic funds transfer at the time of shipping or delivery?
- Are bills and accounts receivable in amounts exceeding the cost of processing excluded from the system?

Purchasing and Accounts Payable

- Are all items that are less than the cost of purchasing excluded from the purchasing system—with an efficient system used for these items?

- Are all repetitive high-volume and -cost items (e.g., raw materials and manufacturing supplies) negotiated by purchasing with vendors as to price, quality, and timeliness?

- Does the production system automatically order repetitive items as an integrated part of the production control system?

- Has consideration been given to reduce these functions for low- and high-ticket items, leading toward the possible elimination of these functions?

- Does the company consider paying any vendors on a shipment or delivery basis as part of its vendor negotiation procedures?

- Does the purchasing function only purchase those items where economies can be gained through a system of central purchasing?

- Is there a direct purchase system for those items that the purchasing function does not need to process, such as low-dollar purchases and repetitive purchases?

- Are purchasing and accounts payable systems simplified so that costs are at the lowest possible levels?

- Do purchasing personnel effectively negotiate with vendors so that the company obtains the right materials at the right time at the right quality at the right price?

- Is there a vendor analysis system present that objectively evaluates vendor performance?

Other Costs and Expenses

- Are all other costs and expenses kept to a minimum? Remember, a dollar not unnecessarily spent is a dollar directly to the bottom line.

- Are selling costs directed toward customer service and strategic plans rather than maximizing salespeople's compensation?

- Is there a system in effect that recognizes and rewards the reduction of expenses rather than rewarding budget increases or increased expenditures?

- Are all non-value-added functions (e.g., management and supervision, office processing, paperwork, etc.) evaluated as to reduction and elimination?

If you keep your eye only on the operations, you'll miss the results.

If you do not know where you are going and the results to be achieved, there is nothing to control against.

ECONOMY, EFFICIENCY, AND EFFECTIVENESS

In establishing effective operating practices for small business success, such practices must embrace the concept of conducting operations for economy, efficiency, and effectiveness. The following is a brief description of each of the *three E's* of effective operations:

1. **Economy (or the cost of operations).** Is the small business carrying out its responsibilities in the most economical manner—that is, through due conservation of its resources? In appraising the economy of operations and related allocation and use of resources, you may consider whether the organization is:
   a. Following sound purchasing practices
   b. Overstaffed as related to performing necessary functions
   c. Allowing excess materials to be on hand
   d. Using equipment that is more expensive than necessary
   e. Avoiding the waste of resources

2. **Efficiency (or methods of operations).** Is the organization carrying out its responsibilities with the minimum expenditure of effort? Examples of operational inefficiencies to be aware of include:
   a. Improper use of manual and computerized procedures
   b. Inefficient paperwork flow

    c. Inefficient operating systems and procedures

    d. Cumbersome organizational hierarchy and/or communication patterns

    e. Duplication of effort

    f. Unnecessary work steps

3. **Effectiveness (or results of operations).** Is the organization achieving results or benefits based on stated goals and objectives or some other measurable criteria? The review of the results of operations includes:

   • Appraisal of the organizational planning system as to its development of realistic goals, objectives, and detail plans

   • Assessment of the adequacy of management's system for measuring effectiveness

   • Determination of the extent to which results are achieved

   • Identification of factors inhibiting satisfactory performance of results

A graphic way to look at the effect of economy, efficiency, and effectiveness on the small business's growth and profitability is shown in the formula below in Exhibit 1.5.

EXHIBIT I.5   **Small Business Success Formula 2**

$$G + P = E_1 + E_2 + E_3$$

G = Growth

P = Profitability

E_1 = Economy

E_2 = Efficiency

E_3 = Effectiveness

For the small business to be successful and grow and prosper in a profitable manner, the small business owner must operate the business using the least amount of scarce resources (economy), using sound business practices in its operations (efficiency) to achieve the optimum results of success (effectiveness).

THE INITIAL SURVEY

To develop effective operating practices for a small business that desires to operate properly using sound business practices and grow and prosper in a successful manner, an initial survey form can be used to identify present practices and effective controls over operations. A sample initial survey form is shown in Exhibit 1.6. The purpose of the initial survey is to identify areas of major importance in the total organization or specific operations to be improved.

EXHIBIT 1.6   Initial Survey Example

Planning and Budgeting

1. How does the company plan? Describe the system of planning.
2. Does a long-range plan exist? Attach a copy.
3. Do current short-term plans exist? Attach a copy.
4. What are plans for expansion or improvement?
5. What are plans for physical plant development?
6. What are plans for future financing?
7. What are personnel plans?
8. How does the organization budget? Describe the budgeting system.
9. Does a current budget exist? Obtain or prepare a copy.
10. Do budget-versus-actual statistics exist for the last five years of operations?

Personnel and Staffing

1. Does an organizational chart exist? Obtain or prepare a copy.
2. Do functional job descriptions exist for each block on the organization chart?
3. Do staffing statistics by functional area exist? Obtain or prepare a copy.
4. Is there a system of employee evaluations? Describe the procedures.
5. How are employees recruited, hired, evaluated, and fired? Describe.
6. How are new employees oriented and trained? Describe.
7. What are promotional policies? Describe.
8. How are raises and promotions determined? Describe.
9. Is there a grievance mechanism? Describe.
10. What type of personnel records are maintained? Obtain copies.

(Continued)

EXHIBIT I.6 (Continued)

Management

1. Does a board of directors or other governing group exist? Attach a list of names and credentials.
2. Who is considered "top" management? Attach a list of names and credentials.
3. Who is considered "middle" management? Attach a list of names.
4. Who is considered "lower" management? Attach a list of names and credentials.
5. How adequate are existing reports in furnishing information for control purposes and making management decisions? Describe.
6. Are there tools for internal downward communication to the staff? Describe.
7. Is authority effectively delegated to management and lower levels? Describe.

Policies and Procedures

1. Do written policies exist? Obtain a copy.
2. Are written policies current?
3. Are systems and procedures documented? Obtain or provide a copy.

Accounting System

1. What is the chart of accounts used? Obtain or prepare a copy.
2. Is the accounting mechanized? Obtain documentation.
3. What financial and operational reports are produced? Obtain documentation.
4. Is there an internal audit function? By and to whom?
5. Are internal operating reports produced? Obtain copies and determine uses.

Revenues

1. What are the sources of revenue for the last five years? Obtain or prepare statistics.
2. Have there been any substantial changes during this period? Document them.
3. Is actual-versus-budgeted data available? Obtain or prepare a copy.

Expenses

1. What are the major expense accounts used? Obtain or prepare a copy.
2. What are actual expenses for these accounts for the last five years?
3. Have there been any substantial changes during this period? Document them.
4. Is actual-versus-budgeted data available? Obtain or prepare a copy.

Information Technology

1. Where is computer processing presently located in the organization? Obtain or prepare a copy of information technology organization.

2. What computer equipment is used? Obtain or prepare a copy of equipment list and locations.
3. What is total cost of equipment rental or purchase price?
4. What are the major applications computerized? Obtain or prepare a copy of the list of applications, with general systems descriptions.
5. Are management, operational, control, and exception reports provided?

Purchasing

1. What is purchasing authority? Obtain or prepare a copy of policy relative to purchasing authority.
2. Is purchasing centralized or decentralized? Describe operations.
3. How are purchase requisitions initiated? Describe general procedures.
4. Who determines quality and quantity desired?
5. Are purchase orders used? Describe the procedure.
6. Are competitive bidding procedures used? Describe the procedure.

Manufacturing Systems

1. Is a computerized manufacturing control system being used? Describe.
2. What types of manufacturing processes are being used? Describe processes.
3. How are jobs controlled in manufacturing? Describe procedures.
4. Is a manufacturing cost system used by job? Describe the system.
5. Are operational and management reports provided to control manufacturing operations? Obtain or prepare copies.

Production Control

1. Is a manufacturing control system being used? Is it computerized? Obtain or prepare a copy of general procedures.
2. What types of manufacturing processes are being used? Describe.
3. What is the location(s) of manufacturing facilities? Document.
4. Are production control cost centers used to control the routing of manufacturing orders? Obtain or prepare a copy of cost centers.
5. Is a manufacturing cost system used? Obtain or prepare a copy of cost accounting procedures.
6. Are operational and management reports provided to control manufacturing operations? Obtain copies.

Inventory Control

1. Is an inventory control system being used? Is it computerized? Obtain or prepare a copy of general procedures.
2. What types of inventory control procedures are being used? Describe.
3. Where are inventory storeroom locations? Obtain or prepare a copy of locations and describe storeroom procedures.

(Continued)

EXHIBIT I.6   (Continued)

4. How are inventory records maintained? Describe procedures.
5. Are inventory statistics and data maintained? Obtain data as to items in inventory, dollar value, usage, on-hand balances, etc.
6. What is the basis for reordering inventory items, and how are reorder quantities determined? Describe procedures.

Responsibility and Authority

1. Are responsibilities clearly defined and understood by managers and staff personnel? Describe procedures.
2. Has authority been delegated effectively to managers and lower levels within the organization? Describe the process.

Adequate operating practices are present if management has planned, designed, and organized in a manner that provides reasonable assurance that the organization's risks have been managed effectively and that the organization's goals and objectives will be achieved efficiently and economically, producing desired results.

CHAPTER 2

Strategic Concepts

The process of developing and implementing strategies has been in existence for a number of years and has been referred to by numerous terms such as *strategic management, strategic planning,* and *strategy development.* Strategy development focuses on anticipated growth and managing the uncertainties and complexities found in most organizations—maybe more so for a small business with less resources and planning expertise. One of the basic assumptions is that historical trends (for the business or the industry) will continue into the future. Strategic planning focuses on the identification and use of strategic thrusts and competencies within the organization in developing plans for future growth. An underlying assumption is that extrapolations made from past data and experience alone are inadequate bases for future growth.

As environments—internal and external—change, departures from past patterns are expected, requiring strategic adjustments such as new or changed products or services, facility changes, and new markets. Strategy development focuses on the entire environment of the organization, requiring knowledge of all the factors that have an impact on the business. The emphasis is on continued recognition of current business conditions but adding to it the ability to anticipate the need for strategic changes. What is needed is strategic flexibility so that the business can respond quickly to sudden changes—on a real-time rather than a periodic basis. In addition, strategies need to be proactive, allowing the business to create change rather than just respond to or ignore such changes. While strategy development is an excellent academic business exercise, it is a sore point, not only for the large corporation that may go through the steps but not follow through, but also for the small business that typically manages on a seat-of-the-pants basis.

Strategy development is a continuous process.

Strategy Development

The development, evaluation, and implementation of business strategies is the heart of successful and effective small business management—even though in most instances small business management disregards such concepts. Strategy development is the cornerstone of a management system that assists small business management to:

- Develop vision for the business.
- Understand the dynamic and changing environment in which the business is managed.
- Consider and decide on strategic alternatives that are responsive to the changing conditions that affect the business.
- Adopt strategies that are based on competitive advantages and that will be sustainable.

A small business strategy that is often referred to as its *competitive strategy* takes into account the following elements:

- **Products or services.** The scope of the business is defined by the products or services it offers or chooses not to offer, by the market (customer or client base) or population it seeks to serve or not serve, and by the competitors it chooses to challenge or avoid.
- **Strategic investment thrust.** Although there are many different investment options and variations that can be considered, the following represent the range of possibilities:
  - Growth/expansion: investing to enlarge or enter a new market
  - Stability: investing only to maintain the existing position in the market

- Retrenchment/harvest: minimizing and/or reducing investment to deplete or downsize the business
- Divestiture/liquidation: curtailing investment by recovering as much of the asset base as possible by closing down or selling off the business
- **Functional competence.** Specific methodologies on which to compete may be based on one or more functional area strategies such as:
  - Products or services offered
  - Pricing considerations
  - Distribution methods/logistics
  - Manufacturing, retailing, or service delivery
  - Technological competence
  - Quality/reliability
- **Unique competitive advantage.** A strategic skill is something that a business does exceptionally well, such as manufacturing, service delivery, customer service, quality control, or marketing and promotion, and that has strategic importance to that organization. A strategic asset is a resource such as a recognized name (e.g., brand name like Starbucks) or well-satisfied customer/client base (e.g., Wal-Mart shoppers) that creates an exceptional advantage over competitors.

The organizational planning cycle is shown in Exhibit 2.1 and the strategic planning and management cycle is shown in Exhibit 2.2.

Seek the competitive advantage and then surpass it.

Strategies for Competitive Advantage

There are many different strategies that the small business can adopt to achieve an advantage over the competition. However, many types of strategies share similar characteristics that drive the strategy and provide the

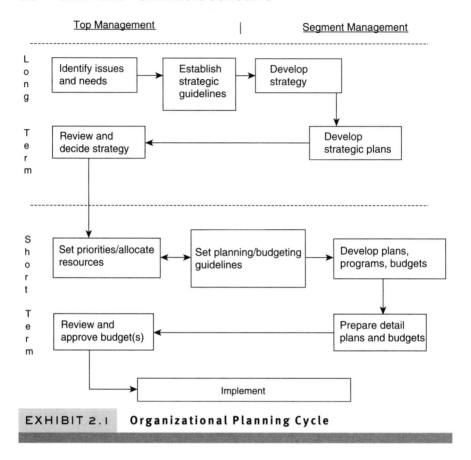

EXHIBIT 2.1 **Organizational Planning Cycle**

competitive advantage. Among the various strategies to consider, many fall into the following two categories, as shown in Exhibit 2.3.

1. **Differentiation strategy.** This is when the product or service provided is differentiated from the competition by various factors that increase the value to the customer/client, such as enhanced performance, quality, prestige, features, service, reliability, or convenience. Differentiation strategy is often but not always associated with higher prices. The desire is to make price a less critical factor to the customer.

2. **Low cost strategy.** This strategy achieves a sustainable cost advantage in some important element of the product or service.

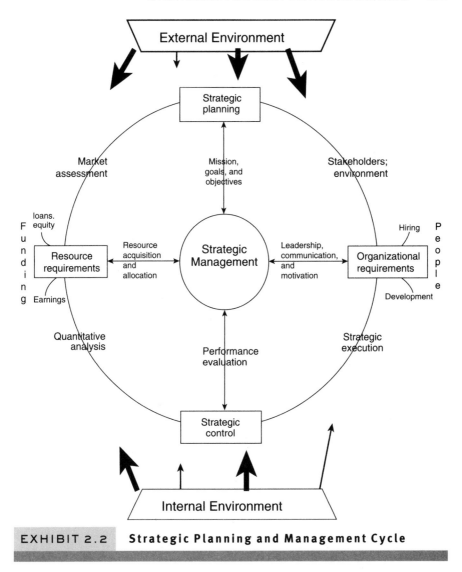

EXHIBIT 2.2 Strategic Planning and Management Cycle

Low cost leadership position can be attained through high volume (high market share), favorable access to lower cost materials or labor markets, or state-of-the-art manufacturing or product/service-delivery procedures. Low cost strategy need not always be associated with charging lower prices, as lower product or service costs could also result in increased profits or increased marketing, advertising, promotion, or product development investment.

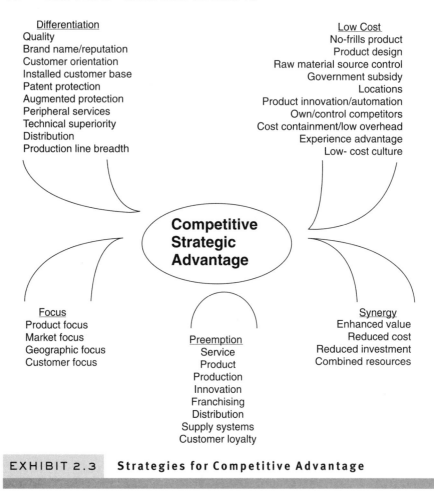

Differentiation
Quality
Brand name/reputation
Customer orientation
Installed customer base
Patent protection
Augmented protection
Peripheral services
Technical superiority
Distribution
Production line breadth

Low Cost
No-frills product
Product design
Raw material source control
Government subsidy
Locations
Product innovation/automation
Own/control competitors
Cost containment/low overhead
Experience advantage
Low- cost culture

Competitive Strategic Advantage

Focus
Product focus
Market focus
Geographic focus
Customer focus

Preemption
Service
Product
Production
Innovation
Franchising
Distribution
Supply systems
Customer loyalty

Synergy
Enhanced value
Reduced cost
Reduced investment
Combined resources

EXHIBIT 2.3   Strategies for Competitive Advantage

OTHER STRATEGIES TO EXPLOIT

Although most strategy development involves differentiation and/or low cost strategy, there are many other kinds of strategies that can be exploited. Examples include specific organizational competencies such as creativity and innovation, global perspectives, entrepreneurialism, research capability, sophisticated systems, and automation and computerization. Within this framework the following three strategies, which are not easily categorized as differentiation or low cost strategies, can be considered in small business strategy development.

1. **Focus.** This strategy involves businesses that focus on either a relatively small customer base or a restricted part of their product or service line. For example, a retailer selling to tall men or small women, or an investment advisor offering personal financial planning services to highly wealthy individuals employs a focus strategy. The particular focus is usually the driving force in the businesses' strategy development—although differentiation and/or low cost may also be part of the strategy.

2. **Preemption.** A preemptive strategic move is the first implementation of a strategy into a business or service area that because it was first produces a distinct competitive advantage. Normally, for such a preemptive move to create an advantage, competitors are prohibited or precluded from matching or countering the move. Some examples might be tying up the major distributors in a new market area before the competition can make a move, or becoming the sole source for a particular product such as a new computer software package, electronic device, or enhanced electronic processing of an existing device. Being able to pull off such a preemptive move can put your competition at a substantial disadvantage for some period of time.

3. **Synergy.** The benefits of synergy (where the total is greater than the sum of its parts) can occur when an organization has an advantage due to its connection with another business entity. The two entities may share sales and marketing efforts, research and development capabilities, office and support staff, and facilities, warehousing, and so on. With the element of synergy, the two or more entities may be able to offer the potential customer/client the products or services that are desired that neither might be able to do alone. For example, a traditional computer electronics retailer might link together with a computer software development company to provide clients with full hardware and software computer systems development services.

First the strategy, then the execution.

Business Models

Business strategies often dictate and define a specific business model on which the business operates its business activities—for instance, business models of pay first (in whole or partial payment), and then provide the goods or services afterward; or a business model of knock-your-socks-off customer services. Examples of nationally known business models related to strategic thrusts are:

- **Quality differentiation.** Maytag appliances and Michelin tires
- **Low cost, minimal frills.** Wal-Mart and Target stores, Kia automobiles, Southwest Airlines
- **Discount clothing stores (focus).** Ross for Less, TJ Maxx
- **Customer service focus.** Old IBM, more recent Dell, Caterpillar farm equipment, office supply catalog/Internet companies (Quill, the old Viking)
- **Technological position (preemption).** Microsoft operating systems (Windows and Vista), Apple Ipod, RIM BlackBerry
- **Owner/employee satisfaction and gratification.** Old Ben and Jerry's, Tom's Toothpaste, alternative energy
- **Innovation and creativity.** Cisco systems, software development and video game companies, and computer animation
- **Synergy.** Office Depot and Gateway, AT&T and Cingular, Johnson & Johnson and McNeil Labs (Tylenol), Adobe and Macromedia
- **Stock brokers focus.** Charles Schwab, E-Trade as opposed to Smith Barney and Merrill Lynch
- **Internet preemption.** Google, e-bay, Amazon, Priceline
- **Outsourcing.** Electronic manufacturing (Solectron, Flextronics), call centers (First Data, Dubai, India)
- **Food service.** Fast food (McDonalds, Burger King, Taco Bell, Pizza Hut), restaurant chains (Olive Garden, PF Chang's, TGIF, Applebees, Cracker Barrel)
- **Brand recognition and preemption.** Starbucks coffee, Polo and Chaps clothing, Nike athletic gear
- **High-end status.** Mercedes, BMW, Lexus, Range Rover, JennAir, Sub Zero

It is important to understand the various existing business models so that you can take the best advantage of their strengths and be able to avoid or remediate their weaknesses. And remember, it is the second mouse that gets the cheese. As you probably will be starting or are operating more of a local business it is also a good procedure to analyze the business models of those businesses operating in your local area—as to which models seem to be successful and which are not. Keep in mind that you may be competing with these local businesses, but that those national concerns are also your competition and may be more formidable competitors.

FRONT-END STRATEGY ANALYSIS

In developing specific strategies for an individual small business, unique characteristics and qualities relevant to the business's operations must be identified. This normally requires some front-end analysis to determine exactly what strategies will be most effective. Some factors to consider relative to developing specific strategies include the following:

- **Market orientation.** This is the business's awareness of its external environment, including customers, competitors, and the marketplace. The goal here is to develop customer-sensitive strategies that utilize the business's market strengths.

- **Proactivity.** This means attempting to influence events in the environment as opposed to merely reacting to forces as they occur. Examples are lobbying for changes to a law that will significantly affect the business, or trying to exploit a situation that at first glance appears to have totally negative implications (e.g., providing environmental cleanup, toxic waste disposal, or waste management services).

- **Information systems.** There is need for the identification of existing information systems and their capability to provide accurate and timely data to make the strategy development process operate effectively. This includes the determination of what information is required, how to provide it, and processing and analysis requirements. Another factor to consider is the ability to provide online data so that strategic changes can be made more responsively.

- **Entrepreneurial style.** This emphasizes the business's need to be more responsive to opportunities and not let an unwieldy management system bog down the decision-making process.

- **Multiple strategies.** Use of multiple strategies rather than a single strategy with related financial projections may help in the development of the most effective overall strategy. The focus, however, should be on the strategy development and not on the financial projections.

- **Implementation capability.** While proper strategy development is extremely important, it provides no more than a theoretical set of alternatives unless they can be implemented. For the process to work, the strategy must first fit the business's needs and opportunities and then be capable of being implemented effectively.

For it to work, the strategy must fit the business's needs.

Overview of the Strategy Development Process

An overview of the strategy development process is shown in Exhibit 2.4. It depicts the external and internal analyses that provide the inputs into strategy development, strategic decisions, and related strategic management.

External Analysis

External analysis involves a review of the relevant elements external to the business, focusing on the identification of opportunities, threats and constraints, strategic questions, and alternatives. Inasmuch as there are many external factors that can be considered, it is important that the external analysis not be overdone, since this could result in substantial cost in terms of time and resources. Some elements that could be reviewed in an external analysis include:

External Analysis
· Customer analysis
· Competitive analysis
· Industry analysis
· Environmental analysis
  · Technological
  · Regulatory
  · Economic
  · Cultural/social
  · Socio-economic
  · Geographic
· Opportunities, threats, and
  strategic questions

Internal Analysis
· Performance analysis
  · Return on investment
  · Market share
  · Product line analysis
  · Cost structure
  · Systems
  · Personnel capability
· Determination of strategic
  options
  · Past and current strategies
  · Strategic problems
  · Organizational capabilities
    & constraints
  · Financial resources
· Strengths, weaknesses, and
  strategic questions

Strategy Identification and Selection
1. Define the corporate mission
2. Identify the strategic alternatives
   · By product or service
   · By strategic investment thrust
   · Growth/expansion
   · Stability
   · Retrenchment/harvest
   · Divestiture/liquidation
   · By functional competence
   · Fuctional area strategies
   · By unique competitive advantage
   · Organizational proficiency or competence
3. Select the strategy
   · Consider strategic questions
   · Evaluate strategic alternatives
4. Implement the strategy
   · Develop operating plans
5. Review the strategies and replan as required
   · Install timely and accurate information/control systems

EXHIBIT 2.4   **Overview of the Strategy Development Process**
External Analysis

- *Customer analysis* involves identifying the business's customer/client base and their needs. Particular emphasis is placed on products/services desired, special requirements, quality, and service considerations.

- *Competitive analysis* includes the identification of competitors, both existing and potential. Areas that could be included in competitive analysis are intensity of competition, competitors' performance, their objectives (i.e., are they the same as yours?), strategies employed, strengths, weaknesses, and so on.

- *Industry analysis* focuses on determining the potential of the industry in general and the products/services within the industry. For instance, will your business and others be able to earn sufficient profits, or is the industry or product/service so competitive that attractive profits are unlikely to be attained? Elements that can be included in the analysis are industry size or potential, growth prospects, competitive intensity, barriers to entry (or to exit), threat of substitution, the power of suppliers and customers, cost structure, distribution/marketing channels, industry/product/service trends, and key success factors (such as quality, customer service, customer relationships, etc.).

- *Environmental analysis* focuses on factors outside the business that may create opportunities for or threats (and constraints) to the business. This analysis is limited so that it does not become excessive in terms of time and scope. Areas to include are:
  - Technological changes (i.e., impact of new developments)
  - Regulatory issues (effects of new or pending legislation)
  - Economic factors (effects of general economic conditions)
  - Cultural/social considerations (what's "in" or "hot" in the market)
  - Demographic trends (ages, patterns, socioeconomic changes, population patterns)
  - Geographic factors (rust-/sunbelt patterns, urban/suburban/rural changes, transportation considerations, weather, etc.)

No small business is an island.

Internal Analysis

Internal analysis involves achieving a detailed understanding of areas of strategic importance within the organization. An examination of the business's strengths and weaknesses and their impact on the strategic issues is a relevant part of this process. The appropriate considerations can be categorized as:

- *Performance analysis,* which evaluates the performance of the business in terms of financial results (e.g., return on investment) as well as other performance measures such as market share, product line analysis and performance, cost information, product development, management systems, personnel capabilities, and so on.

- *Determination of strategic options,* which focuses on a review of those elements of the business that influence strategy choices, such as past and current strategies; strategic problems that, if uncorrected, could cause significant damage (e.g., insufficient professional staff or other resources); organizational capabilities and constraints; financial resources/constraints; flexibility to change; strengths/weaknesses (build on strengths or neutralize weaknesses); and so on.

Look inward for the right strategies.

Strategy Identification and Selection

There are three basic steps in the strategy identification and selection process:

1. Define the business's mission.
2. Identify the strategic alternatives.
3. Select the strategy.

The recommended first step in an effective external and internal analysis is to *define the business's mission:* "Why is the business in existence and what is its purpose?" A good mission statement usually defines the areas in which business is conducted, how the business is conducted, and what makes it unique. In addition, the mission statement can state growth directions, business philosophy, behavioral standards and ethics, human relations philosophies, financial goals, and so on.

The mission statement is unique to the business.

The second step, *identifying the strategic alternatives*, could include the following considerations:

Strategic Investment Thrust

- Growth/expansion
- Stability (i.e., status quo)
- Retrenchment/harvest
- Divestiture/liquidation

Competitive Advantage Strategies

- Functional areas (e.g., sales, service, quality)
- Use of assets and skills
- Differentiation
- Low cost
- Focus
- Preemption
- Synergy

There is always a best strategic alternative.

Some criteria to consider in the third step of the strategy identification process include:

- Responsiveness to opportunities and threats
- Use of competitive advantage
- Consistency with mission statement and objectives
- Feasibility and realism

- Compatibility with the internal business
- Consistency with other business strategies
- Organizational flexibility
- Use of organizational synergy
- Exploitation of business strengths and/or competitor weaknesses
- Minimization/neutralization of business weaknesses and/or competitor strengths

Select the strategy—then just do it.

Some Basic Business Principles

Once the small business has defined the reason(s) for its existence and its purpose together with an encompassing mission statement, the owners must define the basic business principles on which they desire to operate and have the business function. Small business owners have the right to define whatever business principles they desire and to expect their employees to follow such principles. However, the definition of such business principles provides clear communication to all employees (and customers) as to how the business is to operate. Each small business must determine the specific basic principles on which it conducts its operations. These principles then become the foundation on which the business bases its desirable operations and results.

Examples of such business principles include:

- Produce the best-quality product at the least possible cost.
- Set selling prices realistically, so as to sell the entire product that can be produced within the constraints of the production facilities.
- Build trusting relationships with critical vendors; keeping them in business is keeping the company in business.
- The company is in the customer service and cash conversion businesses.

- Do not spend a dollar that does not need to be spent; a dollar not spent is a dollar to the bottom line. Control costs effectively; there is more to be made here than increased sales.

- Manage the company; do not let it manage the managers. Provide guidance and direction, not crises.

- Identify the company's customers and develop marketing and sales plans with the customers in mind. Produce for the company's customers, not for inventory. Serve the customers; do not sell them.

- Do not hire employees unless they are absolutely needed, and only when they increase the company's effectiveness so that the company makes more from them than it would without them.

- Keep property, plant, and equipment to the minimum necessary to maintain customer demand.

- Plan for the realistic, but develop contingency plans for the unexpected.

With sensible business principles, the business can be clear as to the direction for positive movement and avoid merely improving poor practices. Clear business principles that make sense to all levels of the organization allow the business to identify and develop the proper operational practices. In this manner, everyone in the organization is moving in the same desired direction.

Owners can do it their way—or the right way.

Mental Models and Belief Systems

Many businesses operate on the basis of prevalent mental models or belief systems—usually emanating from present (and past) owners and management. These mental models have an overriding effect on the conditions with which operations within the business are carried out. They can help to produce a helpful working environment or atmosphere or a hindering one. In effect, such mental models become performance drivers—those elements within the business that shape the direction of how employees will perform their functions. Examples include:

- Hard work and doing what you are told are the keys to success.
- The obedient child in the company survives and is promoted, while the rebellious child is let go or leaves the company.
- Only owners/managers can make decisions.
- Power rises to the top—and stays there.
- Employees need to be watched for them to do their jobs.
- Power and control over employees is necessary to get results.
- Owners/managers are responsible; employees are basically irresponsible.
- Those at the top of the organization know what they are doing.
- All functions should be organized in the same manner.
- Higher levels of organization are needed to ensure that lower levels do their jobs.
- Policing and control over employees is needed to ensure their compliance.
- All employees are interchangeable.
- Doing the job right is more important than doing the right job.
- Control the people, control the results.
- Organizational position is more important than being right.
- Owners/managers have the right to set all policies and procedures.
- Owners/managers create results—employees do the job.
- Organizational hierarchies are needed to ensure that things get done.
- Employees cannot be trusted on their own.
- You cannot run a business without the proper organization structure.
- Owners/managers know more than employees.
- Owners/managers have a right to be obnoxious.
- Owners/managers are the enemy.
- Each function needs its own organization structure.
- The more employees reporting to you (and the larger your budget), the more important you are within the organization.

The accurate identification of organizational mental models, belief systems, and performance drivers is extremely important in analyzing the business's operations. If these things are not changed, operational changes will merely change the system and not the business results.

If you believe it, *then it is so.*

Situational Analysis: Planning Questions

In developing the strategic thrusts for your small business there are many questions that must be asked relative to your specific situation. Some examples of the questions that you might ask related to your situation include:

Industry

- Does the organization have a clear idea of the market in which it is operating?

- What is happening to the industry in which the organization is operating? Is it growing or declining? What are the expectations about it, now and compared to last year?

- What is the current size of the market and the organization's market share? Has the organization acquired a greater market share over the past years or has its share declined? Compared with last year, what changes have there been in the organization's market share? Has market share declined or grown compared with last year?

- Compared with last year, has the competitive position changed?

- How much of an idea does the organization have of the impact of political and economic trends on their prospects?

- What are the chances of legislative controls changing during the planning period?

- How good an idea does the organization have of the likely changes in the social environment over the planning period?

- Does the nature of the product sold in the industry vary from year to year?
- How do you rate the ability of the company to define likely future sales?
- Over the past years, how closely have the organization's products followed the price trends in the market?
- What degree of seasonality is apparent in the industry?
- How extreme are the long-term fluctuations in the demand for the particular product or service?
- How much money is the company spending on research and development in relation to competition?

Market

- How clear an idea does the organization have of the functional divisions in the market and the type of product or service that it demands?
- When was the last time that the organization sought customers' views on its products?
- What are the effects on the profitability of the business of lowering and raising price on volume of sales?
- Is the organization knowledgeable of the effects of lowering price on volume?
- How does the quality of the organization's products/services compare with competitive products/services selling at more or less the same price?
- How much of the organization's product range is sold at a significant discount (i.e., 25% off list price)?
- How closely has the organization analyzed the potential profitability of a change in credit policy?
- How closely has the organization analyzed inventory levels to achieve the level of service that it considers necessary in the marketplace?
- Has the organization considered potential financial and marketing benefits in its product distribution methods?

- Does the organization know the costs of current delivery methods and of individual deliveries?
- Have alternative distribution methods been considered?
- How much of overall sales are provided by products more than 10 years old? Five years old? Three years old?
- What is the level of control over new product development?
- To what extent are brand opportunities exploited?
- To what extent do major customers (5 to 10) contribute to the organization's sales and profitability?
- What amount of sales is achieved from outside the organization's immediate geographic area?
- What system exists for evaluating the effectiveness of the sales effort?
- What are the specific service standards established for employees?
- What system exists for monitoring operational performance?
- Has the organization considered the potential for improving the speed of service by technological innovation?

Production

- What percentage of production is accurately costed in terms of direct costs like material, labor, machine time, etc.?
- What proportion of the total cost of production of the normal production run is made up of startup or setup costs?
- To what extent is the capacity of the existing plant or machinery fully utilized?
- Are the amounts of raw materials and components effectively evaluated as to minimums required to maintain production?
- Does the organization evaluate the range of products it produces in relation to the effects on production efficiency?
- How much of the finished-goods inventory is over six months old?
- What system of quality control is used over products/services?
- Does the organization evaluate in-house manufacture versus outside purchase opportunities?

- How many suppliers does the organization depend on for the bulk of its raw materials and components?
- How much of the organization's products/services are produced in the most efficient method?
- How much has labor productivity increased over the last year?
- By how much would replacing the current machinery improve efficiency?
- To what extent could production efficiency be improved by better physical layout or a change in facilities?
- Does the organization consider using outside help to improve production processes?

Financial Analysis

- How easy is it to manage and understand the accounting system?
- How accurately is cash flow analyzed and controlled?
- How have overheads, expressed as a percentage of sales, changed over the last three years?
- What measures are used to assess the various elements of operational performance?
- What is the change in the level of bad debts over the last three years?
- What system is used to evaluate capital investment opportunities and how are decisions made?
- Is the tax and pension planning structured to maximize the return to the organization?
- Does the organization have a stated policy relative to additional financing and borrowing?

Personnel

- To what extent are employees involved in the planning process?
- To what extent do employees feel involved in what the organization is doing?

- Is there a form of profit-sharing among the employees?

- To what extent is the nature of each individual job defined (and the authority and responsibility that go with it)?

- How does the organization review personnel requirements for the future?

- How many (number and/or percent) have done exactly the same job over ten years? Five years? Three years?

- What are the organization's recruitment procedures?

- How many employees have received no training over the last year? Two years? Three years?

- What is the level of absenteeism for illness over the past few years? Level of accidents?

- What are the employee grievance procedures?

- How well does the organization understand its legal obligations relative to personnel concerns?

CHAPTER 3

Planning and Budgeting: Identifying the Right Direction and Staying on the Path

A good starting point in understanding the operating processes of the business is to understand the organization, why it is in existence, and what it is trying to accomplish (i.e., its goals and objectives). To accomplish this, there needs to be an understanding of the business's planning methods and related budgeting and control processes. Focus should be on the business's approach to planning and its integration with the budgeting process. The business's planning and budgeting techniques should be a means of achieving improved organizational effectiveness. There should be an awareness of the elements of an effective planning/budgeting system to compare with the business's present practices. Keep in mind that many small businesses, as previously stated, do very little planning (and no budgeting) except on a crisis or day-to-day basis. Whatever plans might exist live in the head of the owner or on an informal basis.

For the small business to be most effective in its efforts to grow and be profitable, there should be interaction and interdependence of the strategy development, short-term planning (what directions do we want to move toward?), detail planning (how are we going to get there?), budgeting (what resources do we allocate to the plan?), and monitoring (how are we doing?) processes. The planning process should be an essential first step in the preparation of an effective budget or profit plan for the business. By learning effective planning and budgeting procedures, the small business owner and management team will be able to more effectively review and analyze operating procedures on an organization-wide, departmental, or specific function basis.

*The plan—*long and short term*—begets the budget.*

Relationship between the Planning and Budgeting Process

Although small businesses may plan and budget, many consider these processes as separate. In reality, they should be one process. Planning comes first until the business defines its goals and objectives. Knowing where to allocate resources, including financial resources, constitutes the budget process. All organizations plan; all organizations budget. Some do it formally, others informally (or even furtively); some are effective, others ineffective or even counterproductive in their methods. But all organizations do it! The advantages of formalizing and throwing open the planning and budgeting process provides an open, integrated, and reasonably structured process that significantly benefits the long-term visibility of the business. It is for these benefits that this area is considered a critical function to include in the small business's striving for success.

Planning is a management function that should not be ignored because the business is small.

Every organization must plan for its future direction if it desires to achieve its goals and objectives—whether a manufacturer, service provider, wholesaler, or retailer. The organizational plan is an agreed-on course of action to be implemented in the future (short and long term) and directed toward moving the business closer to its stated goals and objectives. The planning process, if exercised effectively, forces the business to:

- Review and analyze past accomplishments.
- Determine present and future needs.
- Recognize strengths and weaknesses.

It also enables the organization to:

- Identify future opportunities.
- Define constraints or threats that may get in the way.
- Establish business, departmental, and functional goals and objectives.
- Develop action plans based on the evaluation of alternatives.

Prioritize the selection of action plans for implementation based on the most effective use of limited resources.

> Planning on the front end produces results on the back end.

The first step in the planning process is to determine why the organization is in existence. Once the organization has identified all of the reasons that it is in existence and has articulated them by means of a *mission statement*, the next step is to define related organizational goals, both long and short term. Owners and top management typically formulate these organizational goals, although it is a good practice to obtain feedback from lower-level managers, supervisors, and operating personnel as to the appropriateness, practicality, reasonableness, and attainability of the stated goals. A good rule to keep in mind in the development of an effective business plan is that in most businesses it is the employees closest to day-to-day operations that usually know most about present problems and what needs to be done to correct them. Accordingly, the business that wishes to be most successful over the long term must have everyone (i.e., representatives from many levels) in the organization involved in the planning process from beginning to end. Many small businesses have been unsuccessful in their planning efforts and their ability to survive because of lack of foresight and their inability to use employees' input creatively.

The small business planning process encompasses everyone—from top to bottom.

In addition, operating personnel need to know how to plan properly and operate according to such plans (putting the plans into action) in order to conduct their operations successfully in an integrated and coordinated way. Operations personnel cannot plan for their own areas effectively unless they understand and agree with the organization's long- and short-term goals and have had the opportunity to provide significant input and feedback concerning these plans. It is not sufficient that operations personnel be allowed merely to provide input and feedback; top management must actively encourage their input and seriously consider it in the finalization of goals. The development of goals must be internalized as a system of top-to-bottom agreement for it to be most successful.

Graphic depictions of the organizational planning process are shown in Exhibits 3.1 and 3.2.

Owners have decision-making power, but employees know what is going on.

However, it must be understood that owners and management have the ultimate decision-making power and therefore may still decide to do whatever they desire, regardless of operations personnel input. The result of such exclusive top management decision making, however, is goal setting by directive rather than by participation. Because operations staff will see these goals as the owner's and management's and not their own, they not only will

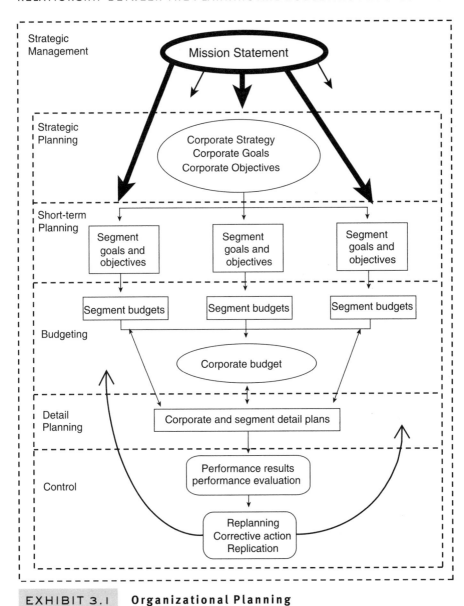

EXHIBIT 3.1   Organizational Planning

be less inclined to direct efforts toward their achievement, but may work openly against or even sabotage their accomplishment. In an effective planning system, it is extremely important to have everyone in the organization working toward the same goals. In this manner, management

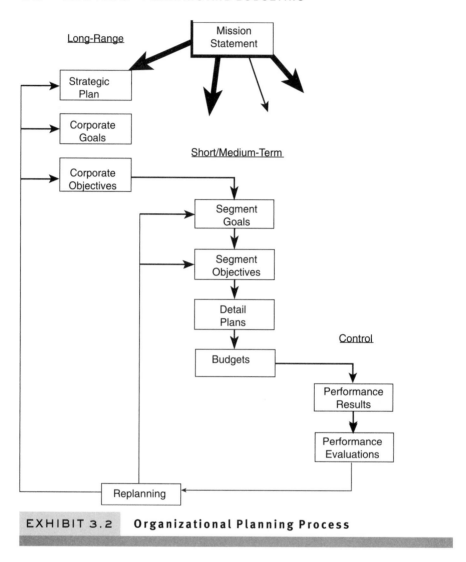

EXHIBIT 3.2   **Organizational Planning Process**

and operations staff are far more likely to make decisions that are consistent with overall plans and direction.

PLANNING PROCESS

Within this framework, how then does a small business plan effectively for its future? The planning process is shown in the organizational planning process exhibits (3.1 and 3.2). Note that in the development of long– and short–range plans, which includes the development of detail plans and related budgets, a *top-to-bottom* approach is used, whereby owners and top management and operations management and staff interact and communicate, resulting in an agreed-on set of overall business plans (strategic plans, business goals, and objectives) and functional objectives, detail plans, and budgets.

The strategies and long-range goals established by top management then have to be translated into more specific functional goals and objectives. Definitions of goals and objectives are:

Goals: Statements of broad direction that describe future states or outcomes of the business to be attained or retained that indicate ends toward which the business's effort is to be directed—which may or may not be attainable.

Objectives: Measurable, desired accomplishments related to one or more goals where attainment is desired within a specified time frame and can be evaluated under specifiable conditions.

Characteristics of objectives are:

- **Measurable.** Attainment (or lack thereof) can be clearly identified.
- **Explicit.** There is clear indication of who, what, when, and how.
- **Time Specific.** They are to be accomplished within a stipulated period of time.
- **Realistic.** They are capable of being attained within the time frame specified and with the expenditure of a reasonable and cost-effective amount of effort and resources.

Note that goals are broad directions or targets that the business or function desires to move toward and that they may or may not be achievable. Objectives are specific desired results, relating to one or more goals, that can be attained within a given time frame. Normally, short-term goals and objectives are developed for a specific planning cycle (often annually) for both the business as a whole and each functional unit. As the owners and management are responsible for developing the long-term goals, so operating managers and staff should be responsible for developing and implementing the short-term goals and objectives within the framework of the overall long-term plans.

> ## EXAMPLE: LONG-TERM GOALS AND SHORT-TERM GOALS AND OBJECTIVES
>
> This example demonstrates the relationship between long-term goals and short-term goals and objectives.
> A long-term goal of the business may be:
>
> "To become the industry sales leader for product line YY."
>
> A related short-term goal might be:
>
> "To increase sales in units of product line YY."
>
> A specific short-term objective for this planning cycle then could be:
>
> "To increase sales in units of product number 3 of product line YY by at least 10 percent over last year."
>
> The short term supports the long term; the detail plan supports the short term.

This specific objective can then be translated into specific detail plans (i.e., how to go about achieving the specific objective) and related performance expectations for sales, manufacturing, accounting, and other functions. In effect, these short-term objectives and related detail plans become the starting point for the budget process. The beginning budget will then reflect what is necessary (in terms of labor, materials, facilities, equipment, and other costs) to meet the agreed-on short-term objectives. When the owners and management approve each budget, it will reflect the authorized level of expenditures needed to fulfill the objectives by following through on agreed-on detail plans. At this point, each manager/supervisor and other employees have theoretically been delegated the authority to incur the expenditures to make each detail plan workable. Finally, each employee is responsible for a detail plan, and a budget can be evaluated based on his or her ability to effectively work the plan to achieve established short-term objectives.

The short-term planning cycle is shown graphically in Exhibit 3.3 and short-term planning steps are shown in Exhibit 3.4.

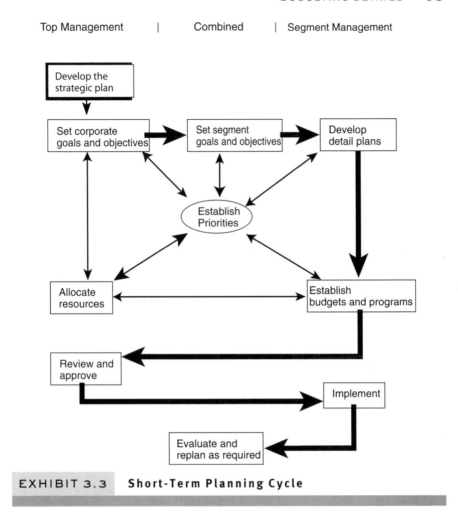

Top Management | Combined | Segment Management

EXHIBIT 3.3   Short-Term Planning Cycle

BUDGETING DEFINED

In a business, no matter how small, functional disciplines (e.g., sales, manufacturing/service delivery, marketing, purchasing, information technology [IT], accounting, etc.) are all interdependent. Therefore, all these functions must work together to successfully achieve business goals and objectives—and operating results. The overall plans and direction of the business must be clearly communicated so that owners and managers in functional areas are aware of what needs to be done to ensure smooth integration with other areas and for the entire business. Effective profit

EXHIBIT 3.4   Short-Term Planning Steps

planning and budgeting are among the tools used to coordinate the business plans and the detailed activities of each of the disciplines.

The budget is a detailed plan depicting the manner in which monetary resources will be acquired and used over a period of time. The budget is a quantitative manifestation of the next year of the business's strategic, long- and short-term plans, and the related detail plans. It is part of the short-term operating plan. The overall budget summarizes the business's plans (i.e., goals and objectives) for the future time period, providing for the allocation of financial resources to agreed-on operating plans. It is a statement of owner/management expectations and establishes specific targets relative to such things as sales, operating costs, production/sales levels, general and administrative expenses, and other monetary transactions for the time period covered. Budgeting should result in projected revenues by type of sale (e.g., product/service and customer) and expenses (e.g., product/service, functional, and customer). In effect, the budget reflects owner/management short-term plans for the operating period—and how these plans are to be carried out expressed in financial terms.

DEVELOPING AND MONITORING THE BUDGET

Effective profit planning and budgeting are among the tools used to coordinate the business plans and the detailed activities of each function. The budget is then a detailed plan depicting the manner in which monetary resources will be acquired and used over a period of time. The budget is the quantitative manifestation of the current year of the company's strategic plan. It is an integral part of the business's short-term operating plan.

The business's budget system, within the preceding definitions, can be initiated and maintained through the computer system. Revenue transactions can be automatically posted through the recording of sales transactions. These sales data can be compared to sales forecasts (e.g., by sales person, customer, product, customer, etc.). Expense transactions can be automatically posted against the budget system with suspect items flagged and automatic budget adjustments processed. The budget should be considered as part of the company planning process and as a continual process (not once a year) with flexible budgeting concepts considered. In this manner, the plan can be continuously reviewed and updated along with the corresponding budget.

Once goals, objectives, and detail plans are determined throughout the business, the allocation of scarce resources—that is, budgeting—can take place. An example of a static budget system monthly report for a small business's two manufacturing divisions is shown in Exhibit 3.5. Such budgeting concepts are based on static conditions and operations, with no changes in operations or activity levels during the budget period.

As no business conducts its operations totally according to its plan and budget, as planned activities change, so must the corresponding budget. Thus planning and budgeting are ongoing and ever-changing processes. Reflecting budget changes based on activity changes is known as *flexible budgeting*. An example of a flexible budget for manufacturing operations is shown in Exhibit 3.6.

EXHIBIT 3.5   Manufacturing Budget Report

(ooo's omitted in dollar amounts)

	Division A			Division B		
	Budget	Actual	Variance	Budget	Actual	Variance
Units produced	20,000	18,000	(2,000)	20,000	24,000	4,000
Sales	$ 1,000	$ 940	($ 60)	$1,000	$ 1,152	$ 52
Costs:						
Material	200	190	10	200	225	(25)
Direct labor	140	130	10	140	160	(20)
Variable overhead	135	125	10	135	158	(23)
Fixed overhead	175	170	5	175	173	2
Total costs	650	615	35	650	716	(66)
Gross profit	$ 350	$ 325	($ 25)	$ 350	$ 436	$ 86

EXHIBIT 3.6   Manufacturing Budget Report—Flexible

(ooo's omitted in dollar amounts)

	Division A			Division B		
	Budget	Actual	Variance	Budget	Actual	Variance
Units Produced	20,000	18,000	(2,000)	20,000	24,000	4,000
Sales	$ 900	$ 940	$ 40	$ 1,200	$ 1,152	($ 48)
Costs:						
Material	180	190	(10)	240	225	15
Direct labor	126	130	(4)	168	160	8
Variable overhead	122	125	(3)	162	158	4
Fixed overhead	175	170	5	175	173	2
Total costs	603	615	(12)	745	716	29
Gross profit	$ 297	$ 325	$ 28	$ 455	$ 436	($ 19)

NONMANUFACTURING BUDGETS

Nonmanufacturing businesses, such as retailers, wholesalers, and service providers, have just as critical a need for effective planning and budgeting as do manufacturing businesses. However, the budgeting process is not typically as complex. As in the case of manufacturing businesses, a nonmanufacturer's budgeting process should start with a sales forecast or estimate of revenues. Although such businesses are not concerned with manufacturing issues, they are concerned with the purchase of merchandise for resale and/or provision of labor-intensive services. The amount of these purchases and costs of labor are obviously related to expected sales and must be budgeted for. Some small businesses are more likely to budget on the basis of cash flows (receipts and expenditures) as opposed to revenues and expenses. The budget process is more likely to start with expenditures than with receipts. In effect, the budgeting problem becomes one of determining the amount of revenues necessary to support the level of expenditures desired or perceived to carry out the business's mission.

An expenditures-driven budgeting process normally lends itself to a *line item* type of budget, with standard line item expenses (e.g., personnel, fringe benefits, materials and supplies, equipment, etc.) for each function that expends funds. Such line-item-type budgets normally require a line-by-line expenditure submission and approval. Due to these line item budget constraints, this type of budgeting system usually prevents individual functional managers from exercising their discretion in using budgeted funds to achieve stated goals and objectives. The inherent problem with line item budgeting is the emphasis on individual expense items and types of costs as opposed to concentration on objectives and results to be accomplished.

An example of a static and flexible budget for a service organization is shown in Exhibit 3.7.

CONCLUSION

It would be nice to think that every small business, from the largest to the smallest, has an effective planning and budgeting system as described in this chapter. However, in reality you may find that very few small businesses come close to planning and budgeting in this manner. In cases where such planning and budgeting systems do not exist or are found to be deficient, one must superimpose such concepts on the business or area under study to establish desired results. You must also keep in mind that the task is to determine not merely the existence of such planning systems, but the effectiveness of these planning systems in moving the business in the right direction toward growth and profitability. To be most effective, the planning

EXHIBIT 3.7	The Example Agency-Counselling Component

Static Budget Report

	Budget	Actual	Better (Worse) than Budget
Revenues			
• Units of service	600	540	$ (1,800)
• Average charge per hour	$ 30	$ 26	(2,160)
Total revenues	$ 18,000	$ 14,040	(3,960)
Expenses			
• Personnel	13,968	12,440	1,528
• Materials and supplies	767	1,682	(915)
• Rent	500	500	0
• Utilities	667	783	(116)
• Insurance	300	1,460	(1,160)
• Transportation	100	180	(80)
• Contracted services	50	400	(350)
• Other expenses	60	12	48
Total expenses	16,412	17,457	(1,045)
Excess of revenues over (under) expenses	$ 1,588	$ (3,417)	$ (5,005)

Flexible Budget Report

	Original Budget	Adjusted Budget	Actual	Better (Worse) than Budget
Revenues				
• Units of service	600	540	540	0
• Average charge per hour	$ 30	$ 30	$ 26	$ (2,160)
Total revenues	$ 18,000	$16,200	$ 14,040	$ (2,160)
Expenses				
• Personnel	13,968	12,351	12,440	(89)
• Materials and supplies	767	690	1,682	(992)
• Rent	500	500	500	0
• Utilities	667	600	783	(183)
• Insurance	300	243	1,460	(1,217)
• Transportation	100	90	180	(90)
• Contracted services	50	400	400	0
• Other expenses	60	12	12	0
Total expenses	16,412	14,886	17,457	(2,571)
Excess of revenues over (under) expenses	$ 1,588	$ 1,314	$ (3,417)	$ (4,731)

Financial Approach to Budgeting

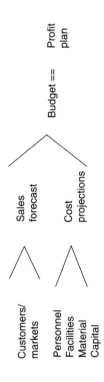

Customers/
markets

Sales
forecast

Personnel
Facilities
Material
Capital

Cost
projections

Budget == Profit
plan

Budget calculated . . . goals, objectives, etc. may or may not be developed to support it.

Planning Approach to Budgeting

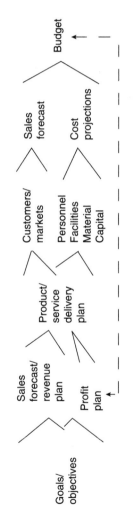

Goals/
objectives

Sales
forecast/
revenue
plan

Profit
plan

Product/
service
delivery
plan

Customers/
markets

Personnel
Facilities
Material
Capital

Sales
forecast

Cost
projections

Budget

Budget flows from goals, objectives, and the organization planning process.

EXHIBIT 3.8 **Approaches to Budgeting**

system must be continually attended to and the related budget flexible so that it supports the plan rather than making it more difficult to achieve results. The budget is alive, not static.

Exhibit 3.8 is a schematic that shows the difference in approaches to the budgeting process as follows:

- Financial approach to budgeting
- Planning approach to budgeting

The first step in planning is to determine why the organization or work unit is in existence in the first place.

CHAPTER 4

Improving Customer Service

*C*ustomer service is the business you are in*. Without customer service you have no business. Whether you believe your customer service is good, bad, or indifferent—it can always be improved. Outstanding customer service does not need to be a cost center, but rather a profit center that develops a quality customer base that pays huge dividends in customer loyalty, repeat business, and referrals—which results in increased real profits. The purpose of this chapter is to discuss how you and your business can achieve results-oriented customer service.

> A customer in the hand is worth two in the future.

Perhaps you have found that lucky niche (the small-business Holy Grail) and manufacture or sell a one-of-a-kind product, one that is very technologically advanced and available nowhere else on Earth, and your handful of specialty customers all need the product. If that is the case, you probably do not need to really worry about customer service—until the inevitable competitor pops up. However, it is a good idea to service the customer now, as you do not know what the future will bring. For the vast majority of us, though, ignoring customer service is akin to ignoring a goldmine at our feet—*because customer service can make or break your business*. The wonderful news is that great customer service is one of the biggest bargains of all time, because it does not cost much more (and usually takes less time and effort) than bad customer service. Just imagine that you can get the Mercedes of customer service for not much more than the Subaru.

What is even better is the fact that great customer service is not that much harder to deliver than poor customer service. Once you know how, and make the commitment to it, it is actually pretty simple. Our task here is to get your business on the track to outstanding customer service—and to keep it that way. Great customer service starts at the top with the owners, and then worms its way into all aspects of the business.

> It is just as easy to catch an employee doing the right customer service as it is to find the wrong.

We are not going to give you lots of *rah-rah* motivational slogans (e.g., "The customer is number 1," or "Customer service is job 1, 2, and 3," or "The customer is always right"). In the long term, that is not going to do you any good. The effect of buzzwords and slogans is fleeting; instead, we are going to show you how to *reprogram the company* so that outstanding customer service becomes an integral part of doing business—second nature for all employees. Although many times it is not the owner or manager who loses a customer, but your lower-level, "nickel-an-hour" staff, the owner or manager can lose a customer just as quickly if not quicker.

Excellent customer service starts with a little pep talk to remind all of us just why great customer service is so critical—together with an understanding of exactly what excellent customer service is and what it entails. A good idea is to look at who is doing it right and who is doing it wrong. Then, evaluate how your level of customer service fits into the spectrum—among the good, the bad, and the ugly.

Looking at your present level of customer service, you will need the right information to formulate a plan for outstanding customer service—laying the groundwork so that your plan will be successful. Incorporate some great customer service ideas using the checklists, exhibits, and quick tips and tricks provided in this chapter. In doing this, you will be better able to sustain that new, great service that you will be offering to your customers.

There is more to be gained from increased sales to existing customers than from continually searching for new customers.

New-Customer Quest

Some business analysts have said that it can cost up to eight times more to get a new customer than it does to increase sales to an existing client. With my consulting firm, for every five to eight jobs that we pitched to prospective clients, I was happy to get one new customer. And it took more than just a pitch—it was a costly and time-consuming process.

Pitching a product or service to a new prospective customer can be pretty exciting. There is the thrill of the chase, travel, wonderful hotels, entertaining in fine restaurants—and there are few feelings that can equate to the rush you get when you land that big, important customer. But, stepping back from the adrenaline rush of chasing the big fish, consider whether that is the smartest approach for increasing your business. It is much more expensive to woo and land a new client than to keep and satisfy the ones you have.

A small printing firm that I worked with did a phenomenal sales and marketing job of getting new customers—they were absolutely ferocious about landing a new account. Unfortunately, once they got those new customers in-house, they were less dedicated to maintaining them, and barely recouped their cost of acquisition before they lost them. This has not put them out of business yet, but it has kept them from being more successful. Eventually, their poor reputation will catch up with them and will make getting new customers that much more difficult.

Customer service means not just getting the customer, but *keeping* the customer.

Customer service invades every aspect of your business, from obtaining new customers through great pre-sale service, to servicing your present customers so that they continue to reorder and refer you to other quality customers—even when they may not have an order in hand.

It is easier to satisfy a present customer than to hook a new one.

Consider what you have to do to get a new customer for your business. You have to:

- Determine who you want to target.
- Understand the target.
- Research the target's needs and wants.
- Determine who in the target's organization is the right person to meet.
- Call the target person.
- Arrange a meeting.
- Travel to the meeting.
- Negotiate with the target company.
- Meet again and again; communicate again and again.
- Sale is consummated, but profits from this sale will be lower to offset the not-insubstantial costs (and do you even know what these costs are?) of getting the initial sale. Of course, the longer the customer remains a customer, the more profitable each subsequent sale becomes (maybe).

Stop looking for the ultimate customer; service your present customers.

SERVICING PRESENT CUSTOMERS

Now consider what you have to do with an existing customer:

- Contact existing customer.

EXHIBIT 4.1   The Satisfied Customer

A small manufacturing business had a particularly satisfied customer named Stan, who liked to give ideas for new products. Surprisingly, a suggestion of his ultimately took the small business into a new and quite profitable line. When the owner, Mike Halloran, called Stan to thank him for his suggestion, he asked him why he had not bothered to do it himself. Stan was a nice guy, but busy running his own successful small business. Mike couldn't help but wonder why Stan had taken the time to worry about new products for his business. Mike assumed that it was because of his supersalesmanship and great personality. Stan simply replied, "I love doing business with your company...it's so easy. The other company I buy from is a pain in the___to work with. I thought, and hoped, it was something you could make, and if I could buy it from you it would make my life easier." Stan also paid his bills on time—actually ahead of time—this is a satisfied *quality* customer.

- Check on level of service being provided.
- Work out new level of service to meet both the customer's and your needs.

Ultimately, it is much easier and cheaper to sell to your existing customers. Treat them well, and in addition to their purchases they may help you in other ways. Exhibit 4.1 shows a situation where an existing customer helped a small business to grow.

At any point in time, a business may have as many as 20 to 50 percent of its customers unhappy with the level of service being provided. For instance, Stan was dissatisfied with the customer service of one business and appreciated another company's outstanding customer service, so he gave the second company his business. Outstanding customer service produces results, although it cannot always be measured. Stan was great (unpaid) advertising for the second company. When discussions of vendors came up, he had high praise for the company, which resulted in new customers. Satisfied customers help your business grow and prosper. Unhappy customers help your business into a slow excruciating bankruptcy.

Happy customers sometimes tell other businesspeople about their positive experience; unhappy ones broadcast their displeasure loud and long and often. And who can blame them? Statistically, customers with bad experiences are likely to tell as many as *eight other people* about that bad experience. So if your five customer service people are in a hurry and each gives poor service to just one customer today, that means that in one week,

200 people will have heard of your poor level of service, and in a month that number is 800. With a bit of effort, you will not be dealing with unhappy customers, at least not as many.

> One unhappy customer can spoil the entire basket.

The vast majority of people want to feel good about their jobs, and even though most of us do not have careers that involve huge contributions to humankind, every cog in the wheel is important. There is great satisfaction and pride in knowing that the service or product you provide has pleased your customer. Satisfying your customers is the *right* way to run a business. Everyone—your customers *and* employees—will be happier.

> Quality customers provide quality profits.

Striving for Outstanding Customer Service

Outstanding customer service goes far beyond a smiling store clerk and a pleasant "hello" and an automatic "have a nice day." Forcing your sales staff to say *please* and *thank you* does not necessarily make for quality customer service, but it is a start.

Outstandingly good customer service means providing a level of service so friendly, so efficient, and so professional that your customer's expectations are exceeded and they look forward to doing business with your company again.

In essence, you want a great first date so that you get a second. Perhaps this is a bit simplistic, but that is what we want—customers that return. If they like your service, there is a good chance they will be back. Each customer must be looked at not only for the current sale but for what their repeat (and referral) business means to your bottom line.

Your customers form their opinion of your business based on more than just employee contact. They will judge your service level before they even set foot in your door or speak with one of your employees. Customer service is much more subtle than that: *It is a package of services and attitudes that is delivered by the organization at the very first instant of contact—and at all future contacts.*

Outstanding customer service is more than just a smiling face.

Customer service can be considered from the following perspective:

- Is it tailored to the needs of the customers?
- Is it reliable and consistent throughout the organization?
- Does it make economic sense?
- Is it tied to the goals of the organization?
- Is it unique—does it make your business different?
- Is there a *wow* factor?

When we talk about customer service, you can see that we are talking about a really big picture. It is much more than just a smile painted on the face of the clerk behind the counter—it is a basic philosophy that permeates every aspect of your business. If your business policies and procedures are not customer friendly, then all the chipper salespeople on Earth will not give you great customer service.

It is not the present sale but all future sales that make the difference.

Customer Service Quick List

Here is a quick list of a few not-so-obvious areas that fall under the heading of customer service. Take good notice of those that apply to your business and determine what can be done to make them into customer service best practices.

Parking   Do you have plenty of it? Is your parking lot easy to navigate? How about when it rains—is it full of big puddles? Is parking for your customers most important, or do you have spaces up front by the door reserved for the manager, or "employee of the month"? Do your employees park on the fringes to save the best spots for the customers? Is the parking lot lighting adequate? Do your customers feel safe? Do customers feel like they need a flashlight to find their car at night?

Signage   Is your outdoor sign big, lighted (if necessary), and easily readable to passersby? Do interior signs make it easy for customers to find what they are looking for? Are your signs confusing the customer rather than being helpful? Are your sale signs overpowering so that the layout looks like a distressed-sale marketplace?

Phone-answering procedures   Are your customers on hold so long that they could listen twice to the long version of *Stairway to Heaven* before they are helped? Do you have an automated answering system that takes longer than 30 seconds to navigate? When someone answers your phone, does he sound genuinely pleased that the customer has called? Is this person helpful, or does the customer feel like she is bothering him?

Restrooms   Do they exist? Are they for employees only? Are they well marked? Are they easy to find, or in the darkest corner? Are they clean? Would you use them if you were a customer? Are the amenities, such as toilet paper, soap, and hand towels, always available? Are the facilities maintained properly and timely? Is the towel dispenser easy to use without water dripping down the customer? Is the restroom also your storeroom?

Pricing policies   Are items clearly marked? Are they fairly priced? Do all prices reflect advertised specials, and do you have sufficient quantities in stock? If prices are not physically marked on the items, does your system clearly display prices to the customer at the time of checkout? Are your specials clearly marked on the customer's receipt? Can the customer easily understand the sales receipt? Do you have an easy return policy?

Merchandise layout   Is it logical? Are items easy to find—by the customer as well as by your employees? Are there pickles next to motor oil, or diapers next to Tupperware? Does the layout enhance the shopping experience or make it more arduous? Looking over the merchandise, is there a *wow* factor? Are the displays clean, current, and stocked with necessary literature? Can your sales personnel answer the questions your customers have—and easily guide them to the correct item? Do you have the range and depth of products that you should?

Employee attitude   Do the employees care, or at least *act* like they care? Are they friendly without being solicitous? Are they willing to go out of their way for a customer? Do they know your products? Do they know how to handle customer concerns and problems? Are they given the authority to handle those concerns and problems?

Operating hours   Are they convenient for your group of customers? If your customers are "ladies who lunch," then 9 to 5 is fine. If your customers work from 9 to 5, is your business available to them evenings and weekends? Are your hours established for the customer instead of for the owners, managers, and employees? Is the best staff working during the high-volume hours, such as before work, during lunchtime, and after regular working hours?

Store lighting   Is it cheerful and bright? Is the light flattering to your products? Does the lighting feel good, or are even your employees depressed? Does it create a pleasant ambiance?

Print size   Do your customers need a magnifying glass to read the print on packaging and/or instruction sheets? The population is aging, small type is no fun, and having to whip out reading glasses is annoying! Are your prices and item descriptions clear and easy to read?

Shipping policies   Are they reasonable and flexible? Do you offer an express option? Do you ship more quickly than your competitors? Who pays for the shipping—is there a policy (i.e., free shipping over a certain amount)?

Is your facility clean and pleasant?   Would you shop there? Does it invite the customer in—is it warm and friendly? Is your staff helpful and courteous to customers—and not officious or pretentious? Is there an inviting "spouses corner" for the nonshoppers, or do they need to stand or walk around aimlessly?

Little things mean a lot—the difference between a customer and a badmouther.

Touchpoints

Touchpoint simply means *any point at which a (potential) customer comes into contact with your business.* That does not necessarily mean human contact; it could mean the point where they walk up to your front door or look in the window, or log onto your web site, or open the phonebook to your ad. When you think about these touchpoints, try to imagine them as actual physical entities—either they are pleasant or they are not. When your customer's call is answered at your office, is that touchpoint a pleasant stroke, or a nasty pinch? When your customer looks at your user-friendly instruction sheet, is that touchpoint a soft pat or a sharp jab in the ribs? Your overall customer service experience is built on touchpoint layered on touchpoint. Your goal should be that when customers think about their overall experience with your business, they remember a pleasant massage, not a brutal beating delivered by a well-meaning employee with a smile on his or her face— "Have a nice day!" (For a checklist of touchpoints, see Exhibit 4.2.)

Wow Moments

There just is not enough of what we like to call *wow* moments, where we walk out of the store or business and think, "*Wow!* That was great; those people really want me to buy from them." When was the last time that you heard from one of your customers that they were just bowled over by your organization? What are some of your *wow* moments? Sharing is great. We are quick to complain about bad-service moments, but what about *wow* moments? When I find a business or an employee doing customer service right, I always make it a point to let them (and the owner or manager) know so that they can incorporate such best practices into their business. Unfortunately, when I have a bad customer service experience, I tend not to say anything (who needs a confrontation?) but walk out and vow not to do business with them again.

EXHIBIT 4.2   Checklist of Touchpoints

Facility Issues
A. Parking lot

Plenty of parking close to entrance?
Well taken care of?
Well lit?
    Paved?
    Safe?
    Employee parking related to customers?

B. Signage

Big and well lit?
Easy to read and see?
Easy to find entrance?
Interior signs allow customers to find their way without being overly obtrusive?

C. Phone service

Automated System:

Does it take a long time to navigate the system?
Is the system particularly complicated?
Can user complete transaction easily and quickly on his or her own?
Length of time on-hold?
Do you tell caller how long they will be on hold?
Is there appropriate on-hold music or information being provided?
Is there a way to bypass the system and reach an extension number?
Is there a way to bypass the system and get to the operator?
How easy is it to leave a message during the day, and after-hours?
Are there instructions on operating/office hours and how to get to the facility?

Nonautomated System:

Does reception/operator sound pleased that customer has called?
Length of time on-hold?
Does someone check back with those on hold?
Can the operator give clear information resolving user's issue?

D. Restrooms

Are they clean?
Good signage leading to restrooms?

(*Continued*)

EXHIBIT 4.2   (Continued)

Safety? No dark corners leading to restrooms?
Are the entrances on video-surveillance cameras?

E. Lighting

Good and clear lighting?
Appropriate to product?
Does it make everyone (customers and employees) feel good, or depressed?

F. Layout

Easy to navigate?
Makes sense to customer?

Employee Issues

G. Employee training

Do they know the products?
Do they know where to get information that they do not have?
Do they know how to handle customer concerns and problems?
Are they given authority to handle those concerns and problems?

H. Employee attitude

Do they care? Are they friendly?
Are they willing to go out of their way for a customer?

Operations Issues

I. Operating hours

Are the hours convenient for your business segments?
Are they clearly posted and understood?
If you adjust hours based on season or time of year, is that clearly understood and communicated to your customers?
If you close at certain times of the year, is that clearly understood and communicated to your customers?

J. Safety

Safe for customers, including children?
No dark corners?
Aisles with sufficient room for customers and shopping carts?
No overstacked shelves?
No surprise end shelves?

K. Cleanliness

Is facility clean?
What happens if there is a spill?
Do products look new—no dust or spiderwebs?
Are products on shelves organized?

Sales and Marketing Issues
L. Displays

Clear and easy to understand?
Brochures available?
Product easily accessible to displays?
Easy to see prices on display and easy to see which products
they correspond to?
Are prices also marked on products?
Print size on display and brochures easy to read?

M. Web site

Print size on web site?
Speed in launching?
Information above and below the "fold"?
Information contained?
Ease of navigating the site?
Contact information available?

N. Materials

Clarity of brochure?
Print size on materials, including Yellow Pages ads?
Amount of "tech babble" in materials?

Product Issues
O. Product(s)

Do you have a range of products?
Do you have depth in your product categories?
Do you examine carefully the quality of your products before you design/
produce/sell them?
Do you have plenty of advertised products in stock?

P. Packaging

Quality and look of packaging?
Clarity/simplicity of packaging?

(Continued)

EXHIBIT 4.2 **(Continued)**

Clearly states what *is not* included?
Print size on packaging?

Q. Instruction/assembly sheets

Is it included or does customer have to go to web site?
Ease of understanding instruction?
Print size on sheets?
Is there an information number to call for after-hours users?

R. Shipping

Shipping policies—are they fair and reasonable for the customer?
Ease of getting product to customer?
Do we always look for the lowest cost for shipping?
On what basis is shipping cost—dollars or weight?
Do you charge a handling fee?

S. Return policy

Do you stand behind your products?
Ease of returns—no questions asked?
Length of time it takes to complete a return and credit the customer?
How difficult is it for the customer to complete a return?

T. Pricing

Fair pricing?
Easy to understand?
Easy to find prices/clearly marked?

U. Payment

Is it easy to pay for a purchase?
Does it take a long time to make payment?
Do you take all forms of payment (credit cards, check, and cash)?
How do you handle international payments?

Other Issues
V. Support

Can I find carts, including ones for larger products?
Can I find employee assistance when needed—in person or on the phone?
Am I forced to correspond via e-mail and then wait for a response?
Are my problems and concerns resolved to my satisfaction, timely, and correctly?

How many times do I have to communicate to get my problem solved?
Is it just as easy to pay and get out as it is to get in?
Are systems customer friendly, or for the convenience of the business?

W. Add your own!

How to Lose a Customer without Really Trying

No company ever sets out to provide poor service (even though it really seems like some do). You are not likely to see motivational slogans posted like "Screw the customer," or "Go away and leave me alone," or "Can't you see I'm on the phone?," but we can all remember times when we have had such poor customer service that we have felt that this was the actual message we were receiving. If you have not given a great deal of thought and consideration to your customers' needs and desires it is entirely possible that they may think you've got a sign or two like these posted in your office. And it is even worse when you publish and post in large letters a mission statement such as, "The customer is our business," or "May we help you?" or "Have a nice day!"

You may think that your business is manufacturing or selling widgets, but in reality, your business is servicing the customer who is purchasing those widgets. If you get too wrapped up in widgets and are not obsessed enough with the *widget customers*, you could end up with tons of widgets and no one to buy them. But all is not lost! Have an inventory clearance sale—at less than the items cost you. Lo and behold, you are now in the markdown business— and these are the prices your customers come to expect.

Being in the business of customer service means that everything you do is focused on providing the customer with the best level of service. Look at every task you do, every way that you interact with the customer, and determine whether you are doing it that way because it makes it easier for you and your employees, or whether it makes things better and more productive for your customers. But even before we look at service excellence, we need to spend some time considering poor service.

I am sure that you could bang out 15 or 20 pages, right this moment, on examples of poor customer service that you have personally experienced. This is a sad commentary on the state of American business, but it will give

EXHIBIT 4.3   Customer Dis-service 1: The Ultimate
              Shopping Site

Susan is an insomniac, and really likes to do late-night shopping through the web site of a well-known home shopping network. Her husband, Joe, tends to shop occasionally for books through a giant and well-known Internet shopping site. It is very upsetting to him that when they both order something on the same day, she gets free shipping and he pays for shipping, and his wife's order arrives in three days and his takes three weeks. Who do you think has more loyalty to their shopping web site? Who do you think looks for other options before shopping? I will give you a clue; it is not the wife.

Susan is fiercely loyal to her web site. If she wants to shop late, it is the only web site she hits. Joe is still looking for a better option, and eventually he may find it, because some company is going to figure out how to take care of his needs.

Susan's web site understands that the customer wants to be taken care of, and that shipping (cost and timeliness) is just as much a part of customer service as answering the phone quickly and pleasantly. The company Joe deals with just does not get it.

your company a huge advantage if you can learn from, rather than emulate, the bad apples. Exhibits 4.3 through 4.6 provide some examples of customer *dis*service.

Poor customer service comes in all shapes and sizes. It can be very insidious, creeping even into a company that is doing lots of big things right. Recall those *touchpoints* we talked about. An irritated customer is not a good customer.

An unhappy customer is not a good customer; a happy customer may be a customer *forever.*

Golden Rule of Customer Service

It may seem simplistic, but if you examine truly great customer service, and distill it to the most elemental level, you will see that it is essentially making it easy for the customer to do business with you.

I like to fly Southwest Airlines. Sometimes I will choose Southwest even if the ticket price is a bit higher. It is not because their employees are friendlier

EXHIBIT 4.4   Customer Dis-service 2: The Rental Car Shuffle

Bob and Sandy rented a car through a very well-known rental car company (that claimed it was trying harder), not at the airport location, but at one of their city offices—with no problems. The problems began with returning the car. The city office was open only until 5 P.M. and Bob was lost at 4:45.

- **Customer service error 1—lack of necessary information.** Only the airport location was identified on their map. Bob had only the city office address. Sandy called for directions and was told they were only a few minutes away and they assured her they would wait. Bob arrived at 5:05, and the office was closed.
- **Customer service error 2—lack of communication.** It turns out that cars can be returned to city offices only during business hours. There was no mailslot in which to drop the keys. Figuring that a big rental car company must have some other return option, Bob called their toll-free number. Their customer service person told him that there were five other city locations, but after putting Bob on hold, told him that all of them were already closed. Bob offered to leave the car in front of their office, locking the keys inside the car. Customer service told him that if anything happened to the car before the next morning, he would be responsible. But the airport location was open all night.

The rental car company made no provision to help customers who really needed their help. Rather than considering how policies could help their customers, they were more intent on creating policies for their comfort, but that frustrated customers and drove them away. Were they really trying harder?

EXHIBIT 4.5   Customer Dis-service 3: Doing the Airline Two Step

On a recent flight out of Boston, an airline would not allow the passengers to carry their normal hand luggage onto the airplane. Most passengers could understand that; the plane was one of those little puddle jumpers, and briefcases and rolling pilot bags just did not fit well. The flight crew took them just as passengers boarded the plane, and assured everyone they would be handed back on disembarkation. You guessed it; someone forgot to put them on board. All the checked baggage arrived, but the passengers' laptops, bags with medicines, car keys, business clothes, and other items too important to check were sitting (they thought) somewhere on the tarmac at the Boston airport. Naturally, this flight was the last of the day from Boston, and the next flight in was not due until after two in the afternoon the next day. The next day when passengers called the airline to check on the status of missing carry-ons, the toll-free number was directed to India. What do you think that airline thinks of customer service?

EXHIBIT 4.6   Customer Dis-service 4: The Great
Orthodontist

Now we have a great orthodontist—and Bill's son has a "Hollywood smile." The receptionist is friendly, the assistants are gentle, and they give free t-shirts or sport bottles with Dr. Smiley's name on it. A wow moment—maybe. Sounds like they have great customer service, Well, it is *good*, but they are missing *great* because of their business hours. Most parents work weekdays and most children attend school on weekdays. Bill has to drive to his son's school, go to the school office, sign him out, drive him to Dr. Smiley's office, return him to school, sign him back in, and return to work. Half of Bill's day is shot, and usually his son has missed something important at school. Obviously, this is not an unusual situation. Orthodontists primarily *treat children* who must be taken to the appointment by parents. Why, then, is Dr. Smiley's office open only weekdays during school and work hours?

The business model the orthodontist is using is more in keeping with 1950s America, where Mom stayed home and the schools understood about kids who missed school for medical appointments. It worked for June and the Beaver, but times have changed. Dr. Smiley's service could be better. If another orthodontist decided to open up evenings and Saturdays, he might get the business even if he did not give away free t-shirts.

(which they are) and it has nothing to do with connections. What I really like is their cancellation policy. I can change flights with no penalty—they make it very easy to do business with them.

When you formulate policies, procedures, rules, physical layout, shipping policies, and so forth, if you ask yourself, "Will this make things easier for my customer?" you will be more likely to make the correct customer service choice. It is hard to go wrong if you keep that in mind—*make it easy on the customer*. If you take away nothing else from this book but the golden rule of customer service—*easy does it*—then you will still improve your customer service.

The golden rule of customer service: Make it *easy* on the customer—easy does it.

Top Ten Things Customers Want from Your Business

1. **Customers want you to make it easy for them to do business with you.** This is the golden rule.

2. **Customers want you to have easily accessible employees.** This one is very obvious; yet all of us have encountered situations where we have had to scour a store or wait on the phone to find someone to help us.

3. **Customers want you to have knowledgeable employees.** It is not enough to have staff stationed every two feet if they cannot answer your customers' questions. It does not do much good for a clerk to ask, "May I help you?" (and have this written on their backs) if he or she *cannot really help you.* Customers not only need to know where to find items, they need to know all about those items or they need to know where to get the answers. Exhibit 4.7 provides an example of good customer service where the employees are knowledgeable about their business.

4. **Customers want you to have well-trained employees.** There is a subtle difference between *knowledgeable* and *well trained.* In the Whole Foods example in Exhibit 4.7, its staff is both. Employees have to be trained in customer service and the company's business policies. An employee can be knowledgeable about the products but ultimately blow it because he or she is poorly trained in customer service.

EXHIBIT 4.7   Less Talk — More Service Delivery

One of my favorite customer-centered organizations is Whole Foods. If you do not have a Whole Foods food market near you, someday when you are traveling, you have to seek one out in order to see for yourself this unique shopping experience. And *experience* is the right word, because this upscale grocer really delivers that to you every time you walk in their doors. However, in this context, the next time you visit one, plan on spending time asking questions. Go to the wine department and ask them for a good dessert wine. Or ask them for half-bottles of wine and see what they suggest. Looking for a good bread to go with the stew you are making for dinner? Ask the bakery, because they will have a good suggestion. Or ask the guy stocking the soup aisle where the Panko Bread Crumbs are and you will get a surprise—he will not just say "Go to aisle 10"; rather, he will stop what he is doing and *take* you to aisle 10 and show you where the bread crumbs are. And if, for some reason, the Panko has been moved, he will then find out where it has been moved to and take you there. He will talk about service; he will deliver it. Are they perfect? Absolutely not; but their level of service helps you forget about less-than-perfect lighting, overstimulating shelves, narrower aisles than you prefer, and other missteps that might otherwise drive you away from the store.

EXHIBIT 4.8   **Overnight Promises**

Bill recently had a package FedExed to him. His "overnight" package was sent on Monday. One week later, he got a call from a Federal Express representative claiming that they had tried to deliver the package Friday morning but the road was too bad. He called the station manager and pointed out that he had received a different FedEx package that same morning, and wondered why the second driver could not make it up the road. The FedEx employee promised to check into it. He said they would redeliver on their next delivery day, which was on Friday. Bill pointed out that he paid to have the package shipped "overnight" one week ago because it was urgent. He also requested a refund of the exorbitant extra fee he had paid for overnight delivery. The FedEx employee said he could not do anything about that; Bill would need to call their 800 number. The previous day, when Bill was attempting to track the package using the 800 number, he requested a credit and was told *they* could not handle it—Bill would have to talk to the station manager. Pretty clever.

5. **Customers want you to take ownership of problems.** "Sorry, that's not my department," "I'd like to help you, but it's against our policy," "Sorry, you'll have to contact the manufacturer"—I am sure some of these cop-out statements sound familiar to you. These are timeworn phrases of companies that refuse to take responsibility for solving customer problems that they have created. Such a situation is shown in Exhibit 4.8.

   One of the basic credos of good customer service is that if you promise the customer something, you need to deliver. If the company cannot deliver, it is the company's concern to make good on its promise. Avoid the customer runaround. Admit your mistake and do what has to be done to make it up to the customer. In Exhibit 4.8, FedEx should have afforded a full refund with its sincerest apologies—without the necessity of having the customer bring such a situation to its employees' attention. Be proactive in your customer service or you will not get the chance to be active.

Be proactive in your customer service or you will not get the chance to be active.

One of the largest companies to follow the credo of owning the problem is Ritz Carlton Hotels. If a guest with a problem approaches an employee, Ritz management expects that employee to fix that problem, even if it falls outside their regular job description. No passing the buck.

If you mention to the check-in clerk that you would like goosedown pillows in your room, and the hotel is out of goosedown pillows, that clerk will tell you that he will get you one as soon as possible, and then, if necessary, he will go to the store, buy a goosedown pillow, and deliver it to your room. What is really amazing is that this policy applies regardless of whether the problem is the hotel's fault. *Think Ritz-Carlton.*

There are any number of Ritz stories about employees of the hotel chain who have gotten on airplanes, given away their own shoes, and done many other things, all with a similar theme—taking ownership of a problem to take care of their customer. Ritz further allows its employees to spend up to $100.00 without management approval to solve a guest problem. Think about that for your small business.

Wait a minute, you think, and rightly so. If I charged what the Ritz charges, I could give that kind of customer service, too. That is a valid point. There is a balance in the cost/customer service equation. But, the focus here is that any organization can at the least take responsibility for problems they create for their customers. This will inevitably cause you some headaches, and it will take more time, but you must own the problem so that it will be *easy for your customers to do business with you.* And do not forget to correct the cause of the problem, not merely the symptom, so you do not spend even more time correcting the same problem over and over again.

6. **Customers want you to value their business.** It is human nature; we all want to be loved. In your customers' case, they just want to be appreciated. Do not take them for granted—*especially not repeat customers.* As we have studied and worked with clients on customer service, we have learned that organizations have a tendency to ignore problems with customers, waiting until they are really upset to try and rectify matters. They wait until the customer has made the decision to switch to a competitor, or even worse, until after he has already switched, to reach out and help—as depicted in Exhibit 4.9.

EXHIBIT 4.9   Are You a New Customer?

Here is how a satellite TV company handled a recent situation. They had been running a huge advertising campaign to attract new customers. They were offering free receivers and special packages, anything to attract new business. A customer called them to request an extra receiver, which they were advertising for free, naively assuming that they would be happy to provide a long-time customer with an extra receiver at no cost. "Sorry," replied the apologetic phone rep, "that offer is only good for *new* customers. However, if you cancel the service for three months, you could then resubscribe and as a new customer get the free receivers."

7. **Customers want you to deliver what you promise.** If you advertise that you sell or manufacture a quality widget, make certain that it is. Occasionally, you will end up with a defective product, so it is important to have a fair return policy—you want to make it easy for your customers to get a new one. That should not be happening too often, however. If your purchasing department (or manufacturing facility) is doing its job, defective products should be few and far between. Do not make the mistake of thinking that a liberal return policy will make up for an inferior product. It is irritating and time-consuming for your customers to return an item; the best customer service is to *deliver what you promise in the first place.*

If your staff tells customers that your widget will pare an apple perfectly and easily on the first try, then it had better do just that. When they use their new widget, and it mangles their apples and their fingers, because in reality it required lots of practice to get it right, you will have an unhappy customer. Your staff has given them unrealistic expectations that the product cannot meet. A well-trained staff will eliminate that type of problem. Exhibit 4.10 depicts just such a situation.

It is pretty simple. Give your customers what you say you will—and something extra. Do not promise more than you can deliver. You will all be happier.

Deliver more than you promise; do not promise more than you can deliver.

EXHIBIT 4.10   Small Print—Big Promise

Tom ordered a remote-control helicopter for his son as a Christmas gift. The item was advertised in a prestigious catalog as easy to use and guaranteed to fly. He was disappointed Christmas morning, when, despite his best efforts, it remained earthbound. Upon examination of the fine print buried deep in the instruction manual, Tom discovered that it "could not be operated in temperatures below 55 degrees." Further reading also pointed out that the helicopter could not operate at altitudes above 5,000 feet. Tom lives at 7,500 feet. It was a bust as a present. Someone at the catalog company did not do their homework—those restrictions should have been mentioned before Tom ordered the helicopter. While the altitude might be unusual, there is no excuse for the 55 degree restriction. Most U.S. temperatures are lower than that in December—even the catalog company was located in the snowbelt. Someone did not take the time to make sure that they *delivered what they promised.*

8. **Customers want you to meet their expectations—and hopefully exceed them.** This is similar to delivering what you promise, but this area is subtler. Your promises are overt, defined in your marketing and advertising, while your customers' expectations may differ. A consumer entering a Sam's Club to purchase a new TV will have a different set of expectations than he would if he were stopping into Nordstrom's to make the same purchase. He will expect a different level of facility, sales help, and shopping experience. As long as you provide at least the minimum level of service expected, you are okay. Deliver more than that level and customers will be really satisfied. It is somewhat of a balancing act, so take a look at your customer service "see-saw."

   As the seesaw moves up and down, there is always a balance between the level of service and what your customer pays. If you provide them the *best* service and then charge them a lot (think Ritz Carlton Hotels), in most cases your customers are happy, or at least they are content knowing they got what they paid for. Customers are okay with *no frills* service if they do not have to pay a lot or you are selling convenience (think a 7/Eleven store). If you provide them with the *best* level of service in an *inexpensive* cost structured business (think providing a Ritz level of service inside a Sam's Club), your customers are thrilled. But woe to you if you provide them with a no-frills level of service and you charge your customers an arm-and-a-leg. There is always a link between the level of experience you provide and

EXHIBIT 4.11   **Meeting Expectations**

Trudy will shop in Target for t-shirts and jeans, and she will also shop in an expensive, "upscale" department store at the local mall. She does not expect the same experience. At Target, she will have to get that little plastic tag with a number from the fitting room clerk, no one will bring her a different size, and she will have to bring the merchandise out of the dressing room to the clerk. She does not mind; that is just part of the expected Target experience. She feels like she is getting a deal on the clothes, so it is a trade-off. She still has a minimum standard as to what she expects out of the store: courteous sales clerk, clean and fairly well-lighted dressing room, and efficient checkout.

At the upscale department store, she expects to pay significantly more, and while she expects the merchandise to be of a higher quality, she also expects her shopping experience to match. On her last visit, the lighting was dim, and the carpet in the fitting room was dirty. She was not happy, and did not buy anything. She said it was kind of depressing, everything seemed overpriced, and she did not like trying on clothes there. The funny thing is, the dressing rooms are not much different at Target—but, she *expected* the dressing rooms at the department store to be better. When her expectations fell short, her experience was out of sync with the reality.

what your customers are willing to pay for it. Ride the customer service seesaw, but watch out how you end up.

Pricing, facility, depth of product mix, quality of product, and service level are all a factor in determining whether your customers' expectations are met. Every store or business is not a Ritz—nor do they have to be. There are lots of consumers who are looking for quality services and products with no frills. It is when part of the experience is out of sync that customers are unhappy, as shown in Exhibit 4.11.

Businesses seem to know how to get the customer in, but do they know how to keep the customer there and to get the customer out?

9. **Customers want you to meet their needs.** What do customers want?

- Products they want to purchase—not what you want to sell them.
- High quality—that minimizes the customer service calls, eliminates merchandise returns, and creates real *user friendliness.*

EXHIBIT 4.12   **An Office Supplier Makes It Easy for the Customer**

The following is a summary of the terms and policies of an office supplier:

- Call us: [toll-free number], 24 hours a day, 7 days a week; and **talk to an actual person**
- Ordering: Internet online (weekly e-mail special offers), 800 number, catalog (with monthly and specific specials), fax orders—and **free gifts**
- Choice of free gifts when ordering
- Best available price from any of our specials
- Fast shipping (next day in most cities; same day in over 900 cities) and free delivery (orders of $40 or more—if less than $40, only $3.92)
- Thirteen full-service distribution centers around the country
- Thirty-day free trial on anything you order
- One-year guarantee on every product you order (technology excluded)
- Handling and processing fee: $1.98 on all orders

  - Thirty-day free credit to most businesses

- Availability—when they want to purchase. If you offer a special, make sure you have enough on hand. An item on hand is better than two rain checks lost in the customer's drawer or wallet.
- Reasonable prices—related to quality and value. Some customers are shopping price only, while others will pay more if they get more.

    Too often items are out-of-stock or back-ordered. You cannot sell from an empty shelf—and if your shelf is empty, your customers may find a competitor with a full one.

10. **Customers want you to make it easy for them.** I cannot say this enough—customers want you to make it easy for them! Look at the example in Exhibit 4.12.

Can the office supplier do any more to get the customer's business?

Looking at Your Own Rules and Policies

Think about your own business. Are there ways that your strategy is not working in tandem with your customer service? The organization's approach to customer service has to be an outgrowth of its business strategy. Of course, rules and policies are necessary. But when you are examining yours, make sure that they are customer friendly. If you take care of the customer, that will be what is right for the organization. All too often, companies create a series of rules that are designed to make sure that the company wins, and if the customer does not—well, that is just too bad.

Examine the rules in your business, and bring your staff into this process as well. Look at the rules you have in place, and determine those that can be eliminated. Over time, just like we accumulate junk in our home, every organization develops a series of rules that are nothing but junk. Take those out and trash them immediately!

Then, consider the rules that remain and look at them more closely. Are they absolutely important to the health of the organization? Are they critical to allowing you to deliver the products and services to your customers? Do any of them prohibit you from delivering over-the-top outstanding customer service? If they do, immediately trash those rules as well. If you find it upsetting to just eliminate a rule, substitute this rule in place of any you toss: *If a rule does not make it easy for the customer to do business with us, get rid of the rule!*

Looking at Customer Service from a Fresh Perspective

Just because "it has always been done that way" does not mean it needs to be done that way. Rethink the way you do things in regard to what your customers want. Examine everything from your company entrée to your company policies, being sure that your employees, especially your lower-level ones, are not the gatekeepers that are killing the process.

It is not just what you say to your customers, but every interaction with them...every touchpoint. In other words, something as simple as the hours your business is open to the public or how your phone is answered is a part of how your customers think of your level of service. Banks and the medical profession have traditionally been rated very low on service surveys, primarily because they have chosen to keep their service and hours for themselves—back in the age of *Leave It to Beaver*. It is a whole new world, but you would never know it based on how bankers, dentists, and doctors operate. They use the philosophy of letting the *customer* adjust to how they do business.

Changing for Your Customers—Empowering Your Employees

Let us think for a moment about the success of Internet companies like Amazon.com and eBay. They have been successful because they have changed the way *they and others* operate to accommodate their *customers.* What a radical idea, and it appears to be working. How about your business? Has it changed to accommodate the needs and wishes of your customers? If you were a customer of your own business, what would you like about it, and how would you want to change it? A good example of such poor customer service is shown in Exhibit 4.13.

The company was more into control than customer service. Had they only empowered their frontline employees (those with direct customer contact), the situation would have been salvaged. The clerk *knew* the right thing to do. He *wanted* to do it. Unfortunately, he could not do it. His company had not given him the power to do it because they mistrusted whether he would do the right thing.

It is a fine line, deciding just how much to empower your staff. Ultimately, it is a judgment call based on your evaluation of their readiness to accept responsibility. If you are aware of the importance, though, and look for ways to give them that extra measure of empowerment, you will end up with happier customers and happier employees. And if you give up your power and control to your employees, how does that affect your comfort and trust levels?

Think of the last time you went into your local bank. With whom did you talk? Was it the CEO of the bank or one of the tellers? How about the

EXHIBIT 4.13   **What Does Commitment Mean?: Power to the Customer—and the Employees**

My cell phone charger stopped working less than five months after it was purchased. So back I went to the store to exchange it for one that worked. Of course I had no receipt, but the charger did have the name *Verizon* on it in big, bold letters. The clerk looked it up in the computer to see when it was purchased. However, their system sorts data by cell phone number, so when he looked it up, he found no record of it being purchased. It was purchased from his store right before Christmas. The employee told me they get really busy right before the Christmas holidays and the person who sold me the charger probably did not have time to enter it in the computer. So he could not honor the warranty and exchange the broken charger for a good one.

last time you went to that chain restaurant to eat? Did you talk to the Vice President of Strategic Planning or did you deal primarily with the server?

Those who have the most impact on direct customer service are usually the ones with the least impact on decision making. So even when they recognize changes to improve customer service, in all likelihood their comments and suggestions are not heard. But, chances are, they are more expert on customer service: They know what the customers want, what makes them happy—and what makes them unhappy.

Establish a customer service network from bottom to top. Meet to review company rules—especially those that get in the way. Make it a fun event, where employees gather to eliminate anything that keeps them from delivering great customer service. Have a rule-burning party. Besides eliminating rules deadwood, it also emphasizes the importance of placing the customer first. Your staff will know that you trust and value their input—that they are part of the process—and that you are serious about delivering *wow*-factor customer service. Remember:

- Push the decision-making authority down to the customer-interaction level.

- Let your customer service staff determine when something has to be returned to you for a warranty claim, and when the customer can just junk it. Give them the credit—no questions asked!

- Empower employees at all levels—make each one an entrepreneur.

Empower your employees to provide *wow* customer service.

Tips for Terrific Touchpoints

Tip 1: "How are we doing?"

- The first question to ask when calling on a customer should be "How are we doing?" Then comes the hard part: to shut up and really listen. Pretend you are a therapist, and create an open and honest atmosphere. It is a fairly open-ended question, so the

EXHIBIT 4.I4   How Are We Doing?

On a sales call to an important customer, Joe asked his standard, "How are we doing?" and settled back, assuming he would hear wild and wonderfully positive things about his customer service. The customer bought a lot of product from Joe, and Joe felt that his company really took good care of him. He was stunned when the customer absolutely blasted him over a technical problem with one of the products. Joe was a bit deflated, but he listened carefully, and told the customer he would check into it. Joe did exactly what he told him he would do. However, Joe did not solve the problem, presenting the customer with a new and improved product. It turned out that he could indeed improve the item, but unfortunately not at the price point he needed to hit. Joe went back to the customer and walked him through what he had found out. He explained that the company could change some hardware to fix what he did not like, but the price would be higher. Ultimately, Joe let the customer decide. The customer decided it was not worth the extra cost to him, so he stayed with the status quo. Did he now love the product? No, but he was more satisfied with it—and with Joe's service.

---

customer can really tell you what she thinks of your business. You will learn a lot; some of it (hopefully) will be glowing praise, and some of it will be things that have you cringing. But you will know what you need to work on. Be prepared; if you ask the question, you will have to be ready to listen, and then, if appropriate, make changes, as shown in Exhibit 4.14.

Tip 2: Two heads are better than one.

- Have discussions with friends who are also in business. It does not matter whether it is the same type of business; you will find you have a lot of concerns in common. Sometimes, one of the best ways of getting advice is a get-together after hours (or at lunch). After a long day of work, you can go out and talk about business problems.
- Maybe it is just human nature, but it is always easier to see the flaws in someone else's business than in your own. Others can look at your business and see ten things you could improve, usually things you have not noticed. So, using the after-hours approach, toss ideas back and forth about problems that each of you are having with inventory issues, hiring, firing, pricing, marketing, and so on. And since you are not with competitors, but rather with friends whose business judgment you trust, it is not that difficult to talk to them about problems.

Tip 3: You can snatch victory from the jaws of defeat—admit your mistakes and overcome them.

- We all make mistakes. In the area of customer service, the key difference is what happens after you make that mistake. If you want to salvage your customer service, admit the error quickly and fix the mistake immediately. Interestingly, your customer may come away from the problem thinking that you have even better service than he thought you did before the problem. This may be due to the fact that so many businesses today handle their mistakes so poorly. It is downright refreshing when a business says, "You're right; we're wrong."

- Admitting the mistake is not the killer; trying to cover it up is. When your business makes a mistake, admit it, apologize, and if it is not obvious, ask your customer what he wants you to do to fix it. Say you have a home service business, installing air-conditioning systems, and an employee breaks a customer's lamp. You might ask, "Would you like us to try to find another one, or would you like us to deduct the cost from our bill?" Or perhaps you manufacture rope. If you ship a customer the wrong rope, ask him whether he wants to cancel the order, wants the correct item shipped with his next order, or would like you to ship the rope express at your expense. If it is appropriate to the situation, as they say in New Orleans, give customers a *lagniappe*, just a little something extra that they do not expect. Perhaps the customer with the broken lamp would appreciate a coupon for an extra 10% (or more) off her next preventive maintenance. These customers will now trust you (*Aha!* An honest person!), and be even more loyal to your business. Examine the error, and take steps to make sure that it will not happen again.

Tips for Avoiding Traps that Trip You Up

Trap 1: "I've fallen and I can't get up"—the glued-to-your-desk syndrome.

- A manager of a large resort hotel believes he needs to spend at least 80% of his time out of his office, walking around the facility, talking to employees and guests. He feels that this is the best way to, as he puts it, "take the temperature of the hotel." He says that "managers too often feel that they should be sitting behind their desks" and dealing with issues like budgeting, hiring, firing, marketing, and so forth. Instead, this business leader feels that his time is much better spent being out with the guests and staff. When he does this, he is effectively setting the tempo for the organization. Whenever his staff sees him interacting with guests, they understand where the real focus of their efforts needs to be—with the guests. And he avoids the trap of being caught in his office.

Trap 2: "All customers are created equal."

- *Wrong*: They are not all equal. I know, it almost sounds un-American, but you do not need to treat every customer the same. Service level for any business should be set very high. Every one of your customers receives at least that level of service. Top customers receive an even higher level. Special treatment and extra favors go to the biggest accounts that may never be offered to other customers.
- It is a fact of business life; some customers provide more volume or more profits than others. As the owner or manager of an organization, it is up to you to know and understand which customers are your bread-and-butter. For those, you go above and beyond. Remember that when you are considering your best customers, you also want to look at those that have the most promise.

Trap 3: "It's okay to screw the little guy."

- Now while it is true that all customers are not created equal, they are all important. Be very careful, though, not to make the mistake of letting your service standards slip just because a customer may seem insignificant. As your company is dedicated to outstanding customer service, you never want your staff to get the message that *any* customer is not important. Outstanding customer service is a culture, a habit, and an underlying philosophy that has to be ingrained into every employee. Treat every customer well, no matter how small they are. If you're willing to take their money, they deserve good service. An example of how not to treat a small customer is shown in Exhibit 4.15.

EXHIBIT 4.15   The Little Customer Is Not Important

Dave is in the woodworking business, and he typically gets his products from a local distributor. They know his needs, deliver to his doorstep, and back their products. Recently, he decided to try out a new supplier. This new supplier has been in business for years, and generally deals with larger businesses. Dave placed an order with them, but when the order came, it was the wrong species of wood—the supplier's mistake. The truck driver did not know what to do, and so Dave accepted the delivery, assuming that the company would make an exchange and give him the correct wood. When he called them, they told him that since he had accepted the delivery, it was his. When he called the salesman he had ordered from, the salesman told him there was nothing he could do, they did not typically deal in such small orders and it would be too much trouble to exchange it. In a perfect world, someday our small woodworking company will become a huge lumber customer who will never purchase from that supplier. In the meantime, their "screw the little guy" mentality will creep into other aspects of customer service. Every employee involved in that transaction has received the message: Small customers are not important.

The "little guy" does not matter; he will never be a customer—or will he?

Trap 4: "Death of a Salesman"—how reprimands are handled.

- If someone in customer service makes a mistake, *because he is trying to provide outstanding service,* do not make it a federal crime. Exhibit 4.16 depicts a situation where the sales force does the right thing but it turns out wrong.

Trap 5: "Let's take a meeting."

- I ran into the Home Depot early one morning, figuring it would not be crowded. The store was indeed empty, not only of all but a few customers, but also of employees. I finally went to the checkout clerk, after searching in vain for any staff on the floor. It turned out that they were all in a customer service meeting. And it is not just meetings that are at fault. In another case, there were checkout lines snaking through the store because only one clerk was ringing up sales while three others were counting inventory.

EXHIBIT 4.16   **Empowerment Made Me Do It**

Say that you own a business that produces items for the lawn and garden industry—pink garden hoses. *Here we set the stage:* You have recently instituted a brand-new policy that allows your customer service/salespeople to spend up to $500 to solve a problem for a customer. No prior approval is required. Frank's Garden Center has been a good customer, but payables has informed you that they are past-due 60 days, so you have them on a shipment hold—no money, no product. Unknown to you, Frank is getting close to going out of business, but is doing everything he can to keep the creditors at bay.

The scene opens: Frank calls, and tells your customer service rep that "a check is in the mail," but he has to have some pink garden hoses rushed to him because he has a tradeshow coming up. He tells your rep that this is his most important show of the year, and he expects to sell hundreds of pink hoses. Your customer service rep remembers that new policy and agrees to send him $500 worth of pink garden hoses. After all, he has been a good customer, and your business is noted for its outstanding customer service. The curtain drops two weeks later, when Frank's Garden Center files for bankruptcy. How does the scene end for your intrepid customer service employee?

Is it "Exit, stage right"? Or do you discuss the situation calmly, keeping in mind that he was trying to provide great service? Your other employees will be watching this one as people are bound to make mistakes, and it is better that they make the mistake trying to do the right thing for the customer.

They know how to get customers in, but not how to get them out.

- And here is a classic that I encountered recently: There was one clerk ringing up sales in a discount store, there were seven unhappy customers waiting on line, and two aisles over, there was a table set up under a large banner emblazoned CUSTOMER SERVICE. A clerk sat there, totally alone, waiting to sign customers up for the store's bonus-points card. She looked pretty bored, and evidently entertained herself by watching the customers endlessly waiting on line at the register. Do not fall into the trap of letting meetings or slogans about customer service interfere with actual customer service.

Trap 6: "The customer will tell you what he wants."

- Now you have been learning to listen to your customers, find out what they want, discover their needs and fulfill them, and so forth. But, sometimes, they will lead you astray. Remember the customer in

Exhibit 4.14 who wanted the product change, but then decided that it really was not necessary if it was going to increase his price? Here was a case where the customer was right (sort of). He wanted the new product; what he told the company about the product was correct; he just did not want to pay what he would have to for the new version.

Trap 7: "We want every customer we can get."

- As it turns out, sometimes you should not keep some of your customers. Some customers are just too expensive to maintain. They may take too much time of your salespeople and purchase too little product, they may return products too often, or they may be doing things that are outright fraudulent.

- In an old business, it was decided that they could not afford Home Depot as a customer. They sold a good amount of product to them. But taking into account everything they needed to do to keep them as a customer, they would be in the situation of losing money on every transaction. You cannot make that up in volume. At the time, they needed customers, and it was a touch decision, but they decided that the best move was to not take on a large customer like Home Depot. They could not provide them with the level of customer service that they demanded at the prices they were willing to pay, and they were not going to make promises to them that they could not keep.

- From a customer service perspective, you have got to look at your customers and ask yourself which ones are taking up too much of your time and are too costly. Are they calling with too many requests? Are they changing orders late in the game, causing manufacturing difficulties? Are they sending returns back when you are certain it has nothing to do with the product, and more likely has to do with their cash flow? You have got to figure out who are your best customers, after you take into account *all* the costs and charges that go into dealing with them.

Trap 8: "The customer is always right."

- This is not true. The customer can be, and often is, wrong. But the issue here is how you deal with customers when they are wrong. It can be a touchy subject. You will need to deal with them carefully because perhaps the source of their problem is coming from your confusing brochure, your unmarked prices, or your sales flyer that was outdated before it was printed. But if the customer is truly wrong, you have to tell her that without making her go running to the competitor. One should not mind being told that one is in error as long as it is done with the grace to save face. This is a great place to include role-playing in your staff training. Give them a typical place where the customer can be wrong and let them work through ways to tell customers that without alienating them.

Trap 9: "Technology is always cheaper than people."

- In regard to using technology to replace or eliminate people as customer contacts, look at what happens today when you call the "customer service" or "customer care" hotline.

Tips for Watching Out for Traps

Keep an eye on:

- How much time you are spending mediating problems with rules in your business

- How much effort is going into the design of your bonus program—the simpler the better

- Anything that is keeping you from talking and visiting with your existing and prospective customers

Making that Great Customer Service Last: Keep the Romance in the Relationship

What ultimately separates the Wilson's store from Dillard's, the Bobby's World from the Sears and Kmart, is the culture of the organization. Successful businesses keep those warm and fuzzy feelings alive with their customers, trying to get that *wow* factor back.

I know this may sound like a *rah-rah* slogan, but it is true. Organizations with outstanding customer service have it because at the core of the business is the belief that the customer is the number-one priority. This is not just a trite, overused phrase that should be posted on the wall with a picture of a sunset and a seagull. You could wallpaper your entire office with that phrase and it would not help your customer service one iota. It is ironic that, although the lower levels of our hierarchal organizational pyramid have the most contact with customers, it is top management that sets the tone for outstanding customer service. A culture evolves from the top down. Not only will your employees pick up top-level attitudes; eventually employees that do not emulate that attitude will leave or be "helped out," and the new hires will be more in tune with your company philosophy.

The key to a customer service culture is to provide the customer with the best service possible. That means a lot of things, including delivering the best-quality product at the lowest price. To do that, you have to watch your costs very carefully, but that does not mean you let service slide to accomplish that goal. Your actions and words give rise to both of them. Customer service culture is created and maintained the same way. The owner might occasionally ask a customer service rep how orders were shipping. Were they going out fast enough? Are there any backorders? Now, the owner might already know the answers but want customer service to know that those things are important. After a sales trip, you might visit customer service to report back to them about customer comments—good or bad. When a customer calls, the owner should interrupt a meeting with an employee or supplier to take the call. Everyone in the company knows that *customers are our number-one priority.*

Provide the customer with the best service possible—*customers are our number-one priority!*

CONCLUSION

Memorizing the customers' top-ten list and analyzing your business will not do any good if you do not set the example. Remember the incident with the woodworker who received the wrong lumber from the big company in

Exhibit 4.15? They may offer good service to their big customers, but they will eventually go astray because they have no culture of service. If they had, that incident would have been less likely to occur, because the employees would have known that every customer was deserving of a certain level of service. An incident like that is actually a great opportunity to set the example. When the office manager heard about the problem, he should have sent a truck with replacement wood out immediately—even if they lost money on the order. What a great learning experience for all the employees involved. They would have understood that outstanding customer service is an intrinsic part of the business; it should become ingrained in their culture.

You have the tools and knowledge to elevate your service level, but when the first flush of memos and meetings subsides, it will be your attitude and commitment that will keep it flourishing. *Your* actions and focus will become the example for the culture of outstanding customer service that you want in your business.

You are the starting point for outstanding customer service. *Wow* them!

CHAPTER 5

Cash Conversion

A s mentioned previously, one of the businesses that the small business is in is the cash conversion business, which creates an emphasis on:

- Obtaining quality sales that result in timely cash collections that provide for a desired profit after deducting for all relevant costs such as product/service, functional (such as purchasing and accounting), and customer costs.

- Collecting cash on sales as quickly as possible through cash advances or upfront cash payments, payment at the time of shipment or customer receipt, effective use of electronic funds transfer (EFT), and pricing adjustments for those customers who desire to pay within a shorter collection period.

- Effective vendor negotiations that ensure lowest possible prices while still guaranteeing 100 percent quality and on-time deliveries.

- Procedures for ensuring that materials and supplies are not ordered, received, and paid for until absolutely necessary.

- Continual program to reduce all costs that are unnecessary or of a non-value-added nature (that provide no add-on value to the product or service).

In this manner, the cash conversion process becomes a tool to maintain the business in the most economical, efficient, and effective manner possible. In establishing operating controls that monitor the goals listed above, the business must keep in mind those operational areas that affect cash in and out. With these principles in mind, operations can be analyzed to identify areas for improvement in which best practices can be implemented that maximize cash inflow and minimize cash outflow.

Maximize cash inflow; minimize cash outflow.

Although the primary focus of ongoing cash conversion and continual operational analysis is on the manner in which cash is used by the business, considering the sources and uses of cash and the policies and procedures used to deal with over- and under-cash conditions, all other operational areas that have a direct impact on cash conversion also need to be addressed. Effective cash conversion analysis may result in the analysis of many of the business's major operations, as cash affects every function and activity. To ensure that the business operates with effective cash conversion procedures, it must understand that every dollar expended and every dollar collected must be evaluated as to its appropriateness to its plans and operations.

Cash is the fuel that powers the company.

Profit can be thought of as an emergency number created by accountants. Having enough cash allows business management to concentrate on growth, finding new businesses, acquiring new customers, locating new business partners, developing new products, installing new processes, and so on. Not having enough cash forces the company to fixate on getting more, sometimes to the exclusion of growth and development.

CASH CONVERSION BASICS

Effective cash conversion management is essential to the success and survival of the business. It may be even more important than producing goods or services or generating a sale. Most businesses can lose a sale or a customer and still continue operations. However, miscalculate the availability of cash when needed, for example, for payroll or taxes or a critical vendor, and the business may very suddenly be out of business. Cash conversion management helps to avoid such operational crises by applying some basic principles to the business.

The business needs cash to pay its bills—business expenses (i.e., service or manufacturing costs, selling expenses, general and administrative costs, etc.)—and to pay off scheduled liabilities on time (e.g., loans, accounts payable, taxes, etc.). Cash generally comes from four sources:

1. **Sale of equity.** In the form of company stock or ownership of the business

2. **Borrowing.** From a variety of sources such as friends and relatives, customers, vendors, employees, and financial institutions

3. **Conversion of assets to cash.** Sale of idle or unneeded facilities or equipment, reduction of excess inventory, or collection of accounts receivable

4. **Reinvested profits.** Those resulting from real cash collections add to the bottom line, not just from recorded sales that may or may not be collected

Keep in mind that every business has to be continually in the *cash conversion business.* The process starts with a cash infusion, produces or purchases products or services for customers, sells and delivers the product or service, bills, collects payment, and adds the resulting cash to the business coffers. A successful business collects more cash from customers than it expends for providing and servicing its products and services. The positive difference is called *profit* and a negative difference is called *loss.*

The business is concerned not only with managing its cash conversion in a positive manner but also with closing the gap in terms of time between cash infusion and the ultimate collection of cash. The *cash gap* can be considered the number of days between when it pays for materials and services and when it receives payment for the sale of the product or service. The longer the gap, the more time the company is out of pocket for cash. The company must have cash generated from other sales to take up this cash slack. If this is not possible, the company must finance the difference. Thus, the unavailability of cash can become expensive to the business in terms of cost of borrowing as well as the inability to operate most economically, efficiently, and effectively. In my mind, each sale is a profit center and the significance is whether the sale is profitable, how quickly the money for the sale is collected, obtaining the desired selling price, and minimizing the costs (product/service, functional, customer) of the sale.

Maximum results at minimal costs close the cash gap.

Every business is continuously in the cash expansion and conversion business; whatever business the company is in starts with a cash infusion and eventually ends in cash liquidation. If the business is successful, ending cash will exceed starting cash by more than enough to cover the time value of the cash infusion(s). The business cannot be selling to nonpaying customers or selling products that generate less cash than their costs. Furthermore, investing in accounts receivable, sales backlog, or inventory should be avoided since these cannot be spent or reinvested until they are converted back into cash. Inadequate cash is often the principal limiting factor in the growth of the business, and the business's goal should be to accelerate the cash conversion process—and close the cash gap—as much as possible.

Effective cash conversion management maximizes cash generation for the business. This means, in effect, generating positive cash flow by applying effective techniques for collecting cash due to the company, expending no more cash than necessary, and delaying (within limits) the payment of cash due others. For the business to survive, it must have cash when it needs it. In addition, a positive cash buffer provides a safety net against unforeseen business crises, emergencies, or management errors, and allows the company to take advantage of opportunities that may arise. Sufficient cash availability is also necessary for the business to grow and survive. Businesses typically fail not from lack of growth or lack of profitability, but from lack of cash to pay the bills.

Create a cash buffer; have cash when you need it.

Also keep in mind that an overinvestment in cash can impose opportunity costs on the business by loss of earnings on that "excess" cash that would be available from investment in profitable alternative opportunities. However, excess cash does not normally lead to serious business problems, while insufficient cash is always a problem. Effective cash management allows the business to control its cash and manage its business economically, efficiently, and effectively. In this way, the business can reduce business disruptions, operate in a smooth and efficient manner, and provide for its ongoing growth and profitability.

Managing the company means managing its cash conversion.

Flow of Cash Funds

Any business—manufacturing, service, financial, not-for-profit, government, and so on—begins with an infusion of cash. The fundamental operating cash flow process within the business then operates in a continuous loop of short-term asset transformation. This flow of funds in a business is shown in Exhibit 5.1.

From cash to cash as quickly as possible.

A business starts with cash—the owner's investment and usually some borrowed funds. The purchase of goods or services, together with the manufacturing process or service provision, transforms the cash into inventory or services to be delivered. As the goods or services are provided to the customer, they are converted to accounts receivable or cash receipts. The collection process then transforms the accounts receivable back into cash. If the business process works properly, the cash received is greater than the cash laid out, and the resulting excess (i.e., profit) provides the business

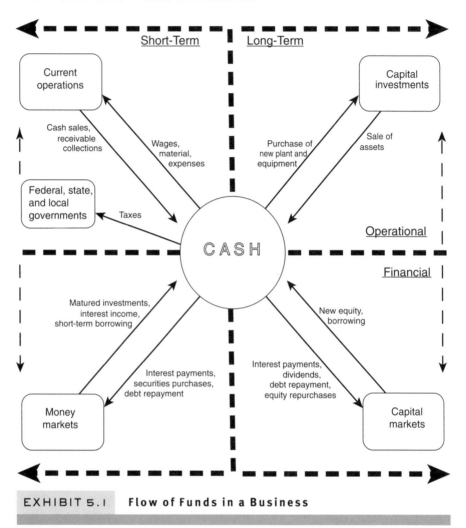

EXHIBIT 5.1   **Flow of Funds in a Business**

with additional funds to reinvest and grow. The process then needs to repeat itself in an ever-increasing continuous cycle. A major planning step must always be to have sufficient cash available to allow this series of activities to continue unabated. This is the cash conversion process and it must be controlled to work effectively.

The cash received should be greater than the cash out.

Factors that typically increase the amount of cash resources available include:

- Accounts payable increases
- Outside financing
- Asset conversion
- Profits from operations

Factors that decrease the level of cash include:

- Accounts receivable increases
- Inventory investment
- Debt repayments
- Dividends or distributions paid to owners or investors
- Operating losses

In addition, most businesses require periodic purchases of fixed assets—property, plant, and equipment—in order to maintain or expand their business activities. These are not part of the normal cash conversion cycle, but do require an outlay of cash, often quite significant.

In reality, the cash conversion process does not operate simply or smoothly, but is subject to numerous disruptions. Changes in the level of inventory retard or increase the flow of cash as do changes in the level of accounts receivable and accounts payable. Payables are free short-term loans from vendors or suppliers that represent a source of cash for the business. Inventory and accounts receivable, however, are idle assets reducing cash availability until they can be converted into sales and collected. Chronically high levels of inventory or accounts receivable can easily threaten the survival of the business. While cash itself contributes only minimally (through possible interest earnings) to profitability, it does make possible the acquisition of the goods and/or services that create profitability.

Simply stated, if each sale represented by cash inflow exceeds the amount of cash outflow needed to pay for the costs associated with the sale (i.e., product or service, functional, and customer costs), the organization produces a profit. Under this concept each sale could be justified as being a profit center and controlled as such. The sale and cost relationship of the cash conversion process is shown in Exhibit 5.2.

EXHIBIT 5.2   **Small Business Success Formula 3: Cash Conversion**

$$CI - CO = P/L$$

CI = Cash in: cash infused into the business through investment by owners and others, borrowings, and cash generated by sales and profits
CO = Cash out: cash paid out by the business for materials and supplies, personnel, cost of borrowings (e.g., interest), taxes, and other administrative costs
P/L = Profit or loss from each transaction or the business
   The rule for successful cash conversion is that cash in should exceed cash out, resulting in a remainder to the company in the form of operating profits.

The problems associated with too little cash are obvious. Too little cash means problems of survival, while too much cash can result in lost opportunities and inefficient utilization of limited resources. Cash conversion management is a continual effort to smooth out fluctuations and focus on the Goldilocks Cash Conversion Principle—"not too much; not too little; but just the right amount."

There is no formula to make this determination, but there are several factors that need to be considered:

- There needs to be enough cash to pay the business's bills.
- There needs to be enough cash to meet any banking requirements such as compensating balances, minimum cash balances to cover service charges, or loan covenants.
- There needs to be enough cash to handle unanticipated opportunities or emergencies.
- There needs to be enough cash to provide the owners of the small business with sufficient *sleep insurance*—that is, to provide a sufficient margin to meet the safety needs of the business and its operations.

How much cash is enough? *How much is too much?*

CASH CONVERSION OBJECTIVES

Cash conversion operations focus on making the asset transformation process of the business work smoothly. To accomplish this, the small business owner needs to be aware of the objectives of effective cash conversion operations:

- Control and track cash flows—cash in and cash out.
- Maximize sources of profitable cash in.
- Minimize uses of cash out—reduce or eliminate all unnecessary costs.
- Maximize revenues and minimize expenditures.
- Collect for sales as quickly as possible.
- Expend cash only where necessary (i.e., primarily value-added functions and activities).
- Pay creditors no sooner than necessary, and minimize the costs associated with vendor purchases and payments.
- Provide for adequate external sources of funding.
- Properly manage external short-term borrowing and/or investment activities.
- Effectively utilize any excess differential cash generated.
- Keep the cash conversion gap at a minimum.

Effective cash conversion management and control is necessary due to a lack of synchronization between incoming and outgoing cash flows, a lack of reliable forecastability of cash inflow amounts and timing, and costs of holding cash balances or borrowing to cover cash shortfalls. What cash conversion techniques should be designed to do is shorten the cash conversion cycle by effectively managing the assets, liabilities, revenues, and costs of the business.

Cash in procedures can be maximized, borrowing minimized, and return on assets enhanced by:

- Selling profitable products or services to quality customers who pay on time
- Speeding collection of accounts receivable, or collecting in advance of or at time of shipment or delivery of the product or service

- Getting material and purchased parts inventory into production and out the door as quickly as possible, or getting out of the inventory business entirely by letting the suppliers carry the inventory

- Reducing or eliminating finished goods inventory by shipping immediately from production to the customer

- Maintaining work-in-process inventory at minimum levels by effective production scheduling and control techniques that ensure maximization of real customer orders into production, minimizing production time, eliminating rework and rejects, and minimizing production costs

- Taking maximum advantage of accounts payable and other interest-free loans by not paying sooner than required

- Reducing or eliminating expenditures whenever possible

- Avoiding accounts payable entirely where payable costs exceed the amount of the invoice or where vendor price reductions for fast payment exceed the cost of processing the payments

- Operating the business efficiently in the use of fixed assets, or increasing results with the use of fewer resources

- Operating the business in the most economical and efficient methods by keeping costs and non-value-added functions and activities to a minimum by diligent management of the cash assets of the business by minimizing investment in property, plant, and equipment

- Operating with the least number of personnel possible

- Incurring costs and expenses for only necessary value-added functions and activities

- Maximizing sales to real quality customers, which can be produced and delivered at real cash profits

Small business owners understand the importance of cash and the benefits of collecting in cash at or before the point of sale. Exhibit 5.3 demonstrates how this cash principle may in fact put the business in jeopardy.

PROFITABILITY VERSUS LIQUIDITY

We have all heard the outcry from small business owners, "If I'm making so much money, how come I don't have any cash?" This exemplifies the

EXHIBIT 5.3   Cash Discounting

Roy is the owner of a small building-supply business. He has been in business for over 40 years, and knows most of his major customers personally. For these customers, he offers a 20 percent discount if they pay him directly in cash, bypassing the regular recording of sales. He personally loads the merchandise onto the customer's trucks from the back of the store. There is no paperwork trail. The cash goes directly into the owner's pocket.

This is probably a familiar scenario for a small, closely held business. Sometimes others are not aware of such practices being in existence and spend unnecessary time in attempting to provide guidance and advice to the owner as to how to improve his or her business operations and profitability. Other times, others are aware of such practices but decide to ignore their existence.

What would you do about this practice?

Suggested Response

- The owner's practice of offering a 20 percent discount on "off-the-books" sales to preferred customers is, of course, an improper business practice, resulting in tax fraud. This is a practice that should not be approved of as to proper operations and reporting controls. You must convince the owner of his or her folly and prove that this is a bad business practice as to:

  - Making sales that may be putting cash in the owner's pocket but may result in a loss
  - Being able to determine profitability of the business
  - Determining the effectiveness of cash conversion procedures and controls
  - Monitoring cost and pricing policies as well as product, sales, and customer profitability
  - Proper inventory control procedures as to inventory on hand for future sales

- To effectively control operations and provide guidance to the small business owner, as to what needs to be done to grow and prosper. there must be access to all business transactions. The practice of unrecorded sales only works to the detriment of the owner.

The owner must be educated as to proper business practices, the need for such operating controls, the effect on ongoing cash conversion controls, the positive effect of setting a proper control model for the company, and the benefits of operating the small business in an acceptable control environment.

---

difference between profitability and liquidity. Profitability has to do with making an adequate return on the capital and assets invested in the business—sometimes reported as sales and profits but never collected or collected at a greater cost than the profit. Liquidity relates to having an adequate cash flow that allows the company to make necessary payments and ensure the continuity of operations.

The main reason profitability does not always ensure liquidity is the system of accruals used by some small businesses in accounting for profit and loss. Small businesses that maintain their financial records on the cash basis do not have these concerns. The accrual accounting system records revenues and expenses as they are incurred, sets up accounts receivable and inventory, establishes accounts payable, capitalizes and amortizes assets, and so on to arrive at profit or loss based on the timing of the economic event, not on the flow of cash. Because of accounting judgments required and flexibility permitted, profit can be determined in part by the accountant's imagination and legitimate creativity; but cash is cash—it is real and it is precisely measurable.

Cash conversion controls look at actual cash receipts and disbursements to arrive at the amount of cash available. Business survival is much more a matter of adequate cash than that intangible thing called profit. Cash, not profit, is used to pay the bills. You pay with cash, not with profits.

Recording profits is not the same as collecting cash.

There are as many ideas as there are so-called experts as to what needs to be done to conserve and control cash. Some ideas for you to use in establishing effective operating practices relative to cash conversion are shown in Exhibit 5.4.

Cash is king; manage your business accordingly and convert cash quickly.

A small retail business may start its existence as a cash-only or a cash-and-carry-type operation; that is, the customer pays cash at the time of the purchase. However, as the business increases or changes the way it operates, it may need to offer credit terms to its customers to grow and survive. Exhibit 5.5 exemplifies such a situation.

EXHIBIT 5.4   Cash Conversation Checklist

Cash

- Conserve what you have and invest any excess.
- Use the concept of float (money in the system but not yet taken from your account) for cash disbursements.
- Negotiate with the bank for quicker availability of deposited funds.
- Use lockboxes for quicker bank recording of deposits if they make economic sense.
- Centralize cash and use sweep accounts or like devices.
- Invest excess funds as early and as long as possible.
- Do not spend unless you must.
- Use electronic transfers for incoming cash whenever possible.
- Offer discounts for cash sales, but the resultant amount should be the desired sales amount.

Accounts Receivable

- Get invoices out no later than time of shipment.
- Establish and stick with credit limits and terms.
- Age and monitor your receivables.
- Follow up regularly and persistently on overdue accounts.
- Consider (but do not automatically implement) cash discounts or other incentives to pay.
- Make the sales amount net of the discount the desired amount to be received.
- Consider shortening payment terms to customers.
- Control the accounts receivable-to-sales ratio.
- Factor receivables where it makes economic sense, if not collateralized.
- Use collection agencies if necessary.
- Implement penalties for late payments.
- Get cash payment for invoices where cost of billing, receivables, and collections exceeds the amount of the invoice.
- Establish a cash-only policy for low billing amounts (i.e., under $500).

Inventory

- Stay out of the inventory business as much as possible as to raw materials and finished goods.
- Concentrate on work in process (WIP): Enter customer order into WIP as late as possible to meet customer's delivery schedule and maximize throughput of all.
- WIP customer orders.
- Buy for bonafide customer sales orders rather than for stock.
- Use vendor consignment inventory.
- Negotiate blanket purchase orders for large repetitive requirements with flexible delivery schedules that meet your customers' needs.
- Consider effective disposal of obsolete inventory without jeopardizing future sales or overloading your market—convert to cash where possible, otherwise scrap the obsolete items.
- Stratify your inventory items as to value and usage using an ABC-type system, and then control the categories based on criticality and value.
- Continually improve inventory turns over raw materials and finished goods with the goal of pushing toward zero inventory by item, by category, and in total.

(Continued)

EXHIBIT 5.4   (Continued)

- Consider unloading dead or dying inventory for cash without sacrificing present and future sales (e.g., fire sales, parking-lot flea market, etc.).

Prepaid Expenses
- *Don't!*
- Always make sure to get your deposits back.
- Avoid salary and expense advances.
- Consider monthly, quarterly, or semiannual insurance payments rather than annual payments.
- Do not overpay or prepay taxes.

Fixed Assets
- Buy only what you need, not what you want.
- Consider used equipment.
- Use finite facility capacity effectively—use only what is necessary, rent out extra space.
- Consider leases to conserve cash.
- Sell off idle assets—do not keep around for extreme backup.
- Refurbish or rehabilitate rather than buy new.
- Use outside contractors for temporary excess production requirements—establish ongoing contractual arrangements.
- Use excess capacity to do contract work for others.
- Negotiate favorable payment or financing with suppliers of necessary new equipment.
- Defer purchases of equipment until absolute necessary.
- Borrow to finance plant and equipment purchases based on sound capital investment return decisions and follow up to ensure compliance.
- Continually review and change plant layout for optimum efficiency.
- Consider making employees responsible for maintaining their own equipment.

Accounts Payable
- Pay only what you owe based on quantity ordered and agreed price.
- Make sure that you pay each vendor's invoice only once—do not double pay.
- Pay only properly authorized vendor invoices.
- Do not pay vendor invoices any earlier than necessary—and then only for very good reasons.
- Take advantageous vendor discounts based on sound economic factors, even if you have to borrow for large amounts.
- Negotiate effectively with critical and large suppliers based on price, quality, and on-time deliveries, as well as your willingness to pay earlier and commit to long-term purchases.
- Make effective use of your computer accounting system to schedule and manage payments.
- Establish plans and budgets for payments; review and analyze variances.
- Pay slow if necessary, but communicate with your suppliers about your payment plans—especially your critical vendors.
- Use bartering if possible to conserve cash.
- Slow down spending, question each dollar to be spent, and spend only what you have.
- Pay off small invoices on time to reduce amount to be managed.

- Pay cash for small invoices where the cost of processing exceeds the amount of the vendor invoice (e.g., an invoice for $34 where the cost of processing is $58).

Borrowing

- Negotiate for the lowest interest rate and the best terms.
- Obtain deferrals when necessary on interest and/or principal.
- Analyze totality of loan costs—interest, compensating balance requirements, restrictive covenants, repayment terms, and so on.
- Borrow as little and as late as practical.
- Match long-term needs with long-term borrowing.
- Do not use long-term debt for seasonal, cyclical, or other short-term needs.
- Establish a revolving line of credit with the best terms possible for periodic short-term cash shortfalls.
- Pay down principal if cash is available based on sound economic decisions.
- Convert to longer-term repayment schedule based on cash situation.
- Do not borrow unless necessary or where the effect of leveraging brings more to the company than the cost of borrowing.

Equity

- Consider if it is best to maintain extra cash from profits in the business for ongoing needs or expansion or to distribute it to the owners.
- Consider some form of deferred compensation plan for employees such as a periodic bonus or profit-sharing plan.
- Consider selling equity to employees, but never sell more than a controlling interest.

Sales

- Make sales based on the business's plan as to what to sell, to whom to sell, when to sell, and at what price to sell.
- Sell to quality customers—those who buy repetitively, refer others, pay on a timely basis, and provide for profitability.
- Sell those products and services that provide desired profits—know your costs.
- Emphasize sales of higher-margin products or services without disturbing your desired product sales mix.
- Negotiate advance payments, payment at time of shipment or delivery, and/or progress payments—use electronic funds transfer for customer payments.
- Remember that only the resultant real profit margin after all costs—product or service, functional and activity, and customer costs—and the bill is collected represents an increase in cash balances.
- Raise prices or lower prices based on market conditions and changes in your cost structure—the lower your costs, the more flexibility in your pricing decisions.
- Increase desired unit sales—remember, once you exceed the breakeven point, the cost attributed to each additional unit sale decreases, allowing for more flexible pricing.
- Use discounts as a viable marketing tool, keeping the after-discount price as your desired price—avoid getting yourself into the markdown business.
- Maximize the amount of cash sales—eliminate the billing and collections process and related costs—set a minimum amount for billable sales, say over $500.
- Direct the sales force to provide the desired level of customer service.
- Analyze sales compensation methods (usually a sales commission) to ensure that such compensation methods encourage the sales force to provide adequate customer

(Continued)

EXHIBIT 5.4   (Continued)

service, sell the desired products or services, and work within the owners' business plans.

Expenses
- Schedule expected expenses (and relate to forecasted sales) to assure positive cash flow.
- Review and control actual expenses to expected expenses or budgets.
- Establish authorization controls and limits (even on the business owners) on purchases.
- Use blanket purchase orders or commitments with flexible delivery schedules for large, repetitive purchases.
- Effectively negotiate with vendors as to price, timely deliveries, and quality, as well as payment considerations as to early-pay discounts.
- Establish an atmosphere of cash conversion and conservation among all employees.
- Control cash disbursements at purchase level as well as actual cash expenditures.
- Remember that each dollar of cost saved equals a dollar of cash to the bottom line.
- Minimize the amount of property, plant, and equipment to the extent necessary to effectively operate the business.
- Minimize the number of employees needed in the business—hire only where the additional employee multiplies the effectiveness of operations and the additional cost of the employee increases the business's real profits.
- Initiate a program of continuous improvements directed toward the implementation of best practices in all aspects of the business.
- Consider a reward program that provides incentives for reducing or eliminating unnecessary costs rather than an emphasis on sales that may be unprofitable.
- Analyze all activities and eliminate any non-value-added activities.
- Operate economically, efficiently, and effectively with only essential expenditures.

EXHIBIT 5.5   Baking the Books

Freddy and Teddy have been bakers for many years, each one owning and operating a small neighborhood bakery. They bake their products at night and their wives sell the baked items during the day in small storefront retail bakeries selling over the counter on a cash-only basis. Both Freddy and Teddy liked the baking part of the business but not the selling part of the business. However, they liked the aspect of owning a cash business that allowed them to pocket whatever cash they desired and report only the remainder. As the bakery business is prone to overbaking in terms of quantity and disposing of unsold product, they were unconcerned as to how much they reported for business and tax purposes. They both kept their own books in a manual ledger.

Eventually, Freddy's and Teddy's wives grew tired of operating a retail bakery. Rather than hire outside employees that made each of them uncomfortable, Freddy and Teddy decided to merge their operations and sell their products directly to other retail stores—such as supermarkets, small grocery stores, employee cafeterias, and so forth. As neither one had ever worked with anybody else, they decided to hire a CPA firm to organize the accounting side of the business and prepare monthly statements for each of the partners. The CPA recommended the purchase of a computer system with proper accounting software and a part-time employee to operate the system.

As neither Freddy nor Teddy had any experience operating other than on a cash business, the CPA had to set up systems of sales orders, billings, accounts receivable, and accounts payable. The CPA spent sufficient time to properly train Edith, the computer operator, whom they had all agreed on hiring, and then came in once a month to review all computer transactions and prepare business statements for the two partners. Edith came in every Wednesday to enter those transactions that had accumulated on her desk.

But the CPA was not aware of Freddy's and Teddy's methods of operations. For instance,

- Freddy and Teddy would take a sales order (whoever was available) from a customer and many times one would fill the sales order without communicating to the other partner or the computer operator.
- Because they liked the baking part of the business, they would overbake and then deliver the excess to the customer as a way of disposing of the extra bakery items.
- They would bill the customer with a copy of the manually prepared sales order at the time of delivery.
- They would receive checks for present or past sales from a customer when making a delivery, or receive checks in the mail, and place the check on Edith's desk for data entry on Wednesday.
- They would place orders with vendors with no communication to Edith. She would only become aware of such purchases when she received an invoice from the vendor. Edith would pay any outstanding vendor invoices when she came in on Wednesday.

Both Freddy and Teddy are concerned that not all business transactions are being entered into the accounting system. They are working more, baking and serving customers, but making less money, even though the combined volume exceeds the previous individual businesses. As the CPA for Freddy's and Teddy's business, what additional operating and accounting controls would you suggest for implementation after realizing the existence of the above operating practices?

Suggested Response

- Establish a more formal sales order system with numerically controlled sales orders that are entered into the accounting system. Educate Freddy and Teddy and implement the necessary discipline as to the necessity of sales order accuracy and submission to Edith. Delegate responsibility to Edith to ensure that all sales orders are accounted for and entered into the computer system.
- Use the computer system as designed to prepare a billing invoice from the data on the sales order. At the same time, establish the sale as an account receivable. Continually communicate with Freddy and Teddy as to outstanding receivables so that they can follow on their next delivery or by phone.
- Deposit checks received (and infrequent cash payments) immediately in the bank— on a daily basis. Record the payment data on the internal copy of the sales orders, reconcile the sales orders to the deposit slip, and securely hold the data for Edith to process.

(Continued)

EXHIBIT 5.5   (Continued)

- Eliminate the practice of overbaking and deliver to the customer only those items ordered. In the rare instances where there are excess items baked, the partners can gift special customers as a sign of exceptional customer service.

Establish a purchasing-type function where all purchases are documented on a numerically controlled purchase-order-type form and entered into the computer system establishing accounts payable. Edith would be responsible for reconciling all purchases, setting up accounts payable, and processing payments based on due-date terms and the availability of cash.

CHAPTER 6

Sales Function

The typical small business is driven by sales, sales, and more sales. The small business owner's major focus on planning, if any, is to concentrate on increasing sales—at any cost. The prevalent theory (or myth) is that if only the business can increase its sales, then sufficient profits will follow. Minimal thought may be given to what products to sell, in what amount, at what price (considering all costs) to produce a real profit, and to whom (i.e., which are our quality customers). If sales, and costs, are included at all in the small business planning process, sales forecasts (usually developed by optimistic sales personnel) tend to be overestimated while cost estimates (even if developed by accounting personnel and/or the CPA) tend to be underestimated. Such quick planning procedures quickly produce an operating scenario where forecasted sales may not materialize but real costs exceed estimated expectations. Such a situation places the small business owner in a crisis situation to generate sales and cash flow, resulting in a business atmosphere that pressures the owner to make quick sales at any cost—making sales and selling off inventory at markdown prices that may not cover the cost of the sale. With such pressures on making sales, sales personnel may wind up trying to sell whatever they can at whatever price they can get. Through the proper control of the sales function, the small business owner should be able to control effective sales flow that results in profitability to the business.

Overestimate forecasted sales; underestimate expected costs.

PURPOSE OF THE SALES FUNCTION

The small business owners and management must define and communicate their strategic plans for the business, including areas of expansion, retrenchment, and status quo. At the same time, owners and management members should identify the businesses they want to be in, the businesses they do not want to be in, their basic business principles and belief systems, and their desires for each function within the organization. For instance, small business management may define a desire for the sales function, which has historically sold whatever it could to customers, to become a more integral part of the planning process and other functions such as product and service delivery. In defining their desires, small business management may identify attributes of the sales function that more closely relate to the purposes of the sales function such as:

- Sales forecasts more realistically related to actual customers and products to be sold
- A larger percentage of the sales forecast (at least 80 percent) matched by real customer orders that can be acted upon
- Sales efforts driven by management's identification in the planning process of what to sell, to whom, and at what quantity—and sometimes at what time
- A sales forecast with a high percentage of real customer orders that allows the business's providing of goods and services to be based on customer orders and expected delivery times, at a specified quality level
- A sales function that is geared more toward providing the right customer service, before, during, and after the sale, than toward making sales that maximize sales personnel's compensation
- A sales function that works within the business's plans together with the other functions of the business, such as manufacturing, engineering, purchasing, accounting, and marketing

The sales function is established to work as an integrated function that supports the business, not as an independent function set up for its own existence and survival. In this manner, the sales function may be seen as the starting point for real profits and positive cash flow—that is, making sales that maximize the collection of cash and net profits.

The starting point for any business is to decide why it is in business. As noted previously, all businesses are in existence to make money—in the right way—through quality customer service and expeditious cash conversion. If a small business desires to stay in business for the long term (i.e., to survive and grow), it must expand its short-term thinking and recognize its present customers (and potential customers) as an integral part of its life cycle. It can no longer use its customers as a dumping ground for excess inventory, a source of quick orders, a place for salespeople to visit and so on. Customer requirements and the company's ability to please those customers keep it in business. The sales function is the conduit between the company and its customers. True customer service starts and ends with the sales function.

The sales function links the customer to the business.

With an adequate knowledge of the purpose of the sales function, the small business owners and management may define their desires for the sales function regarding customer services and making the right sales to the right customers as follows:

- Make sales that can be collected profitably.
- Develop realistic sales forecasts that result in a present or future real customer order.
- Sell products as determined by management at the right time, in the right quantities.
- Actual customer sales should directly correlate with management's long- and short-term plans as to what to sell, how much, and to whom.
- Sales efforts, and corresponding compensation systems, should reinforce the goals of the business.
- Customer sales should be integrated with other functions of the company, such as manufacturing, engineering, accounting, purchasing, and so on.

Do you sometimes get the feeling that your sales function is in business for itself?

Sales Function in Business for Itself

In many small businesses, the sales function is treated differently from other functions of the company. For instance, it may have a different compensation program (salary plus commissions or commissions only), various incentives (trips, cars, meals, vacations, exotic conference locations), flexible hours (both in and out of the office), more liberal expense accounts (customer meals, sporting events, company car), and so forth. In these circumstances, the sales staff may see themselves in business for themselves. That is, their business is to generate sales and maximize their compensation, and the company's business is to provide the goods or services and the other necessary support including the cash to carry out their activities.

There may be limited coordination between the sales function and small business management, and often the sales function and the business end up working at cross-purposes to each other. The results are unacceptable customer order backlogs, products and services that cannot be provided (and billed) on time, accounts receivable that are collected too slowly or not at all, inventory on hand that is not being sold, facilities and personnel that are not being used efficiently and effectively, and ineffective management. The sales function ends up being in the businesses it should not be in—and customer service and cash conversion and making money suffer along with the decline of the business.

In effect, although sales (and possibly recorded net income) may be up, the company cannot pay its bills. This results in panic selling at any cost, a short-term solution that plays havoc with positive cash flow. Realistically, the sales function must then be brought back onto the same path the business is taking, assuming the business knows where it is going. The beginning point is always, "What goods or services should we provide, and to whom?"—that is, what its markets should be. The sales function should provide significant input to this process, as they are the ones who most typically are dealing directly with the customers.

The purpose of the sales function is to service, not just to sell, the customer—that is, to keep the customer in business so that the company stays in business. The goal should be to provide the highest-quality goods and services to customers at the lowest possible price, while still achieving an adequate return for the business. If this can be done successfully, both the business and its customers will grow and prosper. If the sales function can also become an integral and unique part of its customer's businesses, it will enlarge its sales to these customers as well as minimize the effect of competitors. It is usually easier to build a successful business from a core of satisfied customers than by continually searching for new customers, who may be one-time sales or short-term customers. The sales function, then, is the communication link between the business and its customer base.

The purpose of the sales function, therefore, is not just to make sales (and increase the numbers month after month), but also to make the right sales to the right customers at the right time. To do this, the sales function staff must be more fully integrated into the overall company planning system. They need to know the direction the company wishes to follow and then direct their sales efforts along the same path.

> The purpose of the sales function is not just to make sales but to service the right customers.

PRODUCT ANALYSIS

The starting point in the small business's planning process is the sales and market forecast (both short- and long-term forecasts). This is the definition of what goods and services the company desires to sell and to whom. However, because the effectiveness of the organizational plan is dependent on the accuracy of such a market or sales forecast, many small businesses experience planning problems before going any further, a result of their having sales forecasts (if they have them at all) that are more fiction than

EXHIBIT 6.1   Product Determination

Product	Selling Price	Cost	Gross Profit	%	Forecast	Sales	Sales $	%	Total	Gross Profit %
A	$18	$15	$ 3	16.7	800	540	$ 9,720	2.2%	$1,620	1
B	32	20	12	37.5	12,000	9,800	313,600	70.2	117,600	67
C	56	30	26	46.4	3,600	2,200	123,200	27.6	57,200	32
					16,400	12,540	446,520	100.0	176,420	100

reality. So for most small businesses the first step in effective planning is to work toward more accurate sales forecasts on which to base their plans. A good rule of thumb is that an effective sales forecast should consist of at least 80 percent real customer orders or expected sales. This means that the sales function may have to do what it may not have done in years—communicate with and service the customer.

Small business owners and management, together with the sales function, must determine what products or services (or product lines) the business wishes to sell in the coming period. This decision is made by analyzing past sales, present customer (and potential customer) needs and desires, inventory levels, production/service delivery capabilities, future considerations, competitive factors, and so on.

An example of such a product analysis for Products A, B, and C is shown in Exhibit 6.1. Based on the analysis of these three products (or product lines), small business management determines the future goals for these products.

Using the data in Exhibit 6.1, Product A is determined to be a low-cost/ low-selling-price item with low profit margins. Small business management may question whether it wants to stay in this business for competitive reasons—in other words, making a low-cost alternative available for those customers for whom price is a strong consideration—or to get out of this part of the business. The business is not realizing an acceptable level of return, but it is also tying up resources (facilities and personnel, including sales, and cash) that could be used more effectively with other products. It is likely that any cash flow generations and real profits are small.

Product B is the business's bread-and-butter item; it sells these items repetitively at a more than acceptable profit level (37.5 percent), with a high probability of favorable cash flow. Product B is a cash cow, since sales of these items account for more than 70 percent of its total business and 67 percent of its gross profits. These are the items the business is geared for and for which the sales function can easily obtain customer commitments. This is the part of the business's sales forecast that must be accurate. With modest customer service effort by sales personnel this can be achieved, if only the salespeople talk to the customers. Sales goals and respective controls such as how many to sell, to whom, and at what price should be established for this product.

Product C is the high price, top-of-the-line model for those customers who are willing to pay more for a luxurious look or additional options—often a status, rather than price, consideration. Although the business sells fewer items of Product C than Product B, its profits (and usually sales commissions) are greater. Accordingly, there is a likely tendency for sales personnel to spend more time selling Cs than Bs, which may be counter to the business's plans to sell more Bs. Typically, the small business does not know what the real costs (and added costs) are for such top-of-the-line items, and what internal strife this causes in producing and delivering its standard B items. Management needs to consider the business's plans and goals for Product C—increase this business, deemphasize the business, or maintain it approximately where it is at present. Once such goals are established, then the respective controls should be established to monitor compliance. Keep in mind that sometimes selling more than expected can cause an operational problem as well as selling less than expected.

Whatever they decide, small business management must direct the sales function so that its efforts are expended where desired. Cash and net income generated (or lost) by each of the products needs to be an integral part of their decision making.

> The business directs the sales function; the sales function does not direct the business.

SALES AND PRODUCT CONTROLS

Management should be analyzing their product lines and items (or services) on a periodic basis using reporting controls such as those listed below. Such controls are used to compare present sales and customer purchases to the appropriate yardsticks.

- Relationship to sales forecast and company plans
- Products/product lines doing better or worse than expected
- Product contribution to real profits and cash flow
- Customer sales statistics by product and by total sales: comparison to past sales, expected sales, and new sales
- Unforeseen occurrences: lost sales, unexpected sales, returns, inability to deliver, large backlogs, and so on
- Effects of competition: changes in market share, gains and losses in sales to competitors, and sales to competitors customers
- Necessary or requested product changes: to meet customers' needs and related to sales increases
- Relationships to inventory levels: raw material levels moving toward zero, finished goods shipped directly to customers as completed, and work in process containing at least 80 percent real customer orders and all customer orders entered into production at the right time and completed on time

For the typical small business there is little expectation that such product analysis controls presently exist. If this is the case, with very little or no such control analysis in existence, not only is this an operational deficiency, but such sales, product, and customer statistics would have to be developed in order to monitor and evaluate sales function performance. Note that typically, the 80/20 rule applies; that is, 80 percent (or more) of the small businesses sales come from 20 percent (or less) of its customers; and 80 percent of its profits come from 20 percent of its products. These customers and products need to be identified and controlled with regard to their effect on sales, cash flow, net income, and operations. These become the elements of a sales function reporting system.

Working to develop the sales, product, and customer reporting system based on an encompassing sales operation analysis, you might ask:

- On which customers and products does the sales force spend most of its time?

- Is adequate consideration being given to whether the prime customers pay their bills on time?

- Is sufficient emphasis being placed on selling those products that contribute adequately to cash flow and real profits?

- What is the sales emphasis, on the top 20 percent or on the other 80 percent?

- Is the focus on existing top customers, other customers, or potential new customers?

- Is there any emphasis on finding new uses for the top 20 percent of customers and products?

- What is the extent of customer service for the top 20 percent, others, and new customers?

- Are sales personnel aware of customer and product control statistics, and do they actively alter their sales plans based on such statistics?

- Is sales emphasis on dollar sales resulting in sales commissions rather than on business goals and profitability?

- Does sales staff communicate problems with products regardless of the products' salability (high sellers as well as low sellers)?

- What is being done about the 80 percent or so of customers and products that produce only 20 percent of sales and profits? Are there any sales efforts to increase sales of those products and to these customers?

- Are there new products that need increased sales efforts or older products in decline that should be considered for elimination or phasing out?

- Does sales staff provide adequate customer service to all customers— top, middle, bottom, and potential?

- Are opportunities, such as product enhancement, new products, changes in use, and decline in demand, recognized?

Does your sales function know which products to sell to which customers?

SALES FORECASTS

The sales forecast is one of the primary inputs into the small business planning process. It is necessary not only to know what was sold in the past and to whom and at what price and profit margin, but also to know what the company is going to sell in the future. It is this future sales forecast that the business will use to develop its planned profit plan. This becomes the sales budget on which it plans its production budget of goods and services—taking into account what already exists in inventory—and with accurate and realistic costs, its profit plan and cash budget. The greater the number of real customer orders in the sales budget, the more accurate the profit plan will be. With inaccuracies and guesstimates based on prior year's inaccurate sales forecasts in the current sales forecast, the business will produce or purchase more for inventory than for customers, which will in turn result in failure to meet its profit plan and an unfavorable cash position. Small business owners and management together with the sales people must play an integral role in helping to formulate accurate sales forecasts upon which to establish controls to monitor and evaluate against.

The sales forecast amounts compared to actual sales for the past year for products A, B, and C are shown in Exhibit 6.2.

The sales forecast comes from your customers, *not from your sales force.*

EXHIBIT 6.2   Sales Forecast to Actual Sales

Product	Forecast	Sales	Difference	%
A	800	540	260	32.5
B	12,000	9,800	2,200	18.3
C	3,600	2,200	1,400	38.8

Analysis of this chart shows that the sales forecast is way out of line for all three products, but is closest for Product B. With such a sales forecast, it is quite difficult for the small business to plan effectively. It is apparent that the business must have more realistic sales forecasts in order to plan its operations and expected results. This usually means that the sales staff must get closer to their customers. The business must be able to establish realistic sales goals for each product (or product line) in order to direct the sales function and plan its internal operations.

Although maintaining sales statistics by product and customer is important, small business management must learn how to analyze and interpret what these numbers really mean. For instance, they must identify the customers to whom the company is selling products A, B, and C, and determine how these customers are purchasing—that is, strictly by ordering on their own, through the business's sales direction, from its catalog, and so on. In effect, the business must define the relationship of past sales to future forecasts: Will they increase, stay about the same, or decrease, and to what extent? It is only through the sales function that the business can determine this needed information. For the small business, the task of establishing more accurate sales forecasts, effective sales reporting systems and controls, and evaluation and corrective action procedures normally falls upon the owners working together with small business management. The small business needs to move toward more realistic sales forecasts in which the largest proportion possible (e.g., 80% or more) is made up of real customer orders. In this manner, small business management can develop realistic sales, production, cost, pricing, and profit plans working with the sales function to make the plan happen.

The small business sales function staff usually work on their own, basically to sell anything they can, with the owner pressuring them to make sales with little regard to cost of sales and profit margins. The sales force typically (and hopefully) waits for the customer and sales to come to them. Older sales personnel rely on past relationships with ongoing customers for repetitive sales to come in—earning easy commissions—while newer salespeople need to work harder in developing new customers and convincing older recalcitrant customers to increase their business or to reorder from the business. An example of such a situation is shown in the case study in Exhibit 6.3.

The focus is on customer service, not on increasing commissions.

PRICING STRATEGIES

What to sell, how much, and to whom are important planning decisions. Equally, if not more, important is the pricing strategy or decision—that is,

EXHIBIT 6.3   Tale of Three Salespeople

TLDC decided to earmark specific customers and related sales forecasts for its product line, XXX business, by salesperson. For the first quarter of such directed sales planning, the results for the three salespersons were:

Salesperson	Forecast	Sales	Difference	%
Brown	2,500	4,000	1,500	160%
Gray	3,500	3,200	(300)	91%
White	4,000	3,600	(400)	90%
Totals	10,000	10,800	800	108%

Salesperson	Number of Customers	Personal Contacts	Phone Calls	Memos Sent
Brown	18	84	146	63
Gray	26	38	73	28
White	44	26	48	12

After analyzing the data and comparing sales results to efforts, the following can be determined:

Additional Data to Gather

1. Sales data

   a. Seniority of salespeople

      • Years with company: White 12 years, Gray 8 years, Brown 1 year
      • Age: White 54, Gray 46, Brown 27
      • Annual pay: White $124,000, Gray $88,000, Brown $37,000

   b. List of customers and customer statistics/history

      • How long a customer
      • Sales history by product with trends
      • Salesperson assigned
      • New customer/lost customer history

   c. Salespeople history

      • Sales by customer history and trends
      • Sales efforts versus results
      • Forecast-to-actual sales history
      • New customer history
      • Lost customer history

   d. Sales forecast data

      • Sales forecast by customer/products versus actual
      • New customers not in forecast

- Lost customers or sales in forecast
- Amount of sales not materializing
- Amount of sales not in forecast

2. Contacts data

   a. Customer survey

   - Satisfaction with company, products, salespeople
   - Relationship with assigned salesperson
   - If sales have decreased, why, and are customers buying elsewhere?
   - What would help them to buy more?
   - Positive and negative experiences
   - What the company does right—and wrong
   - Competitor relationships and their advantages

   b. Type of contacts

   - Effectiveness—personal contact, phone call, memos
   - Relationship—contacts to salespeople (present and future)
   - Quality of contacts by salesperson
   - Contact procedures by each salesperson

Factors for Improvements

1. Process—sales contact procedures and follow-up
2. Timeliness—How responsive is sales function to customer?
3. Quality—relationship with customer, products, and sales follow-up
4. Cycle—How often is customer contacted—pre-sale, during sale, and after-sale?
5. Numbers:

   - Contacts/sale
   - Sales forecast/actual sales
   - Sales/sales efforts
   - Sales cost/gross sale/net profit on sale

Conclusions/Inferences

1. The greater the sales contacts/customer service, the greater possibility of increased sales.
2. Sales forecasts have little basis in reality and are not related to real sales efforts or plans.
3. The greater the seniority of the salesperson, the less sales effort and fewer customer contacts.
4. Sales compensation is based more on seniority than on efforts and results.
5. Sales forecasts are based on historical sales and cannot be counted on to plan production based on real customer orders.
6. There is little incentive for older sales personnel to fully service present customers and bring in new customers.

what price is to be asked for each item and what pricing flexibility can be tolerated to still cover costs and contribute to profits? Effective pricing strategies, working in consort with the sales function, should enable the business to meet its sales and profit plans. Pricing strategies developed in this manner then become the yardsticks against which to measure. There are various methods or strategies for developing a pricing structure, which include:

- **Percentage markup.** Using a desired percentage of costs (e.g., 40%), usually thought of as a gross profit markup, to calculate the selling price. For instance, an item with a calculated cost of $100, with a 40 percent markup, would have a selling price of $140. Although this method is a quick way to calculate selling prices and maintain consistent profit margins, it has the built-in disadvantage of penalizing customers for the business's cost inefficiencies. For example, if the cost of the same $100 item increased to $150, the new selling price would be $210 (a markup of $60: 40% × $150). The customer is now expected to reimburse the business for its cost inefficiencies and pay an additional 40 percent markup for these additional costs. In many cases, such pricing policies can put the business in a difficult market position and cause the sales function to work harder for each sale and possibly lose customers.

- **Dollars per item.** Using a consistent dollar markup per item over costs. In the previous example, if the business desires to earn $30 per item, the selling price at $100 cost would be $130; and at $150 cost, it would be $180; and at $80 cost, it would be a $110 selling price. This process tends to stabilize profit margins, rewards customers for the business's cost efficiencies (without penalizing them extra for the cost inefficiencies), and clearly identifies the dollar amount of gross profit per item.

- **Market pricing.** Using the marketplace as the starting point for setting your prices. For example, if the standard price for the business's goods or services is $200 in the marketplace, this becomes its basis for pricing. Theoretically, if a business lowers its prices from the market price, its sales should increase; and raising prices should decrease sales. This approach typically stresses sales and may tend to disregard setting selling prices to recover costs and contribute to profits.

- **Competitive pricing.** Setting prices to beat competitors, regardless of whether the additional business is profitable or desirable. Small businesses sometimes get caught up in the "beating the competition" game, losing sight of their real reasons for being in business. If a business finds itself in a competitive selling position—either in total or in part of the business—many times the best approach is to provide the highest-quality product at the least possible cost. This should allow the business to stay competitive, serve its customers, and make money.

- **Unique niche.** Having a product or service that is unique or different from others being offered by your competitors—for example, a unique process (i.e., automatic camera), unique features (i.e., higher speeds), unique uses (i.e., fax and copier), and so on. If a small business can develop such a unique niche, it usually provides a marketing and sales advantage, particularly where there is a high customer demand. A business can decide to take full advantage of this unique advantage by setting higher selling prices and possibly maximizing its return in the short term. However, such a policy (with high profit margins) usually results in other competitors entering the field and possibly driving prices below acceptable levels (or you out of the business—e.g., the microcomputer business). A better approach may be to continually control costs and to keep prices as low as possible and quality as high as possible. This approach may not maximize short-term profits, but it should maximize returns in the longer term and tend to keep competitors from entering the field (e.g., condensed soup).

- **Quality strategy.** Establishing an image in the marketplace for quality of product and/or service (e.g., hotel chains, car rental agencies, auto makers, appliances, etc.). Typically, customers will be willing to pay more for such perceived quality, and this can give you a competitive advantage. However, it may cost the business considerably to establish and maintain the quality image—and it must continuously deliver such quality. If your quality should suffer appreciably, the downward sales cycle may respond faster than the original upward sales flow.

- **Price-sensitive strategy.** Competing based on being able to sell at the lowest price (e.g., Wal-Mart, low-end manufacturers, auto makers, small appliances, etc.). Using this approach to set selling prices requires a business to be closely in touch with its costs, profit margins, and breakeven points. Should it have to raise prices (and customer service, or the lack thereof, remains at the same low level), the resultant loss of sales may grossly exceed the safety level of the business's existing volumes.

Effective pricing strategies can enable the business to meet its sales and profit plans.

There may be pricing strategies other than those described that a small business wishes to use. The important factor to consider is that the pricing strategy fits into the business and sales plan and allows it the flexibility to ensure success. Typically, this means using a combination of the aforementioned techniques, either in total or by individual product line or item. What is most important is that the small business develops effective pricing strategies that enable the sales function to service its customers and maximize the amount of profitable sales.

The lower the cost, the greater the price flexibility.

METHODS OF SALES

There are a number of different ways of selling products and related customer service, for example:

- Direct sales to the ultimate customer
- Selling to OEMs (original equipment manufacturers)
- Industrial sales for additional manufacturing
- Wholesale sales

- Retail sales
- Broker sales
- Manufacturing sales representatives
- Point-of-sale selling
- Goodwill sales
- Combination of these approaches

The small business must understand the different types of sales and desirable practices for each. Small business management may question whether the company is using the right sales technique for each product or product line and the related effectiveness. This is also an area where owners and management can provide some guidance and direction by correlating product lines and products to one or more methods of sales.

Methods of Compensation

The sales function tends to be compensated differently from the rest of the small business—typically, on commission based on sales made. This often places the sales staff's emphasis on selling those products that maximize their commissions rather than on those products and customers that maximize the company's goals. Sales compensation policies must coordinate with the agreed-on direction of the business. Sales compensation must also relate to profitability and collectibility. Many small businesses have instituted commission payments based on profitability and delay commission payment until the sale has been collected.

The method of compensation must also encourage the proper level of customer service, necessary to increase sales from existing major and minor customers, potential new customers, and noncustomers. In addition, the sales force must be available to service the customer after the sale—and after the sales commission has been earned. Many times a salesperson will do what has to be done to make the sale—and earn a commission—but considers other areas of customer service nonproductive. Many older sales personnel (those more than three years in the field) have burned out to some extent and would rather wait for the sales orders to come in and earn the easy commissions than do the full customer service and sales job they were hired to do. Small business management must provide proper supervision, direction, and accountability to ensure that the sales function is performing effectively in accordance with desired direction so that sales performance coordinates with:

- **Company plans.** By customer and product line
- **Sales forecasts.** With a high percentage of real customer orders (80% or higher)
- **Customer service requirements.** Before and after the sale
- **Cash conversion requirements.** Selling to customers with timely payment records
- **Other functions.** For example, manufacturing, engineering, shipping, customer relations, accounting, product service, and so on
- **Product profitability.** Selling the right product for the company, not to maximize commissions
- **Customer satisfaction.** Selling what the customer needs
- **Sales timing.** Selling for the long term, not for short-term sales commissions or sales incentives
- **Internal ability to produce, deliver on time, and service the customer.** During and after the sale
- **Inventory levels.** Items to be sold from inventory, items to be made upon receipt of the order, items to be discouraged

There are numerous methods for compensating sales personnel other than on a strict commission basis. Small business management must evaluate the method of sales compensation on the basis of whether it results in moving the business toward its goals or tends to enrich the sales staff, often to the detriment of the business.

Making the sales function a collection function improves cash conversion.

The method of compensation must motivate the sales force to effectively sell so that owners' and management's, the customers', and the sales personnel's needs are all met. It must support the coordination of all of these factors and encourage the sales function to work together with the business and its plans. Other compensation methods include:

- Salary plus commission (over a specified level)
- Salary based on results (sales level plus customer service)
- Customer calls or contacts
- Variable commission (based on customers and/or products sold)
- Collections (payment based on sales collected)
- Profitability (payment based on sales profit)
- Customer base or territory
- Group compensation based on defined results
- Salary plus profit sharing
- Salary only

Sales Information and Reporting Systems

Small business management must understand what the elements of a desirable sales information and reporting system should include so as to develop such a system for their business. An effective sales information system must provide for integration with the operating components of the business such as manufacturing and production control, engineering, accounting, inventory control, quality control, shipping, credit and collections, and so on. The information system must provide sales personnel with the information they need to properly service the customer and work cooperatively with the other operating areas of the company. In essence, a well-designed sales information and reporting system allows the sales function to provide an effective communications link between the customer and the business.

A desirable sales information and reporting system should include:

- Realistic sales forecasts that integrate with organizational business and sales plans
- Sales forecast versus actual sales reporting by product line or item and by customer, with a mechanism for revisions to the sales forecast

- Sales statistics showing items ordered, sold, delivered, and collected
- Customer statistics showing items ordered, comparison to prior sales, amount of sales, new items, and so on
- Profitability analysis by product item and by customer, indicating plus and minus variances
- Sales staff statistics showing sales by individual, profitability by product and customer, customer sales and projections, orders in process, and so on
- Relationship of sales to other company factors such as backlog, inventory levels, production availability, engineering requirements, other customer requirements, and so forth
- Product line analysis that relates sales to company goals and direction, cost-volume-profit (CVP) and breakeven analysis, expected profit goals, and comparison and trend analysis

Performing the Sales Function Analysis

Typically small business management needs to identify and develop the desired sales reporting and control system. To accomplish this, management analyzes the sales function working with sales personnel. A number of initial questions must be answered prior to the start of an analysis of the sales function. These include:

- **Type of business.** Manufacturing, service, distributor, wholesaler, retailer, and so on
- **Type of process.** Make to order, sell from inventory, direct sales, broker sales, and so on
- **Type of sales.** Direct sales, OEM sales, engineering sales, point of sales, goodwill sales, and so on
- **Type of sales organization.** Company, broker, distributive, manufacturers' representatives, combination, and so on
- **Sales office locations.** Headquarters, remote sales offices, selling from home, individual offices, and so on
- **Organizational hierarchy.** Sales manager, sales supervisors, number of sales personnel and support people, and so on

- **Information systems.** Sales forecasts, planning systems, sales and customer statistics, product line and item profitability, and so on
- **Method of compensation.** Commission, salary and commission, salary only, salary and bonuses, team compensation, and so on
- **Systems and procedures.** How the sales function operates and how it is integrated with the rest of the company
- **Purpose of the sales function.** To sell what they can, customer service orientation communication link between company and customer, goodwill representation

Sales Function Desirable Practices

Management should be aware of various desirable sales function operating practices and efficiencies to effectively assist the small business in developing the sales function reporting and control system. A list of these desirable practices includes:

- A sophisticated sales forecast system that correlates closely with actual customer orders
- Sales forecast procedures that allow for integration with production scheduling techniques
- Sales forecasts and plans that are directed toward selling the desired product or product lines and that allow for monitoring actual versus planned results
- Sales statistics and reporting systems that accurately detail what has happened so that remedial action can be taken
- Effective sales management that properly directs and controls the sales force
- Sales compensation and commission policies that integrate with sales planning and assist in achieving the desired results
- Sales systems that accurately compute sales commissions and ensure that sales personnel are paid at the right time
- Sales statistics by product line, individual product, and customer that enable sales management to make the correct decisions and take appropriate actions

- Sales management procedures that provide for direct supervision of sales staff, including proper training, orientation, and review

- Customer relations policies that are exemplified by direct customer orders, nondependence on specific sales personnel, product and company loyalty, and customer satisfaction

- An ongoing customer base that consistently purchases an expected level of product and can be counted on

- Information and control system that provides the ability to relate sales efforts and related costs to sales levels achieved

- Maintenance of selling costs as an expected percentage or dollar value of total sales

- Selling and promotional techniques that can be directly related to the success of the sales effort

- Customer information system that provides data relative to the sales effort, product quality, timeliness of deliveries, product changes, desired services, after-sales service, and so on

During the sales function analysis, management may uncover various detrimental practices existing within the present sales function. An example of such a bad practice is shown in Exhibit 6.4.

Sales are great, but real profits are better.

EXHIBIT 6.4   Making the Sale

ABC, Inc. is a distributor of health and beauty products. There are six outside salespeople who call on customers. Each salesperson has a quota that must be exceeded each month, with each succeeding month's sales exceeding the one before. While these salespeople are well compensated, the pressure of meeting their monthly quotas has resulted in excessive turnover—at least three of the six every year. One salesperson, in an effort to keep the job, in low months submits a high percentage of sales orders in the last week of the month. In the first week of the next month, most of these sales orders are cancelled. The company pays commissions at the time of sale, and credits back the commission paid if the sale does not go through. However, should the employee leave in the meantime, the company must chase the former salesperson to recover these erroneously paid commissions—they rarely do; it becomes a cost of doing business.

Suggested Response

This is a typical situation for such a small business where the salespeople are continually urged to increase sales from the previous period. Normally, the owners have no sales plan as to what products to sell, to whom to sell the products, what constitutes a quality customer, and what quantities to sell to these customers. The only sales forecast is to beat the previous month's total sales with minimal regard to the quality content of the individual sales. For the salesperson this becomes a pressure cooker, dictating making a sale at any cost, with disregard for customer service and whether the customer really needs the product. For the owners, it is a scorecard system of sales—they are hoping that if they make sufficient sales there will be profits at the end, but have no knowledge of what their costs for each sale are and whether each sale generates a profit.

What operational procedures and controls would you recommend to correct this situation?

Step 1. Develop a real sales plan centralized on the needs of the customers—especially the major customers (the 20% who provide 80% of total sales). This means that the salespeople will need to spend more time on customer service and less time selling the customer. The owners will have to reduce the pressure of making sales and review the present system of sales commissions.

Step 2. Establish controls that encompass the salespeople making quality sales calls to quality customers, increases from previous orders, new products sold, sales profitability, customer collectibility, other customer referrals, and new quality customers added.

Step 3. Redetermine the method of compensation for sales personnel that would encompass the owners taking back control of sales operations and establishing formal sales plans based on customer requirements. The sales personnel would then be held accountable with proper controls and reporting to effectively service the company's customers, especially the major ones. Compensation could be a combination based on providing the desired level of customer service as well as a smaller commission override for total sales—paid at the time the company receives the customer's payment.

Step 4. Rather than going after individual and relatively small sales, the emphasis should be to negotiate with the major customers as to their long-term needs, resulting in a contract that ensures a high level of future sales. If this can be successful, the sales personnel can also be more successful in terms of sales and compensation, resulting in proper growth for the business.

Conclusion

Small business management must consider the sales function as an integral part of the small business's planning process. Owners and management must define the businesses the company is in, its basic business principles, and the products/services to be sold to which customers at which times. It is within this overall planning framework that the sales function develops its plans (or sales forecast) to integrate with management's expectations. Such sales plans must incorporate the maximum level of real customer orders (e.g., 80% of total forecast), so that the small business can exert its efforts on servicing these customers and turning such sales orders into deliveries and cash collections in the shortest time possible.

In addition, each customer and sales order must be looked at as a profit center. That is, the total sales amount must provide a contribution to positive cash flow and net profits. To accomplish this, the small business must exercise adequate control over product, functional, and customer costs. Not only does each dollar of cost savings produce an additional dollar to the bottom line, but it also allows management greater freedom in making pricing decisions. While the cost control emphasis (if any) in most small businesses is on controlling product costs, functional costs (e.g., sales order processing, accounts receivable, and collections), customer costs (e.g., customer service, installation, and after-sale support), and net profit contribution must also be considered in evaluating the efforts of the sales function. Although in many situations sales prices may have to be set based on outside influences such as market pressures and competition, small business management must strive for the greatest flexibility in price setting based on maximizing the differential between real assigned costs and selling price. Accordingly, the sales function must be analyzed as an integrated part of operations. No longer can the sales function operate on its own (as if it is in business for itself) without clear direction from small business management and integration with the other operating areas of the business. It is within this context that small business management analyzes the sales function as part of customer service and cash conversion, and as an effective contributor to positive cash flow and net profits. It is no longer acceptable to make sales that cannot be produced, delivered, or collected in a timely fashion and that may produce a sales commission but do not produce desired cash flow and net income.

CHAPTER 7

Cost Considerations

Although the small business owner typically places major emphasis on increasing sales as the solution to increasing the business or working out of a bad cash or operational situation, most times the cause of the problem is excessive costs or an inadequate margin between costs and selling prices. In addition, the business may be making sales that do not generate a profit or contribution to positive cash flow or making sales to less-than-quality customers who pay late or not at all. In most instances, the control of costs for the small business can put more onto the bottom line than a continual thrust to increase sales. Remember that a dollar of cost savings goes directly to the bottom line, while a dollar increase in sales may in fact produce a loss to the bottom line. However, very rarely will you find a small business with the semblance of a cost accounting system or an effective reporting system that comes close to accurately determining true costs, consisting of product or service costs, functional costs, and customer costs.

> There is more to be earned through the reduction of costs than through the increase of sales.

Cost accounting is a major area of operations that the typical small business owner shies away from. Unfortunately, everything affecting the small business's operations relates to cost accounting. While the small business owner may pay minimal attention to the cost side of the profit equation (i.e., sales less costs equal profit or loss), it is the owners' responsibility to develop effective systems for identifying, reporting, and controlling costs so as to manage the business most economically without sacrificing results and growth.

> Cost accounting affects every activity; business life is cost accounting.

Cost Classifications

Costs can be divided into a number of categories for small business management purposes depending on the business's goals and objectives. Each cost categorization is a separate and distinct method with specific uses different from other classifications.

Manufacturing versus Nonmanufacturing Costs

In the case of a manufacturing business, costs may be divided into two major categories based on the management and functional activities they relate to:

1. Manufacturing costs are product costs related to the business's manufacturing activities—they relate to the following:
   a. Direct materials are the materials and parts that actually go into the finished product. Supplemental materials and supplies such as screws, nails, glue, and so on are usually considered indirect materials and included in manufacturing overhead.
   b. Direct labor is the labor cost directly associated with the manufacturer of the product, such as costs of production workers. Labor costs for manufacturing supervision, material handling, maintenance, quality control, and other support services are usually classified as indirect labor and included in manufacturing overhead.
   c. Manufacturing overhead can be considered as including all other costs of manufacturing except direct materials and direct labor.

Other costs that are usually part of manufacturing overhead include depreciation, rent and/or other facilities costs, fringe benefits, production support costs, indirect materials, and indirect labor.

2. Nonmanufacturing costs are functional costs related to activities other than manufacturing functions of the organization. These nonmanufacturing costs can also be considered as operating expenses such as the following:

   a. Selling/marketing expenses relate to the costs of selling the product or service and keeping it sold. They include sales salaries and commissions, advertising and promotion, travel and entertainment, distribution costs, and sales service costs.

   b. General and administrative expenses include costs of those support functions necessary to keep the business going, such as owners' salaries or draws, staff costs (i.e., accounting, information technology [IT], purchasing), mailroom, insurance, and secretarial/receptionist.

Fixed versus Variable (and Semivariable) Costs

This category measures variability of costs relative to changes in production/service volume or some other measures of activity.

- **Fixed costs.** These are the costs that remain constant in total regardless of routine changes in the business's volume of activity. For example, rent, insurance, taxes, depreciation, and so on are costs that do not fluctuate based on changes in level of activity. They are incurred even if volume drops and remain relatively constant even if volume increases. Variations in these costs come about only as a result of major volume shifts or factors independent of volume changes.

- **Variable costs.** These are costs that vary in direct proportion to changes in levels of functional activities. For example, direct labor and direct material costs will vary approximately proportionately with volume level changes and are therefore classified as variable.

- **Semivariable costs.** These costs vary, but not proportionately, with changes in volume of activity and contain both a fixed component and a variable component. Examples include electricity costs, maintenance, material handling, and so on, each of which will increase as production volume increases, but not on a direct proportional basis.

The concept of fixed, variable, and semivariable costs refers to how the costs behave or react to changes in levels of activity. This is necessary information for activities such as flexible budgeting, profit planning, cost control, variance analysis, and related management-based decisions.

> As the activity changes, *so does the cost.*

Direct versus Indirect Costs

Another way to view business costs is as either direct or indirect in terms of their traceability to a product/service, department, or other segment of the business that represents the activity being costed. This type of cost analysis may be used effectively for product costing, pricing, and profitability analysis purposes or for evaluation of business segments.

- **Direct costs.** These are costs that can be directly traced to the activity being costed. For example, direct labor, direct materials, specific product advertising, sales commissions, and so on can be directly attributed to a specific product/service.

- **Indirect costs.** These are costs that cannot be directly attributed to the activity being costed. Examples include manufacturing or administrative overhead, and other shared functional costs (sometimes referred to as common or joint costs) such as purchasing, IT, personnel, accounting, and legal.

> True product/service costs create the right decisions.

These cost classifications are summarized in Exhibit 7.1 as to manufacturing and nonmanufacturing and in Exhibit 7.2 as to fixed and variable costs and as to direct and indirect costs.

Manufacturing Costs

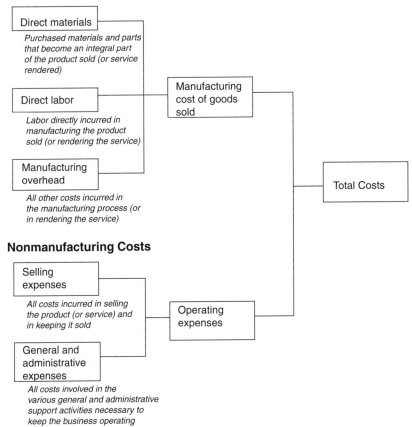

Direct materials
Purchased materials and parts that become an integral part of the product sold (or service rendered)

Direct labor
Labor directly incurred in manufacturing the product sold (or rendering the service)

Manufacturing overhead
All other costs incurred in the manufacturing process (or in rendering the service)

Manufacturing cost of goods sold

Nonmanufacturing Costs

Selling expenses
All costs incurred in selling the product (or service) and in keeping it sold

General and administrative expenses
All costs involved in the various general and administrative support activities necessary to keep the business operating

Operating expenses

Total Costs

Functional Costing

EXHIBIT 7.1   **Cost Classifications: Manufacturing versus Nonmanufacturing**

ACTIVITY-BASED COSTING OVERVIEW

It is probably difficult to convince a small business owner to implement extensive and technical cost accounting systems like traditional job order and standard cost systems. However, one may be successful in convincing the owner to implement a less technical and more easily understood activity-based costing (ABC) system. The most successful cost system for a small business is a simple and helpful one that ABC principles allow.

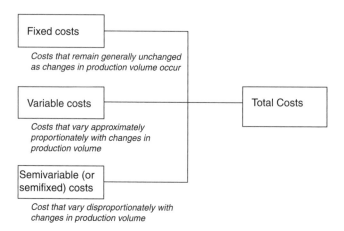

Cost Behavior/Planning Control

- -

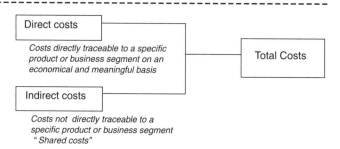

Costing/Profitability/Analyses

- -

EXHIBIT 7.2   Cost Classifications: Costing/Profitability/
Analyses

Such an ABC system enables the owners to implement the cost system that makes sense to them and enables them to operate their business with simple data collection and reporting. The cost controls that are generated are easy to understand, and with effective variance reporting allow small business management to take timely corrective action, preventing the incidence from reoccurring.

ABC is a cost accounting methodology for assigning costs of resources to products or services based on operational activities. Reduce or eliminate the activity and you reduce or eliminate the cost—putting each dollar saved directly to the bottom line. Using ABC methods, it is the activities, not the products or services (as in traditional cost accounting systems), that cause the costs. The ABC approach to cost accounting recognizes the causal relationship between cost drivers, resources, and activities. ABC defines a process, which could occur in the providing of a product or service or in production or the office, in terms of the activities performed, and then develops costs for these activities. ABC does not, contrary to traditional cost accounting techniques, develop costs by organizational cost centers but in terms of the activities performed. In addition, ABC assigns overhead based on the activities (cost drivers) that cause the overhead to occur, rather than allocating overhead via some allocation base such as direct labor hours or dollars. As costs are developed, each activity is appraised as to its necessity and its extent. As activities are reduced or eliminated, their attendant costs are also reduced or eliminated, driving these cost savings directly to the bottom line and to positive cash flow.

Many small businesses are struggling with better methods (or any method) for product/service costing and resultant pricing strategies, together with overall cost management, performance measurement, return on investment, and so on. In this context, ABC is only one of the tools for effective survival, competitiveness, and growth and prosperity, which challenge organizations today in an ever-changing business environment. ABC methodologies, when implemented correctly, can be the central core that provides the elements of an effective organization-wide cost reduction system that enables the small business to identify opportunities for improvement and make best practice recommendations.

Small business management should have a focus as to the purpose for establishing cost controls. It is not merely data collection of numbers but a system to more accurately determine the true costs (product/service, functional, and customer) of a product or service. Some objectives in setting a small business's cost controls based on ABC methodologies are shown below.

Objectives for Cost Controls

Depending on the type of business, such as manufacturing, retail, or service, the following items could be considered for ABC cost control objectives:

- Lower inventories (raw material, work in process, finished goods)—conserve cash and use it where needed in the business.

- Lower product costs (material, labor, and overhead)—increase cash and create pricing flexibility.

- Smaller manufacturing lots (just in time manufacturing)—conserve cash by not spending until needed.

- Improved quality—decrease quality control costs by making employees responsible for quality control, not other individuals.

- Decreased lead times (on-time deliveries)—compress cash conversion period—hold onto cash until necessary to spend and collect quickly.

- Increased productivity—produce more at the same or lower cost (productivity increases while costs do not).

- Improved customer satisfaction—increase customer service business and additional quality sales.

- Identification of value-added cost elements (to product item: direct and indirect)—reduction and elimination of unnecessary costs.

- Report on other than production functions as related to product items (i.e., sales, purchasing, engineering, accounting)—control functional costs and cash outlays.

- Maximize customer service while reducing customer-related costs—include customer costs in your cost formula and continually strive to reduce them.

A dollar saved is a dollar earned.

To identify and implement effective cost controls, the small business owner must be aware of all operational activities and their necessity in the management and operation of the business. It is an exercise to identify not only those costs that directly relate to the manufacturing or providing of the product or service but also those costs, such as functional and customer costs, that are part of operating the business.

Operating Decisions Affecting Cost Considerations

There are many operating decisions that need to be made by the small business owner relative to cost considerations. The small business owner must make many decisions regarding the business's operations as well as what cost considerations need to be implemented to effectively control such operations. Examples of such decisions include:

- Manufacture versus purchase (make versus buy)
- Vendor selection (price, quality, timeliness)
- Single versus multiple sourcing
- Manufacturing or service providing in-house versus outsourcing
- Manufacture versus assembly
- Cost elements and product/service item costing
- Pricing strategies, based on real costs
- Capital expenditures (effective use of facilities)
- Production and service providing processes and use of personnel
- Product line analysis (what products to sell)
- Inventory levels (in-house versus vendors/distributors)
- Lot sizing (how much to produce or services to provide)
- What businesses to be in (expand, status quo, curtail, or disband)

Small business life is cost accounting.

Cost Reduction Targets

Small business management continually looks for areas in which to reduce costs for the business. The focus must not be on strictly reducing costs but on maximizing results with the use of the least amount of resources. To effectively accomplish cost reduction without sacrificing results, the owner must be aware of the elements of the small business's operations. In setting up operating controls directed toward reducing costs and increasing profitability, the owner must be aware of those elements or activities that produce costs to the business.

Based on the type of business and its inherent operating activities, related *cost elements* must be identified, such as:

- Labor—direct and indirect
- Materials—direct and supplies
- Processing time kept to a minimum
- Lead time condensed to the smallest amount
- Paperwork reduced and eliminated
- Setup time—manufacturing and administration—minimized
- Parts and supplies at the best price, quality, and on-time
- Vendors—best prices, 100 percent quality, delivered on time
- Cycle time—manufacturing and administration—kept to a minimum
- Overuse and underuse conditions
- Scrap and obsolescence minimized
- Stockouts—manufacturing and administration—eliminated
- Customer complaints—quality, quantity, timeliness—responded to and prevented from reoccurring
- Uneven production (i.e., 60% of orders shipped last week of month)
- Unplanned downtime reduced
- Excesses (i.e., raw material and finished-goods inventory, work in process, supplies, equipment)
- Not shipping or providing services on time or not meeting customer expectations
- Employee surveys (i.e., anger and frustration) indicating operational weaknesses
- Personnel levels (and related costs) out of sync with what's necessary
- Processes/activities (value and non-value-added) evaluated for necessity
- Duplications/nonintegration of functions—product, functional, and customer related
- Unnecessary activities in any part of the operation—product/service or other

A dollar of cost savings is a dollar to the bottom line.

Areas for Improving Activities

In dealing with the above cost reduction targets, the small business owner should consider the following areas for improving activities to make them more economical, efficient, and effective. Each one of these cost-related areas may become a cost control to monitor and take action on in a developed set of cost controls and reporting system. The area of improvement should be clearly defined so that small business management can effectively monitor these areas to ensure that the business is moving in the right direction and that management takes proper corrective action in fixing the cause and not the blame.

Improve the activity; reduce or eliminate the cost.

Examples of such operating cost controls include:

- Eliminate function/work step on an overall business basis or within an individual function or activity. Management should provide proper guidance as to the direction of the business and each function or activity. For example, eliminate activities where the cost exceeds the value of the transaction (i.e., prepare a purchase requisition and purchase order for less than the cost of preparation, say $50).
- Eliminate duplication of efforts within the same function or across functions (for example, the receiving function checking in materials received as well as the user).
- Combine functions and/or work steps. For example, having employees submit time and expense reimbursement forms through the computer and having the computer software perform the checking and calculations—eliminating the need for further offline manual checking.

- Balance workloads within a function or activity (for example, processing of sales orders by customer or by alphabetic categories). When it happens that one individual is overworked while others are underworked or idle, move the employees to the work and determine whether work loads are shrinking and the function can get by with less personnel support.

> Move the employees to the work; don't wait for the work to come to them.

- Reduce or eliminate bottlenecks that are clogging operations and preventing them from running smoothly (for example, the requirement that the owner must sign and approve all incoming customer orders regardless of the amount, which holds up these customer orders from being entered into the system should the owner be unavailable). This procedure should be eliminated or used by exception for large or special orders.

- Improve process flow so as to maintain customer service and cash conversion goals (for example, a customer order put on backlog because the materials are not in due to the inability of the vendor to deliver on time). This is a vendor reliability problem and either the vendor needs to improve its operations or the business needs to seek other vendors.

- Improve work layout and flow of operations (for example, operating the business out of inventory with insufficient storage space, resulting in excessive time being lost in locating goods for shipment). The business needs to get out of the inventory business through improved reliance on vendors, producing or stocking based on real customer orders, direct shipping by vendors, and so forth.

- Improve scheduling: work and personnel. Work does not always fit the business's hours of operations or the scheduling of personnel. Adjust the hours of operation and personnel to the workflow and do not have employees waiting for work to come in. Normally work does not come in on a straight-line basis but more erratically—adjust work and personnel to the reality.

Queue the employees' work *to the workflow.*

- Eliminate causes of rejects and rework. Set up the control system to identify all incidences of rejects and rework. Ensure the honesty and reliability of personnel reporting so that such rejects and rework are not hidden from the reporting system. Identify and fix the cause, not the blame. For example, the need to rework a production function may be due to faulty tools, equipment malfunction or failure, inadequate training of personnel, poor or sloppy work habits, bad material quality, and so forth. By correcting the cause, such rework or rejects should not happen again in the future.

- Simplify work steps and processes so that minimal room is left for errors or mistakes (for example, an engineering drawing that presupposes that the operator has an adequate understanding of engineering drawings and tolerances). Break the job down into workable steps so any level of employee can easily understand it.

- Improve automation efforts and results. Eliminate manual operations where automation can do the job better and more accurately. For example, rather than relying on manually prepared inventory tags on sellable merchandise, make effective use of bar-code reading and tie it into your point-of-sale system so that the right merchandise is charged to the customer and inventory is automatically relieved, identifying remaining inventory and need for reordering.

- Increase standardization/decrease customization. For example, rather than offer many different options for your product, keep customer choices to a minimum. Know what sells and keep to those items (e.g., vanilla, chocolate, and strawberry rather than mango passion and avocado explosion).

Fix the cause, not the blame.

Some other guidelines that you can use in developing cost controls and maintaining operational efficiencies for the small business include:

- Maintain schedules.

- Practice good housekeeping.

- Strengthen education and training.

- Increase use of coaching and facilitation.

- Continuously improve.

- Meet realistic targets.

- Implement effective planning and budgeting systems.

- Achieve flexibility: doing the right thing.

- Exercise performance measurement and continual review and analysis.

- Take an operational perspective.

- Implement the concept of *economy, efficiency, and effectiveness.*

> Economy, efficiency, and effectiveness (and making money) is every-one's business.

Organizational Concerns

ABC concepts have evolved greatly in a relatively short period of time. Originally conceived as a methodology for product cost improvement and accuracy, ABC is now considered a comprehensive organization-wide performance measurement system supporting a wide range of purposes, such as:

- **Strategic priorities.** Identifying, setting, and implementing; as well as the development of organizational, departmental, and detail plans, together with flexible budgeting procedures

- **Cost performance measurement.** Identifying cost reduction opportunities, quality improvements, product/service design, process improvements, and so on

- **Analyzing cost performance.** Identifying such things as material and labor (and other normal overhead type costs), economy, and efficiency improvements

- **Continuous improvements.** Operating methods, use of facilities and equipment, productivity, use of personnel, vendor and customer relations, inefficiencies, waste, and so on
- **Capital investment.** Using scarce resources in the most economical, efficient, and effective manner
- **Organizational management.** Allowing management to operate and control the organization in the optimum cost-versus-benefit manner
- **Cash management.** Identifying areas for cash conservation, reduction and elimination of unnecessary costs, development of pricing strategies that maximize bottom-line contributions, and implementation of operational economies and efficiencies that result in effective use of resources

The small business owner can use such ABC-system-provided information and controls to improve the management and operation of ongoing activities. The goal of the cost accounting system should be to increase the value of the products/services provided to customers and to increase company profits by providing higher quality/added value to customers at the least possible costs. ABC works toward improving critical organizational decisions in such areas as:

- Product design and mix (what to sell and provide)
- Pricing considerations (what to charge)
- Customer mix (whom to sell)
- Sourcing (vendors, in-house/outsource, markets)
- Improvement priorities (on what areas to concentrate)
- Cash management (where to allocate scarce resources)

In this endeavor to improve the organization and customer service, and compress the cash conversion period through the implementation of best practices in a program of continuous improvement, the cost accounting system looks at the following areas:

- **Products/services.** What to offer, continue or discontinue, expand or contract, as well as cost-volume-profit (CVP) considerations, product/service breakeven analysis, and product line analysis

- **Customers.** To whom and how to sell (present and potential), customer service considerations, profitability, customer statistics (sales, costs, and profits), and sales forecasts

- **Activities.** Those that bring value to the product/service, such as material, labor, and product related (value-added) and those that offer support to the organization at additional cost but provide no value to the product/service (non-value-added), such as administration, support functions, and top management

- **Indicators of poor performance.** Operational measures that provide an indication that there is an area for positive improvement, such as scrap, vendor returns, customer returns, rework, and rejects

ABC provides the information; people provide the solutions.

Financial Cost Measures

In establishing a set of cost controls for a specific small business, there are many activities where costs can be reduced and eliminated. For many of these, immediate agreement with the owners as to the desirability of reducing or eliminating such costs can be obtained—many times resulting in more efficient operations. There are also other activities that should be reduced or eliminated but the owner declares these activities as nonnegotiable—for instance, the owner's son-in-law holding the overpaid position of chief financial officer (CFO) with one computer operator reporting to him and with a limited number of accounting transactions. While this position could be easily eliminated, putting those dollars saved directly to the bottom line, it is an area that is nonnegotiable to the owner as long as his daughter is married to the CFO.

While those activities that are reported through the system that has been established can be clearly dealt with and corrective action taken, there are also various nonfinancial measures that have a positive or adverse effect on small business operations. The small business owner needs to be aware of these measures in the development of operating cost controls due to their impact on operations. While they may not have a present measurable direct cost, they do have a relationship to present and future costs as well as the growth of the business. Some examples of such measures are:

- Customer complaints (returns, rejects, complaints)
- Idle inventory (raw material, work in process, finished goods)
- Late deliveries (vendors, customers)
- Change orders (purchasing, manufacturing, shipping)
- Processing (manufacturing, purchase, and sales orders)
- Recording (purchase requisitions, timecards, move tickets, etc.)
- Quality control (receiving, in process, final)
- Equipment (idle time, setups, maintenance, downtime)
- Production schedule changes (moves, wait time, lost time)
- Customer service (late, inadequate, nonresponsive)

Nonfinancial transactions have a cost.

Cost of Compliance Measures

The cost of compliance measures the dollars associated with *not* doing what is expected. These are considered lost costs or savings and need to be included in an all-inclusive operating control system.

Established standards

- Time (setups, processing, turnaround)
- Cost (i.e., per purchase order, data entry, raw materials)
- Quality (i.e., loss in production, service delivery)

On time

- Vendor deliveries
- Customer deliveries
- Work-in-process moves (to production schedule)

Production/service delivery

- Time commitments
- Quality
- Quantity

Administrative performance

- Goals, objectives, and detail plans
- Sales forecasts/real customer orders
- Budget versus actual versus what it should be

Schedules

- Selling requirements (when to sell)
- Development (i.e., product or service engineering)
- Production schedule
- Production control
- Shipping/delivery schedules
- Billing schedules

Often, it is not what is there but what is not there that creates the cost.

COST ELEMENTS

The elements that should be considered in defining the small business's cost structure are:

Products

- Individual item
- Product group
- Product line
- Specialty/custom product

Functions (distinct areas within an organization structure)

- Departments
- Cost centers
- Responsibility centers
- Profit centers

Activities (within functions)

- Manufacturing (i.e., product assembly)
- Service delivery
- Forms preparation and handling
- Data entry
- Maintenance

Elements (types of costs generated by activities)

- Direct labor
- Direct material
- Repairs and maintenance
- Support work

Customers

- Pre-sale
- During sale
- After sale
- Customer service

These costs are related to four main categories of cost—product/service, functional or activity, unassignable, and customer—and are depicted in small business formula 4, shown in Exhibit 7.3.

Overhead Considerations

Overhead is typically defined as all costs other than direct materials and labor. Traditionally, those costs that cannot be directly associated with product or service costs are classified as overhead and allocated on some basis. Although

EXHIBIT 7.3   Small Business Success Formula 4

$$ABC = P / S + F / A + UC + CC$$

ABC = Activity-based costing, a technique for assigning all possible costs to the product or service to arrive at a more accurate cost on which to base pricing decisions. ABC concepts include the following cost considerations.

P/S = Product and service costs that can be directly attributable to the product or service being provided to customers. Examples of such direct product costs are: **Material costs**, where the goal is to acquire necessary materials at the least possible cost while assuring vendor quality and timeliness of deliveries. Other considerations are to be able to use such materials on delivery, eliminate materials inventory, order just enough for the product or service, use the exact quantity of materials needed to produce the desired output (i.e., a one-to-one relationship between material in and product out, reduce scrap to a minimum, and eliminate rejects and rework).
Labor costs, where the goal is to use the least amount of labor at the least cost. Areas to consider include:

- Setup time (getting the job ready, which is nonproductive time that should be reduced to a minimum or eliminated if possible)
- Processing time (productive time that should be reduced to the extent possible, with efforts made to continually increase productivity)
- Putaway (putting the job away, which is nonproductive time to be reduced or eliminated)

F/A = Functional or activity costs that can be assigned directly to the product or service cost on a direct basis that has a reasonable relationship to the product or service. Examples of such functional or activity costs are receiving, storeroom, quality control, repairs and maintenance, supplies, supervision, facilities, and packing and shipping. In addition, other functions and activities that are less directly related to the product or service may also be assigned as costs, such as purchasing, accounts payable, billing, accounts receivable, and collections.

UC = Unassignable costs that cannot be directly assigned to the product or service. Examples of such unassignable costs include personnel, internal audit, and administrative and top management.

CC = Customer costs that relate to the business's dealing with each customer. These costs need to be added onto calculated ABC product costs to determine the real costs of dealing with each customer. Examples of such costs include before-sale customer service and selling efforts, customer contacts during the sale, and customer contacts after the sale.

---

many of the components of overhead may be necessary, a great number probably are not. Often, the business has hidden such unnecessary or wasteful costs as overhead so as not to attract attention. Overhead costs must be analyzed to determine those components that are unnecessary and wasteful.

Overhead in many organizations, especially the small business, have become the biggest source of costs. Overhead affects product costs, profit margins, resultant profits, and positive cash flow just as direct costs do. Those overhead costs that add value should be directly charged to the activity; those that do not should be eliminated.

The small business owner should review and analyze each function (e.g., sales, engineering, manufacturing, accounting, etc.) and determine which activities are relevant to product or service cost. Those activity costs that are relevant to product costs should be assigned back to the products/ services that use such activities. To accomplish such a functional analysis, each activity has to be fully analyzed to determine which ones are relevant to product costs (and the method of assignment) and which ones are not and should be considered for elimination.

For example, consider some typical activities in an administrative-type department (such as sales, purchasing, accounting, customer service, etc.):

- Telephone calls: incoming and outgoing
- Computer use: data processing, e-mail, Internet, and so on
- Receiving, reviewing, and filing paper
- Memo preparation and mailing
- Expediting/checking/reviewing activities
- Database maintenance
- Meetings: within and outside the department
- Breaks and lunches
- Surveys and audits
- Travel: internal and external
- Processing activities

While it may be difficult to discern how much of the employees' time is spent on some of these nonproductive type activities, and which should be eliminated, resulting in the need for fewer personnel or better use of personnel, you can conclude that there is an amount of time being wasted. By discouraging and eliminating the practice of such activities, you may be able to identify exactly (or pretty closely) the amount of time needed for necessary activities. This can then be the starting point for eliminating unnecessary overhead and minimizing costs to only necessary activities.

Overhead = overboard excess time will always be filled.

Functional Cost Controls

Another important aspect of the cost accounting system and related operating controls is to analyze and control each function of the organization, such as sales, manufacturing/service delivery, engineering/service design, IT, accounting, and so on. The starting point is to review and analyze the function as it is presently being performed so as to identify areas for positive improvement together with recommendations for such improvements. Typically, the small business owners, management, and operating personnel are assigned responsibility for each major function. The goal of this analysis is to begin the cost accounting functional control system with the most economical and efficient systems and procedures possible—and at the lowest cost. From that point, it becomes easier to maintain a program of continuous improvements and create a learning organization.

Some helpful tools for analyzing functions and their related costs are:

- Identifying activities for the purchasing function
- Using functional costs to assign costs to products
- Receiving costs

Identifying Activities for the Purchasing Function

In the analysis of a function it is always helpful to break the function down into its component activities and work steps to assist in determining each one's necessity and possibility of reduction or elimination. The functions and work steps of a typical purchasing function are listed below. Keep in mind that for a specific small business some of these functions or work steps may not exist. In such instances, you need to decide whether (1) they should exist, (2) there are other, better ways to accomplish the same objectives, or (3) there really is no need for them.

Purchase requisition by user

- Preparation
- Review

- Authorization
- Submission to purchasing department

Purchasing department

- Review of purchase requisition
- Vendor review and selection
- Existing vendor
- New vendor
- Competitive bidding
- Contracting
- Data entry
- Purchase requisition
- Purchase order
- Purchase order processing
- Printing
- Forms separation, distribution, and filing
- Purchase order submission to vendor
- Mailing process
- Electronic ordering
- Purchase order filing

Matching process by user

- Open purchase requisition file
- Receive purchase order copy
- Match purchase order to requisition
- File open purchase order

Accounts payable

- Receive open purchase order copies
- File in open purchase order files: by vendor, by purchase order number

Question each activity—is it needed, why is it done, *can it be done better?*

Using Functional Costs to Assign Costs to Products

If you are able to develop a simple ABC cost system for the small business, one of the tools to use is the methodology for assigning functional costs to products or services based on the level of activity of the products or services worked on during a period, as shown in Exhibit 7.4. An example of such a cost assignment is shown in the exhibit for the purchase order (PO) processing activity. Such cost assignments are helpful in determining the added costs of the activity and whether the activity can be reduced, thus saving costs, or eliminated.

EXHIBIT 7.4   **Assigning Functional Cost to Products**

Volume by product—purchase order (po) processing:

Product	Number of POs	%
1	183	6.6%
2	346	12.5%
3	639	23.1%
4	621	22.4%
5	468	16.9%
6	512	18.5%
Total	2,769	100.0%

Total cost for Purchasing Department for period = $88,766.
Assigning functional costs to products:

Product	%	Cost
1	6.6%	$ 5,859
2	12.5%	11,096
3	23.1%	20,505
4	22.4%	19,883
5	16.9%	15,001
6	18.5%	16,422
Total	100.0%	$88,766

Can the activity be reduced or eliminated?

Receiving Costs

Another tool that can be used to develop functional costs for assignment to a product or service cost is to analyze and develop costs for each activity within that function. For example, the development of activity and functional cost for the receiving operation could be accomplished as shown in Exhibit 7.5. Keep in mind that you want to keep your analysis simple and usable for the small business, so use good judgment as to the functions, if any, that you select for such cost analysis.

Based on the calculation in Exhibit 7.5, it costs approximately $24 each time a delivery is received by the receiving department or receivers. This cost is incurred regardless of the amount of the receipt. Accordingly, it does not make good business sense to receive deliveries that amount to less than $24. In addition, each receipt that can be eliminated theoretically saves the company $24, which is money to the bottom line. In reality, such savings

EXHIBIT 7.5   Receiving Costs

Labor Hour Cost: $12 Per Hour

Activity	Time	Cost
1. Receive PO copy from purchasing and file in open PO file	10 min	$ 2
2. Receive delivery and verify that delivery is ours: Check bill of lading, packing slip, and sign	20 min	$ 4
3. Compare delivery to open PO and record receipt on PO	15 min	$ 3
4. Count parts—record on open PO reconcile to PO amount ordered	15 min	$ 3
5. produce receiving report using open PO copy:	30 min	$ 6

- Partial: PO back to open file
- Final: PO to accounts payable
- Receiving report to accounts payable

6. Wait for quality control inspection	4 hrs	—
7. Move—storeroom, shop floor, or internal department	30 Min	$ 6
Total Cost of Receiving		$ 24

cannot be realized until a sufficient volume of receipts can be eliminated to achieve overall efficiency of operations. The cost in the exhibit can be used, however, to estimate the cost of receiving in the ABC cost system and help to convince small business management of the need to reduce such costs.

Taking the small business owner from a sale-at-any-cost philosophy to an only-profitable-sales philosophy is a difficult road. However, you must be diligent and continue to hammer the message across to the small business owner. It is in the best interest of the owner for the business to be successful and grow. An example of such a sales-at-any-cost philosophy is shown in Exhibit 7.6.

EXHIBIT 7.6   Making the Sale (At Any Cost)

Teddy Robbins is the owner of a small machine shop called Robbins Machining. While the business has a number of good repetitive customers, Teddy must submit a quote to get the business on almost every job. Teddy usually assumes that the customer is looking for a better price than he did the job for last time. Some customers have even told Teddy that since he did the job before, he should have greater experience in producing the item and should be able to do it better and less expensively. Teddy does not want to lose a customer, so he automatically reduces his quotes from his last selling price by 8. The 8 has no magic in it; 8 is his favorite number, so he uses it. Teddy controls almost every aspect of his business, from the customer contact through production and shipping. He trusts no one else to negotiate or have contact with his customers. As there is no element of a cost system, Teddy does not know whether these sales are profitable. He believes that if he makes enough sales he will make money. Teddy believes that what he might lose on one sale he will make up on another sale or on volume.

What advice and cost controls should Teddy fellow?

Suggested Response

Teddy is in the sales business. He likes getting the sale and having his machine shop filled with work—he likes being in the shop and keeping busy. However, he is in business to service his customers and make money. The initial step to consider is getting the sale with a large percentage based on bidding quotes. Teddy must get in touch with his costs (product, functional, and customer) to base his bid quotes. There will be bids where Teddy can make a desired profit, those where there is less than desired profit, and those where there is no profit, but a loss. With a proper cost system to be used in his bidding process, Teddy should be able to decide which bids to submit and which ones to pass on. In addition, Teddy should concentrate on customer service aspects such as quality, on-time deliveries, and customer requirements to convince more customers to contract with Teddy on a non-bid basis. Teddy should also release his need for control and allow his employees to service customers. He should develop an effective reporting system that looks at each sales order and customer as a profit center that allows Teddy to make the correct business decisions.

Cost Reduction Analysis: Traditional versus ABC

As has been previously mentioned, the implementation of an effective cost control and reporting system (based on ABC principles) assists the small business owner in identifying costs related to each product and customer in an effort to reduce and eliminate activities that create costs—driving all cost savings directly to the bottom line. In addition, such a cost system enables the business not only to operate most economically, but also to implement best practice efficiencies directed toward organizational effectiveness. To hammer this point home, let us take a look at an example showing the resultant cost structure using traditional cost methods of direct labor and materials with an allocation of overhead costs compared to the cost results and operational information provided using ABC techniques.

ABC Case Study

ACE, Inc., is a small business that manufactures a highly competitive commercial product. ACE was the original inventor of the product and at one time had a 74 percent market share. However, as a small business with strong competition (particularly from the overseas market), market share has dropped to 32 percent over the past few years. While ACE's product is still perceived to be the best quality in the marketplace, its four competitors have been able to basically copy the product and sell it for less than ACE, as follows:

		Selling Price	%	% Market
ACE, Inc.		$129	100%	32%
Competitor	1	$ 89	69%	36%
Competitor	2	$ 98	76%	17%
Competitor	3	$109	84%	8%
Competitor	4	$116	90%	7%

As can be seen, this has become a price-sensitive product, with the greatest sales going to the lowest-price seller. Some customers of ACE are still willing to pay more for what they perceive to be better quality, and there is an indication of some customer loyalty. ACE is implementing ABC cost principles in an attempt to better control its costs, achieve flexibility in pricing, and get back to its previous market share. ACE believes that the public will buy its product instead of the competitors' if it sells the same high quality at lower prices.

The following cost workups for ACE, Inc. show the differences between product costs and selling prices under the following cost concepts:

- Traditional cost
- ABC costs using traditional cost data
- ABC costs integrated with operating efficiencies and cost reductions
- ABC costs with identification of specific elements of other activity costs

Traditional Cost Data

- Material costs: lot size of 100, item cost of $34.68, 120 items into production
- Labor costs: labor rates – direct ($12/hour); indirect ($16/hour)
- Storeroom issues/returns: 2 hours
- Staging/get ready: 1 hour
- Number of setups: 4 @ 6 hours each
- Moves: 4 @ 1/2 hour each = 2 hours
- Queue time = 12 hours
- Processing time: 126.4 hours/lot
- Quality control: 8 hours/lot
- Packing/shipping: 4 hours
- Supervision: 6 hours/lot
- Supplies: $4.80 unit
- Other costs (allocated): $8.40 unit
- Overhead costs: overhead rate: 140% of direct labor costs (setup and processing)
- Selling price markup: 150% of total costs

1. Calculation of traditional cost and selling price per item:

	Total Cost	Unit Cost
Materials	$4,161.60	$41.62
Direct labor		
Setups	288.00	2.88
Processing	1,516.80	15.17
Total labor	1,804.80	18.05
Overhead	2,526.72	25.27
Total cost	$8,493.12	$84.94

Selling price: 150% markup = $127.41; rounded to $129

2. Calculation of ABC costs from the information provided:

	Total Cost	Unit Cost
Materials	$4,161.60	$41.62
Direct labor	1,804.80	18.05
ABC costs:		
Storeroom	32.00	.32
Staging	16.00	.16
Moves	32.00	.32
Quality control	128.00	1.28
Packing/shipping	64.00	.64
Supplies	480.00	4.80
Supervision	96.00	.96
Other costs	840.00	8.40
Total ABC costs	1,688.00	16.88
Total cost	$7,654.40	$76.55

What selling price should be recommended? Assuming the owner can be convinced that ABC costs are more accurate, the new selling price can be calculated in a number of ways such as:

- Add the same dollar difference as used with the traditional cost system, as above, that is, $129 selling price less calculated costs of $84.94 or $44.06. Using the same dollar difference of $44.06 to the new cost of $76.55 results in a new selling price of $120.61.
- Use the same markup percentage of 150 percent of costs as traditionally used, resulting in a newly calculated selling price of $114.83.

- Accept the concept of competitive pricing. It is apparent from the competition that the proprietary product that ACE thought it once had is now working in the competitive marketplace. The question here is how low ACE is willing to go in pricing to meet the competition. Whereas a case could be made to lower the price to $114.99 based on item 2 listed above, what effect would this price change have in the marketplace and would it increase ACE's sales and increase its market share? A price of $114.99 will probably obtain some sales from competitors 3 and 4 (with the smallest sales volumes). It may do little to take sales from its major competitor 1, at a selling price of $89 and a 36 percent market share, or from competitor 2, with a selling price of $98 and a 17 percent market share.

3. Through analysis of operations and processes, the following activities were identified for elimination: *storeroom, staging, moves, queue time, wait time.*

In addition, through effective repurchase negotiations, material costs were reduced to $26.00 per unit and 100 pieces placed into production to produce 100 items.

Direct labor times could also be reduced as follows:

- Setups: 3 @ 4 hours each
- Processing time: 108.8 hours per lot
- Quality control: 2 hours per lot
- Supervision: 1 hour per lot

Calculation of ABC costs based on the preceding data:

	Total Cost	Unit Cost
Materials	$2,600.00	$26.00
Direct labor		
Setups	144.00	1.44
Processing	1,305.60	13.06
Total	1,449.60	14.50
ABC costs:		
Quality control	32.00	.32
Packing/shipping	64.00	.64

Supplies	480.00	4.80
Supervision	16.00	.16
Other costs	840.00	8.40
Total ABC costs	1,432.00	14.32
Total cost	$5,481.60	$54.82

What selling price should be recommended at this cost?

- $54.82 costs plus original differential of $44.06 or a $98.88 selling price
- 150 percent of costs or a selling price of $82.23
- Competitive selling price of $89 to meet its lowest competitor

Further analysis identified elements of other costs of $840.00 to be as follows:

	Output Measure	Per Unit	OM Cost	Total Cost	Unit Cost
Bill of material	Hours	2.0	$30.00	$60.00	$.60
Routing/process	Hours	1.5	20.00	30.00	.30
Purchasing	POs	4	75.00	300.00	3.00
Receiving	Number	4	12.00	48.00	.48
Storeroom moves	Number	2	18.00	36.00	.36
Work-in-process moves	Number	6	12.00	72.00	.72
Inspections	Number	3	25.00	75.00	.75
Packaging	Unit	1	18.00	18.00	.18
Shipping	Unit	1	13.00	13.00	.13
Accounts payable	Number	4	32.00	128.00	1.28
Total activity costs				$780.00	$7.80
Allocated costs				60.00	.60
Total cost				$840.00	$8.40

What activities should be considered for further analysis leading toward further cost reductions?

CUSTOMER COST CONCEPTS

The primary goal of ABC cost systems is to provide more accurate product costs on which management can make proper decisions as to which products/services to sell, to whom and what to sell, what amounts to produce, what to price, and so on. ABC also provides the data on which to manage more economically, efficiently, and effectively. ABC provides for management analysis and performance measurement relative to such things as products/services being provided, functions and activities being performed, justification of costs, and results achieved.

Customer Profitability

Most small businesses use a traditional cost system, some form of rough internal costs, or merely a "gut feeling" of costs (in other words, they have no clue whatsoever as to what their costs are) to determine sale and customer profitability. The basic formula is usually based on total sales amount (not necessarily amounts collected) less a standard product cost that is usually the same for all customers. Their customer service efforts focus on those customers that produce the largest amount of sales. However, should they analyze customer service costs (pre-sale, during sale, and post-sale), they may find that their largest customers are their largest loss customers. For instance, a typical small business found that its largest customer required constant attention (a sales representative assigned full time) and expected the most favorable prices (in fact, dictating prices it would pay). Taking these factors into account, this customer becomes a costly volume loser, forcing the small business to change its sales and customer service policies in relation to this customer in order to continue to service the customer and still obtain a profit from each sale. This necessitated a recalculation of costs to include the special treatment accorded this customer, such as individual attention and price concessions, resulting in reducing internal costs associated with this customer and renegotiating prices so that the customer could continue to receive favorable prices, but those with which the business could realize a profit.

Another customer made many small orders applying just-in-time (JIT) principles at the business's expense. Adding back these processing order costs (approximately $125 per order) based on ABC analysis, this high-volume, profitable customer became a large loser. By addressing this customer's small-amount ordering needs through effective sales negotiations, blanket purchase order concepts, electronic ordering, and production scheduling integration, the business was able to bring costs back into line and continue selling profitably to this customer.

A good starting point for such customer profitability analysis is to develop effective reporting systems that provide customer statistics by product line. An example of such a report is shown in Exhibit 7.7.

EXHIBIT 7.7   Customer Information by Product Line

Customer	Sales $	%	Sales $	%	Sales $	%
Product A						
Peterboro, Inc.	435	14.7%	440	16.2%	460	19.2%
Apex Electric	395	13.4%	440	18.2%	320	13.3%
Kontrol Mfg.	380	12.9%	340	12.5%	240	10.0%
Samson Mfg.	330	11.2%	250	9.2%	280	11.7%
Textron, Inc.	230	7.8%	210	7.7%	180	7.5%
Delta, Inc.	180	6.1%	220	8.1%	250	10.4%
Consolidated Electric	150	5.1%	180	6.6%	160	6.7%
	2,100	71.2%	2,080	76.5%	1,890	78.8%
Other customers	850	28.8%	640	23.5%	510	21.3%
Total Sales	2,950	100.0%	2,720	100.0%	2,400	100.0%
Product B						
Delta, Inc.	225	16.7%	160	15.1%	140	16.7%
Roadway Spas	225	16.7%	160	15.1%	130	15.5%
Samson Mfg.	215	15.9%	180	17.0%	160	19.0%
Peterboro, Inc.	190	14.1%	180	17.0%	220	26.2%
Kontrol Mfg.	165	12.2%	110	10.4%	0	0.0%
	1,020	75.6%	790	74.5%	650	77.4%
Other customers	330	24.4%	270	25.5%	190	22.6%
Total Sales	1,350	100.0%	1,060	100.0%	840	100.0%
Product C						
Katchup Novelties	190	23.8%	90	30.0%	0	
Ace Appliances	130	16.3%	70	23.3%	0	
Sieze the Day, Inc.	110	13.8%	0	0.0%	0	
Eager Specialties	100	12.5%	60	20.0%	0	
Broadway Electrical	70	8.8%	0	0.0%	0	
	600	75.0%	220	73.3%	0	
Other customers	200	25.0%	80	26.7%	0	
Total Sales	800	100.0%	300	100.0%	0	
Product D						
Dept. of Defense	760	66.1%	580	96.7%	0	
Noridge (subcontractor)	280	24.3%	20	3.3%	0	
EPA	110	9.6%	0	0.0%	0	
Total Sales	1,150	100.0%	600	100.0%	0	

Pricing Decisions

Traditionally, pricing policies are a result of some multiplier of product costs (e.g., a 40% markup over total product costs). Most small businesses attempt to allocate as much costs as possible to the product (passing on their inefficiencies to the customer), resulting in increased prices. By analyzing your product costs by product line (and then by individual products) you can get a starting point as to which product lines are profitable and to what extent. However, when you apply ABC concepts, you may find a completely different story.

For instance, let us look at a set of comparative income statement data by product line, shown in Exhibit 7.8.

Based on the numbers shown in Exhibit 7.8, it can be seen that the specialty and custom product lines are comparatively as profitable (i.e., 22.6% and 24.4% operating profit margins), while the basic product line is producing only an 11 percent operating profit margin. However, when we recalculate these statistics using ABC concepts, as shown in Exhibit 7.9, we get a completely different story.

The basic product line business segment is a highly competitive area, but a definite growth area for the business. Under the original cost concepts, the business was pricing these products based on their calculated costs and market-price considerations, resulting in an 11 percent profit margin. The business brings the finished product, which is produced elsewhere, into its

EXHIBIT 7.8   Comparative Income Statement by Product Line

	Specialty	Custom	Basic
Net sales	$2,950	$1,350	$1,150
Cost of goods sold:			
Material	380	180	380
Labor	800	390	180
Mfg. expense	520	200	160
	1,700	770	720
Mfg. profit	1,250	580	430
Gross profit %	42.4%	43.0%	37.4%
Operating expenses	582	250	300
Operating profit	668	330	130
Operating profit %	22.6%	24.4%	11.3%

EXHIBIT 7.9   Comparative Income Statement by Product Line
Using ABC Concepts

	Specialty	Custom	Basic
Net sales	$2,950	$1,350	$1,150
Cost of goods sold:			
Material	320	140	240
Labor	680	340	60
Mfg. expense	500	180	40
	1,500	660	340
Mfg. profit	1,450	690	810
Gross profit %	49.2%	51.1%	70.4%
Operating expenses	500	320	180
Operating profit	950	370	630
Operating profit %	32.2%	27.4%	54.8%

facility mainly to apply identifier materials. Based on ABC functional and activity analysis, the owners decided to make this a sales-distribution-type business, with vendors directly shipping to customers. This resulted in less costs, allowing the business to reduce its prices, capture a larger share of the market, and still maintain substantial profit margins.

In addition, rather than encouraging salespeople to emphasize sales of the custom product line, with more accurate ABC analysis the owners were convinced that while the custom products were still profitable, the specialty products were even more profitable. As specialty products enjoyed a larger sales base, it was easier for the salespeople to obtain repetitive orders for these products from existing customers, resulting in additional production efficiencies and economies that could be passed on to the customer or achieve larger profit margins. At the same time, emphasis was placed on reducing costs in the custom product line to help increase its profit margin.

Customer Complexity Factors

The small business, XYZ Company, sells the same products to both large distributors and retail outlets. Although the retail outlets can order only in quantities specified by XYZ, similar to the distributors, the retailers require a salesperson assigned to each store with related periodic visits. Each store in a retail chain represents a small quantity of the retailer's entire order, requiring individual order identity by store as well as individual shipping, billing identification, and sales statistics. The increased volume of activity that these individual store orders create results in increased costs for each product sold. However, a distributor order is treated as one order its entire way through the system, resulting in less overall costs. XYZ needs to differentiate its costs and pricing policies based on such customer diversity.

Small business management must analyze each customer's requirements and related costs. Through this process, each customer is identified as to its needs, with resultant customer-related costs calculated fairly accurately. These customer costs can then be added to product and functional costs to calculate a final cost that can then be used to negotiate with each customer as to a price that provides a desired profit. Such cost calculations can also be used to determine which customers and products are most profitable and should be emphasized for sales and which customers should not be sold to under present conditions.

Servicing Different Types of Customers

XYZ Company provides its products to a number of different types of customers:

- Large distributors
- Large retailers
- Small retailers (individual stores and small chains)
- Cooperatives
- Wholesalers
- Independent sellers

The large entities (distributors and retailers) require minimal shipments to a few locations with related minimal sales support. The other entities (small retailers, cooperatives, wholesalers, and independent sellers) may generate a large number of transactions with deliveries to multiple locations and larger sales force attention. By looking at these customer costs, the company can avoid selling to the wrong customers and adjust its cost and pricing strategies accordingly.

Such a price-differential strategy is allowed (under the Robinson-Patman Act, which prohibits pricing discrimination) if cost differences occur in the providing of the product or service. ABC customer-driven costs can provide the data to substantiate cost differentials charged. Identified undesirable customers can be transformed into profitable customers if possible, and profitable customers can be planned for to maximize their contribution to profits.

For instance, the customer may be unprofitable because it buys mainly low-margin items, requires large amounts of support, or has negotiated unprofitable (but profitable to them) terms. By identifying these factors, the small business can take the proper remedial action such as refocusing sales efforts, renegotiating sales terms, and updating its pricing policies. By considering customer support and service costs, as well as the allocation of other general and administrative costs to customers and products, the business is in a much better position to make decisions as to costing and pricing, to whom and what to sell, how to sell and market, the level of customer support by customer, and so on. These are the first steps in developing effective sales, marketing, and customer service plans, allowing the small business to use its resources most economically and effectively.

The goals of customer-oriented selling are to provide the optimum customer service to each customer at the least possible cost while maximizing each customer's contribution to profits. ABC concepts provide the tools to accomplish this.

By now, you have come to realize that looking at customer costs can change a seemingly profitable customer into a less profitable or even a net-loss customer. Many times such customers are the small business's higher-sales-volume customers and the small business owner will insist that the business can't lose such a customer. Such a situation is discussed in Exhibit 7.10.

ANALYSIS OF COST BEHAVIOR

The types of costs that we have discussed do not all behave in the same manner. Some costs may vary in proportion to changes in volume or activity (i.e., labor), other costs do not change regardless of the volume (i.e., rent, utilities, insurance), and others vary with changes in volume but not proportionately (i.e., supervision). An analysis of such cost behavior is useful for:

EXHIBIT 7.10   Sales Are Better Than Cost Savings

The Gidget Company produces and purchases many small items for resale in the less-than-a-dollar, impulse-buy, novelty-type merchandise. With such low-ticket items there is not a large profit margin on each item—sometimes less than five cents per item. For the company to add real profits onto their bottom line they must sell large volumes of each item on each sale while containing their costs to a minimum. One of the Gidget Company's largest customers is the biggest retailer in the country, Sam's Mart. Initially, Sam's Mart ordered extremely large quantities from the Gidget Company, all to be shipped to one location. While Sam's Mart asked for and received the most favorable prices where the Gidget company might make less than a penny an item, such a high volume still produced a profit for the Gidget Company. Recently, Sam's Mart told the Gidget Company that they would now have to break up each shipment by individual store location, resulting in multiple shipments rather than one large shipment to a central location, without any additional price considerations. The Gidget Company realizes that such additional costs will not only erode its small profit margins with Sam's Mart but may result in a substantial loss on each sales order.

What would you suggest to the Gidget Company? It does not want to lose Sam's Mart as a customer, due to the volume of sales and potential profits as well as the devastation to their operations should they have to eliminate this volume from their operations.

Suggested Response

A quick answer is to stop selling to Sam's Mart, eliminating their volume from the gross sales amount. The cost of selling such merchandise, including product (e.g., manufacturing and buying), functional (e.g., packing and shipping), and customer costs (e.g., dealing with the company as well as individual store locations), results in minuscule profits and probably losses on most sales. However, since the Gidget Company has expanded its operations to fulfill Sam's Mart requirements, it would be traumatic to retrench its operations and eliminate Sam's Mart. Accordingly, the Gidget Company must look for ways to reduce its costs to maintain the same profit margins or better if it wishes to continue selling to Sam's Mart:

- **Packing costs.** Absorbing and beating the costs of one large shipment as compared to multiple small shipments. One area to be investigated is to determine on purchased items whether the vendor can send the items directly to Sam's Mart. Another area to look at is less costly packing procedures as well as more efficient packing.
- **Shipping costs.** Investigating alternative shipping methods such as bulk shipping, less than truck or rail car shipping, less costly ground shipping (which may require shipping earlier to meet Sam's Mart delivery criteria), and combining items shipped to each store location.
- **Purchasing costs.** For items purchased directly for resale, whether the Gidget Company renegotiates prices based on a long-term commitment. Also, for items manufactured, are there less expensive material alternatives and can they renegotiate with their material vendors for price concessions under a long-term purchase agreement?
- **Manufacturing costs.** Reduction of materials costs and more efficient use of materials, reduction and elimination of scrap, rejects, and rework, reducing/eliminating setup times, increasing processing efficiencies, and eliminating indirect costs such as receiving and incoming inspection, supervision (make the employee self-responsible), quality control (by the employee), repairs and maintenance (each machine operator taking responsibility), and WIP moves (by each operator).

- Variance analysis and cost control
- Cost-volume-profit (CVP) and breakeven analysis
- Short-term decision making such as make-or-buy or the acceptance/rejection of a large special order
- Appraisal/evaluation of managerial performance
- Flexible budgeting reporting

Cost-Volume-Profit and Breakeven Analysis

CVP analysis together with cost behavior information assists small business management in analyzing the effects on profit of changes in volume and costs. CVP analysis considers the impact on profits of such factors as:

- Product prices
- Product mix
- Activity volume
- Variable costs of products
- Fixed costs of the business

Through study of the relationship among costs, sales, and profits, management can more effectively plan and make the correct management decisions. Breakeven analysis as part of the CVP analysis process is used to determine the breakeven level of sales at which total costs will equal total income—and to provide an indication of how rapidly profits will build up as the business's volume exceeds the breakeven point.

CVP analysis can assist management in the following determinations:

- Sales volume necessary to break even
- Sales volume necessary to earn a desired profit
- Profit expected from a given sales volume
- Effect on profits of changes in selling price, variable costs, fixed costs, and level of production or sales
- Effect on breakeven point and expected profit of a change in product mix

Concepts of Contribution Margin   CVP analysis requires that a distinction be made between fixed and variable costs. In addition, semivariable costs must be separated into their fixed and variable components. To perform

CVP analyses as well as compute the breakeven point, you need to understand the following:

- **Contribution margin (CM).** The excess of sales (S) over the variable costs (V) of the product or service. It represents the amount available to cover fixed costs and generate profits.

    Formula: $CM = S - V$

- **Unit contribution margin (unit cm).** The excess of the unit sales price (p) over the unit variable cost (v).

    Formula: Unit cm $=(p - v)$

- **Contribution margin ratio (CM ratio).** The contribution margin as a percentage of sales.

    Formula: CM ratio $= \dfrac{CM}{S} = \dfrac{S - V}{S} = 1 - \dfrac{V}{S}$

- **Unit contribution margin ratio (unit cm ratio).** The unit contribution margin as a percentage of selling price.

    Formula, Unit cm ratio $= \dfrac{\text{Unit cm}}{P} = \dfrac{p - v}{p} = 1 - \dfrac{V}{P}$

Note that in the contribution margin ratio formulas listed above, the CM ratios are 100% minus the variable cost ratio $(V/S$ or $v/p)$. Thus, if variable costs equal 60 percent of the sales volume (or the unit price), the CM ratio is 40 percent.

Calculate the CM, the unit cm, and the CM ratio based on the following:

	Per Unit	**Total**	**%**
Sales: 2,000 units	$40	$80,000	100%
Variable costs	$22	44,000	55%
Fixed costs		28,000	

Calculations:
CM $= S - V$: CM $= \$80,000 - \$44,000 = \$36,000$
Unit cm $= (p - v)$: $\$40 - \$22 = \$18$/unit
CM ratio $=$ CM/S: $\$36,000/\$80,000 = 45\%$
Unit cm ratio $=$ unit cm/p: $\$18/\$40 = 45\%$

Breakeven-Point Analysis   Breakeven-point analysis is used to determine at what level of sales (in dollars or in units) the business's costs will be equal to its revenues. Below that level of activity there will be a loss incurred, while activity above the breakeven volume will generate profits. The business generally will want to have its breakeven point as low as practical to be able to attain profitability as quickly and easily as possible.

The breakeven point assists management in profit planning and can be computed using the following equation based on the cost-volume equation, which depicts the relationship of sales (S), variable costs (V), fixed costs (FC), and net income (NI) as follows:

$$\text{Formula: } S = V + FC + NI$$

At breakeven − point level: $S = V + FC + 0$

To define in units of volume, this relationship can be written in terms of X volume as follows:

$$px = vx + FC$$

where p and v represent price and variable cost per unit, or

$$X = \frac{FC}{p - v} = \frac{FC}{cm}$$

Note that to perform breakeven-point calculations you must know the factors in the formula such as selling price, variable costs, and fixed costs. Also, as the selling price changes so will the breakeven point; that is, the higher the selling price the lower the breakeven point and vice versa. Lowering the costs (variable and fixed) will also lower the breakeven point and raising the costs will raise the breakeven point. The breakeven point is the point where the total sales dollars intersects with the total cost line. This relationship can be charted as shown in Exhibit 7.11. Note that profits are plotted on the vertical axis and volume (units of output) on the horizontal axis and that the slope of the chart is the unit cm. The chart can also be used to analyze profit potential based on various potential sales volumes. The chart focuses more specifically on how profits vary with changes in sales volume.

Other Uses of CVP Analysis

In addition to determining the business's breakeven point, CVP analysis can also be used for other types of analyses, such as:

- Target income value
- Margin of safety

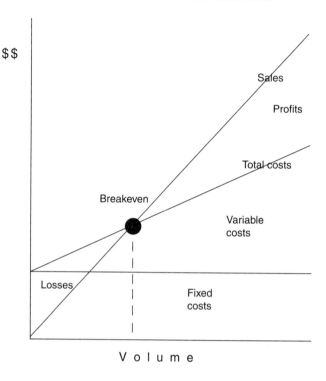

Breakeven calculatiion formulas:

B/E = Breakeven   B/E in units = $\dfrac{FC}{(P- V)}$
P = Unit price
V = Unit variable cost
FC = Fixed costs   B/E in $$ = $\dfrac{FC}{(1- V/P)}$

EXHIBIT 7.11   Break-even Graph

Target Income Value   CVP analysis can determine the amount of sales required to attain a specific income level or target net income. The target net income desired can be expressed as a specific dollar amount, or a percentage of sales.

To determine target net income as a specific dollar amount, the cost-volume (CV) formula to use is:

$$px(ti) = vx(ti) + FC + \text{Target income or}$$
$$x(ti) = \frac{FC + \text{Target income}}{(p - v)}$$

where $x(ti)$ = sales volume required to achieve a given target income, or

$$\text{Target income sales volume} = \frac{FC + \text{Target income}}{\text{Unit cm}}$$

To determine target net income as a percent of sales, the CV formula is:

$$px(ti) = vx(ti) + FC + \%(pxti)$$

or

$$x(ti) = \frac{FC}{(p - v) - \%(p)}$$

$$\text{Target income sales volume} = \frac{FC}{\text{Unit CM} - \% \text{ unit sales price}}$$

Margin of Safety This measures the difference between the actual level of sales and the breakeven sales volume. It can be used for CVP analysis

---

EXAMPLE:

Assume that the business desires to attain:

Situation 1: target income of $50,000

Situation 2: target income of 30% of sales

SITUATION 1: TARGET INCOME OF $50,000

$$x(ti) = \frac{FC + \text{target income}}{p - v} = \frac{28,000 + 50,000}{40 - 22} = 4,334 \text{ units}$$

Proof:

Sales	4,334 units @ $40 =	$173,360
Minus *VC*	4,334 units @ $22 =	95,348
Equals CM		78,012
Minus *FC*		28,000
Equals target income		**$ 50,012**

SITUATION 2: TARGET INCOME OF 30% OF SALES

$$X(ti) = \frac{FC}{p - v - \%(p)} = \frac{28,000}{40 - 22 - [30\%(40)]} = 4,667 \text{ units}$$

Proof:

Sales	4,667 units @ $40 =	$186,680	100%
Minus *VC*	4,667 units @ $22 =	102,674	55%
Equals CM		**84,006**	**45%**
Minus fixed costs		**28,000**	**15%**
Equals target income 30% of sales		**56,006**	**30%**

purposes to determine the amount by which sales revenues may drop before actual losses begin. It is normally expressed as a percentage of budgeted sales:

$$\text{Formula : Margin of safety} = \frac{\text{Budgeted sales} - \text{Breakeven sales}}{\text{Budgeted sales}}$$

EXAMPLE:

Our CVP analysis example projects sales of $80,000 with a breakeven sales level of $62,240. The margin of safety is calculated as:

$$\text{Margin of safety} = \frac{80,000 - 62,240}{80,000} = \frac{17,760}{80,000} = 22.2\%$$

Margin of safety is normally used as a measure of risk. The larger the percentage, the safer the situation—that is, the less risk of dropping to or below the breakeven point.

CONCLUSION

The product/service costs the small business incurs represent the most significant cause of company costs and cash outflows. In order to reduce costs and improve cash flow, it is essential for the business to control these costs effectively. While cost control is a well-accepted way for a business to improve its profitability, its relevance to efficient operations and cash flow is often not understood, not recognized, or (in the worst case) deliberately ignored.

Simple cost systems based on ABC cost principles provide a formalized method that can be used to institute better cost and operating control within the small business. The process allows the business to compare its processes and related costs to objective outside standards—methods developed by others and proven to be best practices. ABC is a method of analyzing small business costs (i.e., product/service, functional, and customer costs) to determine just what drives those costs and assigning the costs to particular products/services based on how many of those drivers are actually used by the particular product/service.

The greatest cause of loss of profitability is operating costs; the greatest opportunity to improve profitability is to control operating costs.

CHAPTER 8

Accounting Operations: Functional Considerations

The small business owner who has seen clearly the value of controlling the sales function and related cost controls to dovetail with the business's goals is well on the way to business growth and increased profitability. However, there is still one area of costs that must also be considered—the area of functional operations whose costs cannot be directly assigned to products or services—such as accounting, personnel, information technology (IT), and overall business management and administration. As stated previously, a dollar of cost savings or a dollar not spent is a dollar that goes directly to the bottom line. Therefore, if the business can accomplish its goals with fewer resources allocated to one of these functional areas, the resources saved remain with the business. Remember, the financial statements and the bottom line do not know where the dollar of savings comes from—a dollar of functional cost savings is just as good as a dollar of product or service cost savings.

> The financial statements do not know where the dollars of savings come from.

These functional areas exist for a purpose, but the purpose can be accomplished in the most economical and efficient manner. Small businesses run the gamut from having these functions at a minimum, possibly to the detriment of effective operations, to an overkill that attempts to emulate the large corporation. With the clear identification and communication of owner/management's expectations, each of these functions has a clear idea of where it is heading, the controls (if any) in place, and the basis for its evaluation. The purpose of effective operations and related controls then becomes one of a helping agent, assisting each function to achieve its stated goals and objectives as related to owner/ management's desires. The performance and evaluation of operations is thus less a critical evaluation of what a particular function is doing and more an appraisal of what needs to be done to help the function achieve its goals and become the best it can be at the least possible cost.

> Effective operations and controls are a helping agent.

As a way of illustrating how to deal with operating efficiencies of functions that have only a peripheral value to the products or services delivered—what is known as non-value-added functions or activities—we will use the accounting functions as an example. This is not to say that accounting is inevitably a non-value-added activity. Properly organized and led, accounting can certainly add value to the business. But it is a function that is often, and sometimes accurately, perceived as not adding significant value to the business—a necessary evil rather than a contributor to profits. As such it is an appropriate representative part of the small business to use as an example of a functional activity. The approach illustrated here can be easily adapted to other non-value-added activities such as personnel, management, and IT within the small business as well.

> The accounting function—turning a cost center into a profit center.

ACCOUNTING FUNCTION

In the current business environment, the accounting function in many small businesses is perceived as a prime candidate for cost reduction, and in extreme situations, for elimination. Small business owners/management view many of the accounting functions (e.g., preparing customer bills, collecting payments, processing vendor payments, and preparing payrolls) as necessary but non-value-added for profitable operations. In other words, these things may have to be done, but can the business accomplish them with as little cost as possible (none, it hopes)—and without the involvement of the owners?

With the nature of most successful small businesses changing from a predominantly mechanical manual operation to a more customer service–oriented approach integrated with effective IT techniques and procedures, small business management must also appraise the accounting function from this perspective. That is, owners/management must not merely review and appraise the accounting function's present activities, but must also be aware of the benefits the accounting function can and should be providing to the business.

Operational analysis is an effective process to use in looking at a small business's activities to measure current economies, efficiencies, and effectiveness of results. In addition, the process assists in the identification of performance gaps—that is, the difference between present and desired operating results as compared with internal goals and external competitors. A thorough understanding of such performance gaps enables owners/management to seize these opportunities for improvement. There has always been a demand, and perhaps more so today, to decrease costs, increase positive cash flow, and improve product/service/customer quality—all directed toward increasing profits.

Ironically, many small business owners see the accounting function as strictly non-value-added overhead (in many cases unnecessary), and such businesses are constantly moving to cut these costs. The operational analysis process assists in reducing accounting function costs through the use of more efficient systems and procedures, along with a clear identification of desired results for such accounting functions. At the same time, the quality of the accounting/financial value-added services provided could be greatly enhanced. In effect, the accounting function can be an active value-added function that contributes effectively to the small business's profit and positive cash flow.

FUNCTION ANALYSIS

The analysis of the accounting functions begins with the review of existing practices within the various accounting areas of the small business to identify activities and areas that can be improved as to best practices. In addition, the causes of work for the accounting function (e.g., all vendor invoices must be verified by recalculation) or triggers (e.g., a customer order) that set in motion a series of activities must be analyzed as to their necessity and whether there is a better, more effective method to accomplish the result. Such work causes and triggers are questioned as to their elimination and the ultimate elimination of the corresponding activities.

With a clear understanding of how the accounting function or activity operates within the small business from full separation of functions and duties to the one-person accounting department, you can begin to identify the following:

- Key aspects of and performance results for the accounting function's activities
- Inherent work causes and triggers
- Critical operational areas and opportunities for improvement
- Channels of communication within the company

In your analysis of the accounting function it is also important to focus on the pockets of good desirable practices (best practices and areas of excellence) and standards for good practices that provide the foundation for best practices.

Defining the elements of each accounting activity, and determining whether it is a value-added or non-value-added activity and what each individual does in the process, as well as why he or she does it, is the basis for analysis as to positive improvements.

> It is not the debits and credits that count—but why they are there in the first place.

Choosing What to Analyze

The accounting functions (e.g., accounts payable, accounts receivable, payroll, and general ledger) cannot be isolated on a linear basis from those other functions that are supported and integrated with the specific accounting function (e.g., accounts payable and the purchasing, receiving, and product/service delivery functions). It is this thinking that has allowed such accounting functions to be drastically cut back in many organizations to the detriment of the aforementioned supported operating functions. In reality, a business operates in a circular or cyclical basis, with each component of the cycle equally important as the others. Therefore, to most effectively analyze one of the accounting functions, it is best to look at it as part of its business cycle. For instance, the analysis of the accounting and financial functions can be looked at in a number of ways, such as:

- **Functional.** Accounting, IT, treasury, reporting, and so on
- **Process.** Accounts payable, accounts receivable, payroll, general ledger, budget, cash management
- **Industry.** Specific manufacturing, retailing, banking, and so on
- **Business cycle.** Based on the concept of closed-loop activities such as:
  - **Sales cycle.** Sales order—shipping—billing—accounts receivable— collections
  - **Purchase cycle.** Purchase requisition—purchasing—receiving— vendor invoicing—accounts payable—cash disbursements
  - **Payroll/labor distribution cycle.** Time and job verification— data entry—payroll/labor distribution processing—pay distribution— record keeping
  - **General ledger/financial statement cycle.** Subsystem data collection—journal entries—general ledger posting—financial reporting
  - **Cost accounting cycle.** Material/labor/overhead data collection— computer processing—operating reports—offline action—reporting by task, job, and period

The accounting function summarizes the results of operations.

Prior to the start of the analysis of accounting functions and activities, small business owner/management's goals/desires for these functions need to be clearly communicated, as well as beneficial results to overall company operations. There must be more than just a desire to eliminate unnecessary costs and increase net profits and cash flow; there must also be a full understanding of why each of these functions should be in existence. For example, management may identify goals and desires for each of the major accounting functions as follows:

Accounts Payable

- The elimination of the function, to the extent possible, where the cost of processing vendor payments exceeds the value to the company in delaying such payments
- The elimination of the processing of vendor payments where the cost of processing exceeds the amount of the payment
- The least costly, most efficient methods of processing those remaining vendor payments
- The ability to computer-integrate accounts payable data with other subsystems such as cost accounting, vendor statistics, manufacturing controls, inventory controls, production controls, and cash management
- An economic balance between necessary controls and the cost of implementing such controls

Accounts Receivable

- The elimination of the function, to the extent possible, where the cost of billing, collecting, and processing of customer payments exceeds the value to the business of extending credit to such customers
- The elimination of the processing of customer billings and collections where the cost of processing exceeds the amount of the billing
- The least costly, most efficient methods of processing those remaining customer bills
- The ability to computer-integrate accounts receivable data with other subsystems such as credit controls, sales forecasts, customer and sales statistics, collection controls, and cash management

Payroll Processing

- The least costly, most efficient methods for processing payroll and the maintenance of necessary records

- The ability to integrate payroll data with other subsystems such as cost accounting, personnel records, and planning and budget systems

- The ability of a computerized payroll system to automatically process labor distribution or labor costs to production jobs (e.g., production employees time processing at their pay rates to job costs), maintain personnel records (e.g., leave records), and post to the budget system as it processes payroll transactions

General Ledger

- Full computer integration with all other subsystems so that the general ledger is automatically updated on a real-time basis

- Automatic generation of all repetitive journal entries, allowing for minimal manual journal entries

- Ability to produce financial statements—balance sheet, income statement, and statement of cash flows—on demand

Accounting and Financial Reporting

- Automatic generation of all accounting and financial reports, showing exceptions to key operating indicator criteria

- Integration of accounting and financial reporting with operating statistics

- Ability to analyze and interpret all such reports so that each report is most useful for both management and operational purposes

- Use of real-time reporting via computer screens, and the requirement for positive action to be taken in all areas

Small business owners/management should also define agreed-on basic business principles as related to the accounting functions, such as:

- The cost of processing should always be less than the amount of the item—the price at which it is sold or the amount of the vendor payment.

- All unnecessary or non-value-added accounting functions should be eliminated.

- All redundant or duplicate activities should be eliminated.

- All necessary accounting functions should be accomplished in the least costly and most efficient manner.

- All accounting processing and data should be fully integrated with other subsystems.

- Accounting and financial reporting should be fully integrated with operational reporting so that management and operations personnel can make the best decisions.

- The accounting functions—accounts payable, accounts receivable, payroll, and general ledger—should be fully integrated into the operations of the company.

- The accounting functions should be value-added providers of financial and operational data so that the value provided exceeds the cost of their operations.

- Accounting function personnel must be able to design, develop, and implement effective reporting systems that assist the company in reaching its operational and profit goals.

- Accounting function personnel must become analyzers and interpreters of data for management decisions, rather than mere processors of data and transactions.

Know what you want to know, not what the system tells you.

Accounting Areas for Control

For each of the major accounting functions, that is, accounts payable, accounts receivable, payroll, general ledger, and reporting, you need to know what are the component activities that may be subject to operating efficiencies. Areas to be considered as related to the accounting functions are:

Accounts Payable and Cash Disbursement Functions

- Accounts payable processing
- Open payables control
- Vendor payment processing
- Cash disbursement processing
- Record keeping and analysis

Accounts Receivable Processing
- Credit policies: establishment and maintenance
- Sales order processing
- Billing procedures
- Open receivables control
- Collection procedures
- Customer statistics
- Record keeping and analysis

Payroll Processing
- Processing procedures
- Payroll statistics: types, frequency, number of personnel, cost, and dollar amount
- Reports produced
- Personnel statistics
- Record keeping and analysis

General Ledger
- Chart of accounts
- Processing procedures
- Journal entry processing
- Reports produced
- Record keeping and analysis

Accounting, Financial, and Operational Reporting
- Reports produced
- Information lacking

- Use of reports
- Analysis and interpretation

FINANCIAL REPORTING

For many small business owners, the most important result of the accounting function is to produce periodic (usually monthly) financial reports. However, in many instances, such financial reporting accomplishes little more than confusing the owner, who is typically not well versed in accounting methodology. For example, for this particular small business (Exhibit 8.1), the only financial reporting that exists consists of a monthly balance sheet and income statement distributed to the owners once the part-time computer operator and the external CPA are sure of its accuracy (i.e., the amounts foot and cross-foot), more than ten days after the end of the month. Most small business owners/management personnel merely file such financial statements; they look at them, but very few understand them, as they have no effect on the reality of their operations. An example of these financial statements for the small business is shown in Exhibit 8.1. These statements are distributed as shown, with no additional comments or explanation.

The external CPA provides no explanations with its submission of these financial statements. Owners and operations management need to know how these numbers affect what their areas are accomplishing—and not accomplishing. They need to know the differences between financial/accounting data and operational data that they can use to improve their operations.

It is not the numbers; it is what is behind the numbers.

OPERATIONAL ANALYSIS SURVEY FORM

The main purpose of a survey form is to reduce large amounts of data into categories or areas that can be more easily compared. The questions on the survey form are developed by members of management and operations

EXHIBIT 8.1   Small Business Financial Statements

Balance Sheet
as of xxxxxxx 31

Assets

Cash	$ 60
Accounts receivable	3,720
Inventory	5,360
Current assets	9,140
Property, plant, and equipment	7,580
Accumulated depreciation	(2,160)
Net property, plant, and equipment	5,420
Other assets	840
Total assets	$15,400

Liabilities and equity

Liabilities:

Accounts payable	$ 1,960
Notes payable	200
Current: long-term debt	840
Other current liabilities	560
Current liabilities	$ 3,560
Long-term debt	7,680
Total liabilities	11,240

Equity:

Retained earnings	4,160
Total liabilities and equity	$15,400

Income Statement
For period ending XXXXXX 31

Net sales	$12,500
Cost of goods sold:	
Material	2,260
Labor	3,260
Manufacturing expenses	2,080
Total cost of goods sold	7,600
Gross profit	4,900
Selling expenses	1,120
General and administrative expenses	1,480
Total operating expenses	2,600
Net income	$2,300

personnel and are directed toward those areas that have been defined as most critical. An initial survey can be used to gather general data and look for patterns in identifying critical areas. A sample survey form related to the accounts payable function is shown in Exhibit 8.2. A similar survey form is

EXHIBIT 8.2   **Operational Analysis Survey Form: Accounts Payable Function**

1. Organizational issues

    a. How is this function organized (hierarchical, vertical, integrated, etc.)? Provide an organization chart showing positions and personnel.
    b. To whom does each activity within the function report? Title and name.
    c. Who manages each activity? Title and name.
    d. How many employees are included in each activity?
    e. What are the major accounts payable policies (e.g., dollar limit for accounts payable)? Provide documented policies and procedures.
    f. What are the total budget and actual allocations for this function?
    g. Do you have a functional job description for each position? Provide a copy of each one.

2. Accounts payable processing

    a. On what basis and what percentage of total payments do you pay vendors?
    • Pre-pay at time of order
    • Payment upon receipt
    • Payment with invoice/receipt within discount terms
    • Payment with invoice/receipt within 30 days: no discount/take discount anyway
    b. How often do you process payables for payment?
    c. Do you make any exceptions between payment periods?
    d. Do you provide for offline manual vendor payments?
    e. What is the amount of new payables at any time? Number? Total dollars?
    f. Is accounts payable processing part of an integrated computer system?
    g. What is the amount of annual payments? Number of payments? Total dollars?

3. Open payables control

    a. Are open payables part of an integrated computer system?
    b. How often do you process payments?
    c. Is there a policy to take vendor discounts? Within/at the discount period/ regardless?
    d. On average, what is amount of open payables? Number of invoices? Total dollars?
    e. Are open payables accessible on an online basis? Only accessible by accounts payable personnel? By others (describe)?

4. Vendor payment processing

    a. Is there a prepayment listing of due bills prior to processing? On screen/listing/ both?
    b. Can an authorized individual select bills for payment? Manually, online?
    c. Can an authorized individual determine the dollar amount for total payment?
    d. How often do you process checks for payment? Do you hold to that schedule? How many times did you go off that schedule last year?

e. Do you automatically combine vendor invoices into one payment?
f. Do you provide detail as to what invoices are being paid?
g. Do you reconcile vendor statements to individual invoices?
h. Do you ignore vendor statements and pay only by invoice?
i. Do you automatically net vendor debits against payments?
j. On average, what is the amount of vendor debits? Number, total amount?
k. Once selected for payments, are checks with payment detail automatically processed? Provide sample of check and detail memo.
l. What is your cost per payment?
m. What is your cost per processing cycle?
n. How many payments do you process at one time? Per run, month, annually?

5. Cash disbursement processing

a. Are payments as processed automatically sent to the vendor? Electronic data interchange (EDT)? Mail?
b. How often do you process cash disbursements?
c. What are the number of checks written? By process, monthly, annually?
d. Do you combine payments by vendor? On what basis?
e. On what basis do you process payment? Receipt of items? Invoice? Both?
f. Do you use a remote bank location?
g. Do you use any methods to slow the receipt of the payment to the vendor?
h. What is your cost per check disbursement? Per disbursement cycle?
i. How many times have checks been processed late in the last year?
j. What percentage of checks have been reported as having errors upon receipt? How many hours are spent in correcting errors, and at what cost?
k. Do you provide EDT for vendor payments?
l. Is timeliness of payment (e.g., EDT) a factor in vendor price negotiations?

6. Record keeping and analysis

a. What records do you keep for each payment?
   • Purchase requisition
   • Receiver/bill of lading
   • Payment voucher
   • Other
   • Purchase order
   • Vendor invoice
   • Check copy
   • All computer maintained
b. What type of analysis do you do relative to payments?
   • Payments by vendor: numbers and dollars
   • Returns by vendor
   • Billing errors
   • Processing errors
   • Other
c. Are there other records/analysis that you keep/do? Describe.
d. What report options do you provide? Standard, custom, user defined?
e. What software do you use for these functions?

(Continued)

EXHIBIT 8.2   **(Continued)**

f. What computer hardware configuration do you use? Provide details.

7. Vendor relations, negotiations, analysis
   a. What is the total number of vendors in your system?
   b. Are your vendors coded by commodity class?
   c. Can you provide a summary of vendors by commodity class?
   d. How often do you negotiate with vendors? Each purchase, monthly, annually, other?
   e. How many vendors make up approximately 80 percent of your total purchases? Can you provide this information by commodity class?
   f. Do you use long-term contracts or blanket purchase orders to lock in price, quality, and on-time deliveries?
   g. Do you integrate purchases of raw materials into your production schedule?
   h. Do you maintain vendor analysis statistics? Do they include the following?
      • Total sales volume
      • Total sales volume by item
      • Quality data
      • Merchandise return data
      • On-time delivery data
      • Other
   Provide a sample report(s) of such statistics.
   i. Are company individuals assigned contact responsibility for major vendors?
   j. How often are long-term purchase contracts renegotiated?
   k. Do you have an ongoing process for identification of potential vendors? Describe.
   l. How many vendors have you added during the past year?
   m. How many vendors have you deleted during the past year?

developed for each of the other accounting functions, that is, accounts receivable, payroll, and general ledger.

ANALYSIS OF FUNCTIONAL COSTS

Another important aspect of the analysis of the accounting functions is to analyze each activity of the function and determine its cost. The starting point is to review and analyze the function as it is presently being performed in order to identify those activities that result in added on costs. This can be done through observation, interviews, workload statistics, and the development and analysis of systems flowcharts. This process not only will allow small business management to fully understand how the function operates, but will also identify areas for positive improvement and generate recommendations for such improvements. The goal of this analysis is to begin the development of best practice recommendations so that each function operates with the most economical and efficient systems as possible.

For example, costs may be identified and developed for those activities that make up the accounts payable and accounts receivable functions, as shown in Exhibit 8.3.

EXHIBIT 8.3   Accounting Activities: Accounts Payable and Accounts Receivable

Accounts Payable

- Receive open purchase order (PO) copies from purchasing department.
- File in open PO files: by vendor, by PO number.
- Receive "receiving report" from receiving.
- Pull open purchase order from file and compare to receiving report.
- If no invoice, hold in open receipts/no invoice file.
- If invoice, pull from invoice/no receipt file.
- Receive invoice from vendor.
- Match invoice to open receipts.
- If match, process for payment.
- If no match, hold in invoice/no receipt file.
- Process any invoice or receiving errors.
- Enter payment data into computer system.
- At time of payment, set up computer system for check preparation.
- Mail checks to vendors.
- File paid/payable voucher.
- Handle vendor inquiries.

Accounts Receivable

- Receive billing information from shipping department: bill of lading, sales order, etc.
- Match to sales order copy in open sales file.
- Prepare bill on computer system.
- Verify accuracy of bill.
- Mail bill to customer.
- Receive payments from customers: usually checks in the mail.
- Match payment to amounts due in computer system.
- Code bill as to allocation to open customer invoices.
- Followup on any discrepancies (e.g., wrong amount, improper discount taken).
- Expedite open customer invoices not paid within time terms (e.g., net/30days).
- Initiate collection procedures for overdue accounts.
- File payment data by customer (e.g., check stub, copy of bill, sales order, etc.).
- Prepare cash receipts for bank deposit.
- Prepare daily cash receipts report.
- Prepare bank deposit.
- Handle customer inquiries.

As each activity in Exhibit 8.3 is identified and its cost determined, each function or activity is questioned as to whether the entire function is necessary (e.g., does it have to be purchased and paid for in this manner?) and whether each activity is necessary (e.g., is it necessary to have customer bills, or can electronic data transfer be used?). The total costs for each activity— accounts payable and accounts receivable processing—are based on the methods presently used to process these transactions. There may be other processes that should be performed that are not being done because of the constraints of time, volume, or limited personnel. In addition, the cost to process an individual transaction may be undercalculated owing to the time pressures to complete each transaction (e.g., in a hurried, incomplete manner). Moreover, if the volume is somewhat reduced, the cost per transaction will probably increase if the corresponding costs of processing are not reduced as well.

An example of such activity costs for the accounts payable and accounts receivable functions and their related activities is shown in Exhibit 8.4.

Eliminating the activity eliminates the cost; eliminating enough activities eliminates the function.

Although the activities and costs shown in Exhibit 8.4 are rough estimates of the processing of accounts payable and accounts receivable, they also represent the expenditure of resources allocated to these two activities. Theoretically, it could be assumed that each vendor payment or customer bill that could be eliminated from processing would result in a $21.00 or a $27.00 savings to the business.

In reality, it does not work that way. A sufficient number of vendor payments or customer bills must be eliminated to provide a significant reduction in work effort resulting in substantial cost savings. However, the costs of processing a vendor payment and the costs of processing a customer bill can be used in the company's internal cost system in convincing small business management that its costs are too high. These figures also can be used to calculate cost savings and increases in positive cash flow and net income.

EXHIBIT 8.4   Activity Costs: Accounts Payable and Accounts Receivable

Accounts Payable Activities and Costs

	Labor hour cost: $20 per hour		
Activity	Cost element	Time	Cost
1. Receive PO from Purchasing and file in open PO file.	Labor	5 min	$ 1.67
2. Receive "receiving report" from receiving, pull open PO from file and compare, hold in open receipts file.	Labor	10 min	$ 3.33
3. Receive invoice from vendor and match to open receipts or pull open PO and compare and hold as open invoice.	Labor	12 min	$ 4.00
4. Invoice/receiving errors.	Labor	—	—
5. Computer data entry.	Labor, IT	12 min	$ 4.00
6. Computer check prep.	Labor, IT, Checks	5 min	$ 1.67
7. Mail checks.	Labor, Envel., Postage	10 min	$ 3.33
8. File paid/payable.	Labor	4 min	$ 1.33
9. Meetings, phone, fax.	Labor, phone	5 min	$ 1.67
Total cost			$21.00

Number of payments processed per year: 16,000
Cost of processing annual payments: 16,000 x $21.00 = $336,000

Accounts Receivable Activities and Costs

	Labor hour cost: $20 per hour		
Activity	Cost element	Time	Cost
1. Receive billing information from shipping department.	Labor	4 min	$ 1.33
2. Match to sales order copy in open sales file.	Labor	5 min	$ 1.67
3. Prepare bill on computer system.	Labor	12 min	$ 4.00
4. Verify accuracy of bill.	Labor	6 min	$ 2.00
5. Mail bill to customer.	Labor, bill, env, postage	5 min	$ 1.67
6. Receive payments from customers.	Labor	—	—
7. Match payment to amounts due in computer system.	Labor	6 min	$ 2.00

(Continued)

EXHIBIT 8.4   (Continued)

8. Code bill as to allocation to open customer invoices.	Labor	4 min	$ 1.33
9. Process payment into computer system.	Labor	12 min	$4.00
10. Followup on any discrepancies.	Labor	—	—
11. Expedite open customer invoices.	Labor, phone	10 min	$ 3.33
12. Initiate collection procedures.	Labor	6 min	$ 2.00
13. File payment data by customer.	Labor	5 min	$ 1.67
14. Prepare cash receipts for bank deposit.	Labor	6 min	$ 2.00
15. Handle customer inquiries.	Labor, phone	—	—
Total Cost			$27.00

Number of customer bills processed per year: 12,000+

Cost of processing annual customer bills: 12,000 x $27.00 = $324,000

Vendor and Customer Statistics

A further analysis of the accounts payable and accounts receivable functions develops additional operating, vendor, and customer statistics, as shown in Exhibit 8.5.

> Accounting is not merely recording transactions, but questioning those transactions.

DEVELOPING RECOMMENDATIONS

The successful completion of the operational analysis of the accounting functions is the development of recommendations on the action that should be taken to correct the present undesirable conditions. These recommendations should logically follow an explanation of why the present condition is happening, the underlying causes, and how to prevent it from recurring. Recommendations should be practical and reasonable so that small business management easily sees the merits in adopting them.

EXHIBIT 8.5   Accounts Payable and Accounts Receivable Statistics

Accounts Payable
Overall data

Total number of payments:	16,000
Total amount of dollars:	$1,800,000
Cost to process a payment:	$21.00
Total cost of accounts payable:	$336,000
Average time to pay invoice:	22 days

Payment Statistics

Payment amount	Number	Percent	Amount	Percent
Under $20	4,760	29.8%	$ 72,000	4.0%
Between $20 and $50	4,440	27.8%	106,000	5.9%
Between $50 and $100	3,680	23.0%	161,200	9.0%
Between $100 and $1,000	1,640	10.2%	533,200	29.6%
Over $1,000	1,480	9.2%	927,600	51.5%
Totals	**16,000**	**100.0%**	**$1,800,000**	**100.0%**

A further analysis of vendors and related payments disclosed the following:

Vendor name	Number	Percent	Amount	Percent
Peterboro, Inc.	2,828	17.7%	$ 306,000	17.0%
Roadway Company	2,630	16.4%	293,400	16.3%
Dellilah Manufacturing	2,448	15.3%	282,600	15..7%
Delta Controls	2,214	13.8%	271,800	15.1%
Eager Specialties	1,832	11.5%	210,600	11.7%
North Facing	1,408	8.8%	154,800	8.6%
Totals	13,360	83.5%	$1,519,200	84.4%
Other vendors	2,640	16.5%	280,800	15.6%
Totals — All Vendors	**16,000**	**100.0%**	**$1,800.000**	**100.0%**

Accounts Receivable
Overall data

Number of customer bills processed annually: 12,000
Cost of accounts receivable function: $324,000
Total sales for the year: $3,500,000
Accounts receivable at the end of year: $ 1,270,000
Average collection period: 48 days
Billing terms: 1 percent 10 days/30 days

(Continued)

EXHIBIT 8.5   (Continued)

Billing Statistics				
Billing Amount	Number	Percent	Amount	Percent
Under $100	5,688	47.4%	$ 252,000	7.2%
Between $100 and $500	4,716	39.3%	801,500	22.9%
Between $500 and $1,000	924	7.7%	406,000	11.6%
Between $1,000 and $5,000	516	4.3%	878,500	25.1%
Between $5,000 and $10,000	72	.6%	322,000	9.2%
Over $10,000	84	.7%	840,000	24.0%
Totals	12,000	100.0%	$ 3,500,000	100.0%

Sales Statistics				
Customer Name	Number	Percent	Amount	Percent
Paul Brothers Company	2,184	18.2%	$ 675,500	19.3%
Apex Industries	1,956	16.3%	651,000	18.6%
Kontrol Manufacturing	1,764	14.7%	437,500	12.5%
Sandstone, Inc.	1,572	13.1%	301,000	8.6%
Textite Industries	1,152	9.6%	269,500	7.7%
Ace, Inc.	1,008	8.4%	364,000	10.4%
Totals	9,636	80.3%	2,698,500	77.1%
Other Customers	2,364	19.7%	801,500	22.9%
Total — All Customers	12,000	100.0%	$3,500,000	100.0%

Many times, a workable recommendation seems to suggest itself, but in other cases some ingenuity may be needed to come up with a recommendation that is sensible and has a reasonable chance of being adopted. Recommendations should be as specific and helpful as possible, not simply that operations have to be improved, controls must be strengthened, or planning systems must be implemented.

Based on the preceding information (beginning with Exhibit 8.1) relative to the accounting functions, the following recommendations were developed for the accounts payable and accounts receivable functions as well as reporting considerations and other operating indicators.

Accounts Payable

Reduce the number of accounts payable payments through consideration of the following recommendations:

- Eliminate all payments for $100 or less by establishing a direct cash payment system such as department credit cards, direct cash system, or telephone orders as a release from a total dollar commitment.

- Reduce the number of payments for larger items by negotiating with the major vendors as to paying at the time of merchandise receipt with the guarantee of on-time quality deliveries. Items to consider in such negotiations include long-term commitments with shorter-term releases, the ability to deliver on-time at close to 100 percent quality (no returned items), the loss of a discount (at present mostly 1% for ten days or an annual rate of 18.4%), and savings in accounts payable processing.

- Solicit other vendors to become part of a similar payment system. The six major vendors were contacted, and they were all interested in developing such a pay-on-receipt system. Two of the business's competitors have already installed such systems. It is estimated that the business can reduce the number of accounts payable payments from the present level of 16,000 annually to fewer than 6,000.

- Work with major (and other) vendors to educate them on how the business operates so that they can be directly plugged into the company's production control system, allowing for 100 percent on-time deliveries and quality of product.

- Integrate the receipt of merchandise with the approval of the payment, which will eliminate the need for computer operator personnel to review the same documentation. In effect, the receipt of the merchandise should trigger the processing of the payment.

Integrate the above cost savings into product cost structures so that the business can effectively reduce its product costs and related pricing to become more competitive.

Deemphasize paying the bills; emphasize eliminating the bills.

Accounts Receivable

Integrate the sales forecast system into the overall company plan so that manufacturing can produce to a greater level of real customer orders, assuring a greater degree of quality on-time deliveries. This will allow the business to better negotiate with its major customers as to long-term commitments and increased overall sales.

- Establish long-term contracts with each of the business's major customers, including the ability to receive payment via electronic data transfer at the time of shipping merchandise. This will require the business to guarantee 100 percent quality and on-time deliveries. If this can be accomplished, the business can negotiate such long-term contracts, locking in price, production and delivery schedules, and future payments for cash flow purposes. This will enable the business to better plan profit and cash flow projections.

- Reduce the number of customer billings through the implementation of the following recommendations:
  - Establish a direct cash payment system for items less than $500, using credit cards, direct cash payments, and similar vehicles.
  - Implement a policy of payment upon shipment or receipt of merchandise for major customers, considering such factors as ability to make on-time quality deliveries, negotiated long-term contracts with adequate notice as to delivery schedules so as to incorporate such deliveries into the production schedule, the loss of a 1 percent 10-day discount for the customer, and the ability of the customer to pay on this basis.
  - Encourage other customers to accept either the direct-cash or pay-on-receipt system. With better control over costs and pricing, the business should be able to lower prices overall to make these systems attractive to its customers. Three competitors are already implementing such systems into their operations.
  - It is estimated that the business can reduce the number of customer bills from the present level of 12,000 annually to less than 4,000.

- Establish effective credit policies so that each customer is sold only that amount of merchandise that they can adequately pay for within the business's payment systems. Such credit policies must be flexible so that each customer's sales can be maximized without sacrificing the risk of lengthy drawn out payments or no payment at all.

- Integrate billing, accounts receivable, and collections into the overall business computer system so that minimal offline processing is necessary.

> Get the cash quickly; get out of the accounts receivable business.

Internal Statements for Profit Improvement

The reporting process in the business is given little attention unless it is unsatisfactory to the recipient. Effective reporting is the means by which the accounting function communicates with the rest of the business. Good reporting can do wondrous things in communicating effectively within the company, while poor reporting can be doubly negative in its impact. First, poor reporting may have unusable, incorrect, or untimely information leading to improper understanding and decisions. Second, poor reports, even if accurate, can cause the reader to turn away in frustration if the information desired is buried deep within a morass of irrelevant (to the reader) or confusing facts and figures. Effective reporting should encompass effective concepts and features, such as:

- **Exception reporting.** Highlighting only those areas requiring attention
- **Flexible budget reporting.** Directed toward a range (rather than a single level) of activity that can be adjusted to reflect changes resulting from variations in activity
- **Summarized reporting.** Providing information for each level within the business so that these activities can be operated effectively
- **Comparative reporting.** Comparing operating results with realistic standards such as:
  - Actual versus budget (or what it should be)

- Current year or period versus previous year or period
- Standard costs and/or revenues
- Company goals, objective, and detail plans
- External benchmarks, such as competitors' results or industry standards

The business's present financial statements, consisting of a balance sheet and income statement, are primarily directed toward the reporting of historical results to owners and management. At present, it is taking the external CPA working with the accounting computer operator at least ten days to complete these financial statements after the end of a month. Although this information may be useful to those who understand accounting principles, it has more limited operational value to the small business owner and management who are responsible for running the business and generating results. The primary reason for this reduced value is that the financial reports are geared toward the expectations and needs of the accounting profession, and these expectations are different from the needs of small business internal users who require data to tell them what is happening operationally at present that will assist them in future planning.

The small business, with the assistance of the external CPA, should develop and provide a financial statement and internal operations control reporting package that:

- Integrates the company's financial statements with the operating needs of the business

- Uses financial data in an operational format to identify operational problems and causes within the business

- Uses financial and operating data for more effective decision making directed toward positive growth

Without recognizing the small business's internal operations (and external environment) and the manner in which it operates, financial analysis alone cannot tell the entire story. The internal operating and external issues that have to be considered include:

- **Product analysis.** What to sell, to whom, product costs, and what to charge (pricing structures)

- **Customer base.** What markets to be in, to whom to sell, how much of which products, how to service
- **Sales forecasting.** How much of which products, to whom, and how to sell
- **Manufacturing or service providing processes.** What to provide, how to provide, and efficiencies to use
- **Integrated systems.** Sales and marketing, engineering, manufacturing, financial, and personnel
- **Planning and budgeting systems.** Strategic, long term, short term, detail plans, and budgets

Accounting is more than financial statements; it is the entire small business's operations.

Other Operating Indicators

In addition to financial data, ratios, and trends, small business management should look at other key operating indicators such as backlog, real customer sales, accounts receivable and collections, inventory changes, personnel levels and use, and so on. It is apparent that sales, accounts payable, and accounts receivable have all increased. Is this the sign of a healthy, growing company? Growing, yes; healthy, not necessarily. Such increases can be interpreted completely differently—for example:

- Increased sales may be the result of sales to existing customers exceeding safe credit limits or to less desirable customers, creating possible collectibility or nonpayment problems.
- Increased accounts payable may mean increases in returned merchandise to vendors, indicating poor vendor quality, production stoppages, and unacceptable vendors.
- Increased accounts receivable may mean recorded sales without corresponding collected accounts and customer returns indicating

poor internal quality and customer dissatisfaction, resulting in loss of future sales.

- Increased backlogs of work may be more an indication of inadequate systems and procedures, poor work practices, improperly trained staff, and so on, rather than actual increases in volume.

The correct interpretation of what is really happening in the small business can well be the difference between recognizing the healthy company with best practices from the sick organization with many operating deficiencies. It is best to identify such problem areas before and as they happen using effective operating procedures—and take quick remedial action—rather than wait until it is too late.

Stop looking at the numbers; understand what they mean.

Conclusion

Effective operational analysis procedures allow a small business to identify its critical problem areas, its need for effective controls, and opportunities for positive improvement maximizing positive aspects of existing procedures and focusing on the most critical areas. Through coordinating activities of various areas, the analysis process achieves positive changes in these areas simultaneously. The process also allows such areas to work together in the analysis of present practices and the implementation of new systems and procedures. In this manner, all areas learn with less reinventing and change within the same time period.

In the review of the accounting function, a number of areas of potential improvement were identified to make the small business operate more economically, efficiently, and effectively. The implementation of such improvements places the business in a better position for future growth and profitability and will enable the business to compete more effectively in the marketplace. Although there are many other aspects of the business's accounting practices that can be addressed for productivity, cash flow, or profit improvements, these materials contain effective examples of the types of conclusions and recommendations that can result from such an operational analysis. Because each small business is different and each analysis is different, the resulting findings, conclusions, and recommendations will also be unique to that particular small business.

In this present business atmosphere, with emphasis on customer service, quality, economies and efficiencies, profit maximization, cash management, and the realization of real profits, such an analysis becomes not a one-time, standalone project, but an ongoing process of searching for best practices in a program of continuous improvements. The application of effective operating procedures is everyone's responsibility within the small business.

CHAPTER 9

Operational Reporting Considerations

This chapter looks at the process of appraising the small business's situation—from both a financial as well as an operational basis—as to determining the level of operational reporting in place, which reporting controls need to be implemented, and which areas of the business need to be improved. Typically, the external CPA exercises due diligence by ensuring that the internal and reporting controls are in place based on asset valuation and income potential as a going-concern small business, and verifying the accuracy and reliability of the numbers presented on the small business's financial statements, such as:

- Balance sheet
- Income statement

In most instances, the small business is privately held, and many times family owned and operated. Thus, these businesses are subject to greater owner manipulation with less reliance on proper internal controls and reporting than a larger publicly held company, which is subject to stricter Securities and Exchange Commission (SEC) legislation and Sarbanes-Oxley requirements. Such a privately held company may operate in a manner that produces questionable nontaxable business expenses that go into the owners' pockets. In addition, there may be unreported cash sales and unreported inventory withdrawals that are in reality proper business transactions that should be recorded in the financial records as such. These factors have an impact on the company's current and continuing operations and must be considered in the development of reporting controls.

Small business owners may have their own financial personnel, but more likely will hire outside financial experts such as a CPA firm to prepare its financial statements. The CPA may reconcile accounts, confirm balances with vendors and customers, verify that transactions such as sales and accounts receivable are legitimate, and perform other tests of the financial records that they deem appropriate. While they may review the company's operations and note some deficiencies, their emphasis is normally focused on financial, not on operating, procedures. Such an emphasis must be moved from a focus only on accounting records to the business operations behind the financial numbers.

> Move the focus from accounting records *to the operations behind the numbers.*

SMALL BUSINESS'S NUMBERS

Let us look at a sample set of small business financial statements as shown in the balance sheet and income statement in Exhibit 9.1. Typically, these amounts will be reviewed as to their validity and whether the business can rely on them as a basis for valuing the small business's financial position. In addition, the amounts and operating trends shown on the statements should be analyzed in regard to producing reliable financial records from proper and efficient operations and internal controls.

Analysis of Financial Statements

As presented in Exhibit 9.1, analysis of the small business company's balance sheet and income statement, besides validating the numbers, might disclose the following concerns:

Balance Sheet: Assets
- **Cash management.** Shows a decrease in cash (from $400 to $450 to $100) with a corresponding sell-off of marketable securities. This is an indication of sacrificing short-term liquidity, making the company

EXHIBIT 9.1   The Small Business

Comparative Balance Sheets as of December 31 ($s in ooos)

	XXX1	XXX2	XXX3
Assets			
Cash	$ 100	$ 450	$ 400
Marketable securities	-0-	500	300
Accounts receivable	1,900	1,600	1,700
Inventory	2,200	1,650	1,600
Current assets	4,200	4,200	4,000
Property, plant, equipment	6,500	3,100	2,800
Total Assets	$10,700	$ 7,300	$ 6,800
Liabilities and Equity			
Accounts payable	$ 1,350	$ 900	$ 750
Other payables	400	350	500
Current liabilities	1,750	1,250	1,250
Long-term debt	3,250	1,100	1,250
Total liabilities	5,000	2,350	2,500
Paid-in-capital	2,200	2,200	2,200
Retained earnings	3,500	2,750	2,100
Total equity	5,700	4,950	4,300
Total Liabilities & Equity	$10,700	$ 7,300	$6,800

Comparative Income Statements for Years Ending December 31 ($s in ooos)

	XXX1	XXX2	XXX3
Net sales	$12,500	$11,000	$10,500
Cost of goods sold			
Materials	3,500	2,400	1,600
Labor	2,200	2,700	3,200
Manufacturing expenses	2,400	2,200	2,000
Total cost of goods sold	8,100	7,300	6,800
Manufacturing profit	4,400	3,700	3,700
Selling expenses	1,200	1,050	1,100
General and administrative expenses	1,200	1,300	1,200
Total operating expenses	2,400	2,350	2,300
Net Income	2,000	1,350	1,400

vulnerable to cash demands, while investing in long-term property, plant, and equipment—hoping for a favorable return on investment. The company barely has enough cash to operate safely on a daily basis and has greatly sacrificed its buffer cash position for emergencies, necessities, and opportunities. It has also maximized its use of accounts payable to satisfy its immediate and short-term operating needs. It has placed itself in a vulnerable position, ripe for a reasonable offer.

- **Accounts receivable.** Shows an increase of 18 percent from $1,600 to $1,900. Based on industry and company norms, this could also be large in relation to sales ($12,500/$1,900 = 6.58 percent). The increase in sales, but not necessarily in collections, has resulted in some corresponding increase in accounts receivable. However, these sales need to be analyzed to determine the presence of poor operating practices such as:

  - Selling excessively to present customers far beyond reasonable credit limits
  - Selling to new customers of a questionable nature
  - Selling inventory at markdown prices to make the sale and turn inventory into cash

    This situation could also indicate ineffective billing and collection procedures.

- **Inventory.** Shows an increase of 33 percent from $1,650 to $2,200. Possibly, to justify the business's long-term capital investment, and once all possible sales have been exhausted, there is still excess capacity, and so the business produces to inventory. This could also indicate weaknesses in inventory control and related purchasing, vendor relations, and receiving and storeroom procedures.

- **Property, plant, and equipment.** Shows a large increase of 110 percent from $3,100 to $6,500, indicating large recent expansion that may have been unnecessary, controlled ineffectively, or used improperly. Based on the decision to invest long term, it appears that the business is trying to operationally justify its decision by hyping sales and creating inventory while devastating its balance sheet.

Liabilities

- **Accounts payable.** Shows an increase of 50 percent from $900 to $1,350, indicating unnecessary purchasing, overextension of expenditures, and weakened ability to pay. Reliance on vendors, especially those critical to its operations, has been weakened, with resultant increases in prices, cash-only policies, and cutoffs of materials. Going to other vendors has resulted in price increases with a resultant stoppage in supply lines.

- **Long-term debt.** Shows a large increase of almost 300 percent from $1,100 to $3,250 that indicates substantial changes in the business, resulting in increased property, plant, and equipment with corresponding decrease in the business's cash position. It is questionable as to whether the business can justify its decision with any semblance of an adequate return on investment. To take this on is a severe burden to this small business company. The owners have to be certain that the business can handle such long-term debt, correct the cash management situation, and produce an adequate return on investment.

- **Retained earnings.** Shows an increase of $650 and $750 for the two years that indicates that the business has increased its net income as the result of changes noted earlier. It needs to be determined whether this is real net income that can be collected or merely booking of sales and accounts receivables. Also, is this significant change expected and should the business have been able to do even better?

Income Statement

- **Sales.** Sales have increased from $10,500 to $11,000 to $12,500 over the past three years. Analysis by product line should be made to determine the causes for such an increase in sales. Should the company have done better, are they all good sales, is it selling to less-than-desirable customers and exceeding realistic customer credit limits? Looking at the entire situation, this is inadequate real growth to justify the devastation of the balance sheet.

- **Cost of goods sold.** Has increased in total from $6,800 to $7,300 to $8,100. However, material costs are the major contributor to this increase, indicating a possible major critical operational area. Factors responsible include price increases and increased production; increased scrap, rejects, and rework; inability to pay timely; and material wastage due to learning curve of new equipment (and possible employee sabotage). In addition, labor costs have decreased over the last three years (from $3,200 to $2,200). This indicates a possible shift in manufacturing, but has the business reduced labor and increased productivity to the extent possible using the new equipment?

Doing the right thing, the right way, at the right cost.

Using Financial Data in Operations

Effective decision making for the small business owner is dependent on reliable and useful information, which may not be forthcoming if all operating transactions are not recorded in the business's books and records. The internal accountant or bookkeeper, and the external CPA, are not the decision makers for the business—especially related to operational concerns and controls. While the internal accountant and the external CPA may provide basic financial information to the small business owner, it must also be determined what else to include in the financial (and operational) information provided to the owners and managers—those who make the operating fixes. Information provided through correct operational reporting becomes a crucial contributor to small business management in the operational problem-solving process. Careful analysis, intelligent problem identification, and accurate assessment of the financial and operational information and controls guide the small business in the right direction.

Financial data must be converted to operational data to be most useful.

Explaining the Difference: Sales versus Cash

Looking at the small business company's statements shown in Exhibit 9.1, the owners were concerned that even though the business was increasing its sales and net profits, they did not have any cash. Obviously, the poor cash position was not due to anything magical, but developed predictably from normal business operations. For small businesses not operating on a strictly cash basis of accounting, but operating with accounts receivable and accounts payable—that is, on the accrual basis of accounting—it must be explained to the small business owner the difference between accrual accounting and actual cash flow. Specifically, the following timing differences must be explained to the owners:

- Sales are recorded when made (at the time when the goods or services are delivered to the customer) and set up as accounts receivable (money due to the company but not paid yet), with the actual cash being received at the time of customer payment (typically 30 days later or more). If the customer never pays for the sale, there is a sale recorded with no corresponding cash received.

- Expenses are incurred on a different timing schedule from cash payments. For example, payroll, material, supplies, and other expenses are paid when due. But the payback from the customer sale will be sometime in the future.

- Profits shown on the income statement are based on accrual accounting (i.e., sales are recorded when made, not when receivables are collected), and expenses are recorded as incurred, not when they are paid from accounts payable.

- An increase in inventory is a cash outlay, but not an expense; an inventory reduction is an expense, but not a cash outlay. That means an inventory reduction program will have a positive effect on cash but a negative impact on profits.

- Some expenses, such as depreciation, are recorded through accounting entries and do not represent cash outflows; similarly, prepaid items are expensed currently, but represent prior disbursements of cash.

- Expenditures for fixed assets are paid for currently, but do not immediately appear on the income statement as expenses; they appear only later through depreciation entries.

- Financial statements do not provide all of the necessary data needed to manage and operate effectively. For instance, the small business owner should know operating facts such as the costs and profits generated for each sales order and for each customer, the number of on-time deliveries, the amount of returned merchandise, and the amount and cost of rejects and rework—in short, those critical operating controls that greatly affect their business.

Analysis of Financial Information

Financial information is usually the starting point for analyzing the small business's operations as to how they work and what controls should be established to ensure effective management over all of their activities. Financial statement and reporting analysis is an effective tool to analyze the small business's operations and reported results. When this is done properly, useful information about the small business's financial status and trends as well as operational considerations will be the result, which will assist the business in establishing effective plans for future growth.

If the owner understands the basic purposes and principles for why the small business is in existence, the owner (sometimes with outside assistance) can help the small business identify why it has gone astray and what can be done to get it back on the right track. In addition, the owner and management must understand the significance of reported financial and operational information, how to interpret such information, and what steps need to be taken to address areas of positive improvement as well as those operational areas in need of improvement and change.

It is not the reporting of information, but the *review and analysis* of information.

A good starting point for such business operational analysis is the timely preparation, analysis, and review of financial statements produced from controlled business transactions to ensure that all transactions are recorded accurately and that no transactions are lost or omitted. However, additional financial and operational data is needed for the small business owner to obtain an all-encompassing picture of what is happening in the business. Remember that every financial transaction processed and reported is the result of some operational activity—accordingly, both financial and operational activities need to be reviewed and analyzed.

The analysis of financial information is the key to what operational areas should be controlled and reported to management. Improving a deficient operational area leads to improving the related financial transactions and reporting.

Financial information emanates from operations.

To illustrate how such an analysis of financial information can assist the small business in establishing an effective path for positive growth, let us take a look at a typical small business, The Lucky Dog Company (TLDC), local producers and wholesale distributors of electronic parts and products, owned by Bob and Dot Wilson.

Initially, let us look at the comparative financial statements for TLDC for the most recent three years, as shown in Exhibit 9.2.

Accrual versus Cash Basis of Reporting

Note: The financial statements in Exhibit 9.2 are based on the accrual basis of accounting, where sales are recorded when made (setting up an account receivable) and expenses are made when incurred (setting up an account payable), and fixed assets are recorded on the balance sheet, but each period's share of the cost is depreciated based on a proration of that period's share of the cost. The purpose of accrual accounting is to record accounting transactions in the period that they relate to, not in the period of the actual cash transactions. Cash basis accounting, which many small businesses use, records each transaction as the cash comes in or goes out. Accordingly, sales are recorded as cash is received, even though customer bills may be outstanding; and expenses are recorded when paid, even though there may be outstanding vendor bills. In addition, if there is inventory, the ending inventory amount is recorded ("plugged in") after the fact, usually by the external CPA, to adjust the recording of net income up or down to meet the desires of the owners for tax reporting. Regardless of the basis of accounting, cash or accrual, such financial statements may sometimes be difficult for small business management to understand.

EXHIBIT 9.2   The Lucky Dog Company

Comparative Balance Sheets as of December 31

	XXX1	XXX2	XXX3
Assets			
Cash	$ 30	$ 200	$ 300
Accounts receivable	1,860	1,080	600
Inventory	2,680	1,200	800
Total current assets	4,570	2,480	1,700
Property, plant, and equipment	3,790	2,840	2,200
Accumulated depreciation	(1,080)	(770)	(600)
Net property, plant, and equipment	2,710	2,070	1,600
Other assets	420	380	370
Total Assets	$7,700	$4,930	$3,670
Liabilities and Equity			
Accounts payable	$ 980	$ 420	$ 250
Notes payable	100	100	100
Current maturities (long-term debt)	420	340	300
Other current liabilities	280	220	180
Total current liabilities	1,780	1,080	830
Long-term debt	3,840	2,600	2,200
Total liabilities	5,620	3,680	3,030
Retained earnings	2,080	1,250	640
Total Liabilities and Equity	$7,700	$4,930	$3,670

A review of these comparative balance sheets discloses the following:

1. Cash has decreased to almost nothing; that is $30.
2. Accounts receivable and inventory have each more than tripled.
3. Total assets have more than doubled.
4. Accounts payable have nearly quadrupled.
5. Borrowing has increased, but less than doubled.
6. Retained earnings have more than quadrupled, indicating good profitability and reinvestment of profits.

Comparative Income Statements for Years Ending December 31

	XXX1	XXX2	XXX3
Net sales	$6,250	$4,680	$3,240
Cost of goods sold:			
Material	1,130	860	480
Labor	1,630	1,170	970
Other product expenses	1,040	860	640
Total cost of goods sold	3,800	2,890	2,090

Gross operating profit	2,450	1,790	1,150
Operating expenses:			
Selling expenses	560	420	260
General and administrative expenses	740	520	270
Total operating expenses	1,300	940	530
Net operating profit	$1,150	$ 850	$ 620

An examination of these comparative income statements shows:

1. Sales have approximately doubled from xxx3 to xxx1.
2. Net income has also approximately doubled from xxx3 to xxx1.
3. Material costs have increased by more than twice while direct labor and other product expenses have gone up less than twice, resulting in a gross operating profit amount that has more than doubled.
4. Selling expenses and general and administrative expenses particularly have gone up by much more than twice, thereby more than eliminating the benefit of the improved gross operating profit and resulting in less than a twofold increase in net operating profit.

Uses and Sources of Funds

An effective and quick way to analyze the effect of operations is to pinpoint the use of funds (what the cash was spent on) and the sources of funds (where additional cash comes from). The Lucky Dog Company's uses and sources of funds from the base year xxx3 to the current year xxx1 are shown in Exhibit 9.3.

This analysis shows confirmation of a large increase in reinvested profits as a major operating source of funds. The company is also using accounts payable as a source of short-term borrowing. The large increase in total borrowing created the investment in net property, plant, and equipment as well as increased inventory and an increase in accounts receivable—resulting in a large drop in the company's cash position.

The small business owner needs to understand the relationship between obtaining a customer sales order and the flow within the business that results ultimately in a positive profit. This process is described in small business success formula 5, shown in Exhibit 9.4.

Each customer and each customer sale is a profit center.

EXHIBIT 9.3	The Lucky Dog Company: Uses and Sources of Funds

Uses of Funds

	$ Change	% Change
Cash	(270)	10.0
Accounts receivable	1,260	310.0
Inventory	1,880	335.0
Net property, plant, and equipment	1,110	169.4
Other assets	50	113.5
Total Uses of Funds	4,030	209.8

Sources of Funds

Reinvested profits	1,440	427.3
Total borrowing	1,760	167.7
Accounts payable	730	392.0
Other liabilities	100	155.5
Total Sources of Funds	4,030	209.8

FINANCIAL AND OPERATING RATIO ANALYSIS

Financial and related operating ratios are relationships between or among numbers that are indicators of how well or poorly a small business is performing. The use of such ratios is an effective tool in the analysis of the small business's performance as to which operations appear to be adequate and which operations need to be strengthened. When measured over a period of at least three to five years, ratios are useful in identifying the *trend of changes* in operations, profitability, and financial position. Ratio analysis also helps to identify operational and financial trouble spots and to focus attention on areas needing management attention.

Ratios are merely indicators—not definitive determinants of "good/ bad," "success/failure," or "survivability/demise." Accordingly, they should be used as indicators of operational concerns, but any inferences drawn need extra investigation to gather more information. Looking at these ratios provides valuable understanding of the small business, its strengths and weaknesses, and how it is changing over time. This is usually sufficient to define where the attention of the small business owner needs to be directed.

EXHIBIT 9.4   Small Business Success Formula 5

$$CO = BL = PO = SR + AR = CR - TC = GP$$

$CO = $ Customer order
Each customer sales order must be entered into the small business records as soon as it is a reality. For major customers, the business's goal is to obtain long-term negotiated commitments from these customers so that the business can plan its providing of products or services in advance. Ideally, for small business manufacturers such negotiated commitments can be automatically plugged into their production schedule. In addition, the small business should attempt to get as much cash advance up front as possible — 100% for agreed-upon small purchases.

$BL = $ Backlog order
If the small business cannot immediately enter the customer's sale order immediately into process, it becomes backlog—that is, a bonafide sales order that cannot be processed. Ideally, backlog should be zero. If a sales order must be entered into backlog, it is an indication that the small business is not operating effectively.

$PO = $ Production order
If the small business does not have the items ordered on site or in inventory, then the order must be processed internally and entered into the system as a production order or order in process. The PO should not be entered into production any earlier than necessary to ensure timely shipment to the customer. The operating controls from this point are to produce the order as quickly as possible using facilities efficiently so that all customer orders are completed to meet customer shipment requirements.

$SR + AR = $ Sale recording + Accounts receivable
If the small business has not received a cash payment in advance or at the time of shipment, the customer will have to be billed and the sale set up as an account receivable. At this point, the customer has the materials and the business has a bill to the customer with payment terms—which may or may not be honored. Accordingly, it is incumbent upon the small business to get out of the accounts receivable where possible and ensure that all bills are paid in a timely fashion.

$CR - TC = $ Cash receipts − Total costs
The cash receipt should be received by the small business as quickly as possible—hopefully prior to shipping or providing the product. However, where billing and collections must be done, the small business must be vigilant in collecting the cash payment as quickly as possible. Note that if discounts are offered for early payment, such cost must be calculated as part of total costs. A good rule is to set prices after deducting for the offered discount, resulting in getting the desired price from those customers paying within the discount terms and penalizing those others by the amount of the discount for late payment. In addition, the cost of money for the period of collection must be considered as part of total costs. Other costs accumulated as part of total costs include direct product or service costs (e.g., material and labor), indirect costs associated with the product or service (e.g., quality control, receiving and shipping), functional costs (e.g., sales, marketing, engineering, accounting), and customer costs (e.g., pre-sales contacts, during sales contacts, and after sale contacts).

(Continued)

EXHIBIT 9.4   (Continued)

GP = Gross profit

Theoretically each customer and each sale to that customer can be looked at as a profit center. If the small business follows this formula, each sale can be controlled as to its contribution to gross profits and any necessary remedial action can be taken at the time of the transaction.

Financial and operating ratio analysis is a very specific process, and the business must develop a comfortable package of ratios that are logical and appropriate for the individual small business. The ratios that follow for The Lucky Dog Company serve as illustrations of the ratios that might be used to provide effective operational reporting for this specific business. Such ratios are used as reporting controls to monitor the small business's progress toward its desired direction for growth. Keep in mind that the most useful ratios are those that truly work for the specific small business, and those ratios may be unique to that business. These calculated ratios are only as valid as the small business's recording of all transactions is accurate.

Survival Ratios

These ratios address the prospective ability of the business to continue as an economically viable entity. Acceptable survival ratios do not guarantee success or even survivability, nor do unacceptable ratios necessarily spell the imminent demise of the business. However, good ratios are indicators of positive change, while bad ratios are indicative of possible problems.

Liquidity Ratios   *Liquidity* measures the small business's ability to meet its short-term obligations (for one year or less), or the ability to convert non-cash assets into cash or otherwise to obtain cash to meet current liabilities. These ratios are of particular interest to short-term creditors of the business.

- *Working capital* is determined by subtracting current liabilities from current assets. It provides a safety cushion for the small business and its creditors. Relatively higher levels of working capital may be desirable if the business has difficulty obtaining short-term borrowed funds.

	Current Assets	−Current Liabilities	= Working Capital
xxx3	1,700	830	870
xxx2	2,480	1,080	1,400
xxx1	4,570	1,780	2,790

The increase in working capital for TLDC is a positive sign, as the business has increased its capacity for meeting its short-term obligations by more than three times.

- *Current ratio* is calculated by dividing current assets by current liabilities. It measures the small business's ability to pay off current liabilities with its current assets. Within reason, the higher the current ratio, the more short-term safety and security the business's balance sheet demonstrates. The ratio may be misleading if, for example, the business has improved its cash position by selling off fixed assets, which improves the current ratio but may possibly result in adverse long-range effects. In addition, too high a current ratio may indicate that the business is not employing its resources to maximum advantage.

	xxx1	xxx2	xxx3
Current assets	4,570	2,480	1,700
Current liabilities	1,780	1,080	830
= Current ratio	2.57	2.30	2.05

- *Quick (acid test) ratio* is calculated by dividing cash and accounts receivable by current liabilities. It is a more rigorous test of liquidity in that it excludes inventory. This ratio represents a comparison of the most liquid assets to current liabilities.

	xxx1	xxx2	xxx3
Quick assets	1,890	1,280	900
Current liabilities	1,780	1,080	830
= Quick ratio	1.06	1.19	1.08

A current ratio of at least 2.0 and a quick ratio of 1.0 or better are considered acceptable as rules of thumb. However, every situation must be evaluated on its merits before any definite conclusions can be drawn. For the TLDC, the current ratio has appreciably improved over the three years. However, when evaluated with the quick ratio, it is apparent that most of the gain is due to the increase in inventory, as well as a gain in accounts receivable, which may not be desirable from an operational standpoint.

Leverage/Solvency Ratios   *Solvency* is the ability of the small business to meet its long-term obligations as they come due. Leverage is a measure of ownership interest—whose money is most at risk, the owners' or the creditors? Long-term lenders and other creditors should have a very strong interest in these ratios. Leverage, in particular, is an issue for the creditors, since they want to see a situation where the small business owners have enough to lose that they will work their hardest to make the business a success. Higher leverage means that the lenders have a greater stake in the business, which is an indication of increased risk to them. Conversely, the owners want to take advantage of leverage as much as possible to maximize the return on their investment.

- *Debt-to-equity ratio* is calculated by dividing total liabilities by total equity and measures the amount of debt relative to equity. Too much debt may cause difficulty in meeting current interest charges and principal payments as they come due and may cause lending institutions to be wary of lending additional money.

	xxx1	xxx2	xxx3
Total liabilities	5,620	3,680	3,030
Equity	2,080	1,250	640
= Debt-to-equity ratio	2.70	2.94	4.73

  This means that for every dollar of equity, outsiders have supplied respectively $4.73, $2.94, and $2.70 of financing for the three years. The TLDC appears to be reducing its debt requirements in relationship to equity, although there is a substantial jump in external financing from $2,200 to $2,600 to $3,840 over the three years— which should cause some concern. As a general rule of thumb, a small business's debt–to–equity ratio should fall within the range of.50 to 1.00. Below that range, the business may not be adequately using the leverage available to it from use of borrowed funds. However, above that range lending institutions may feel there is too much leverage and thus too much risk—as with TLDC.

- *Debt-to-assets ratio* is calculated by dividing total liabilities by total assets. It is a variation of the debt-to-equity ratio and measures similar characteristics of the small business's financial position—namely, what part of total financing needs is being supplied by lenders and creditors.

	xxx1	xxx2	xxx3
Total liabilities	5,620	3,680	3,030
Total assets	7,700	4,930	3,670
= Debt-to-assets ratio	.73	.75	.83

The range of ratios should fall between .33 and .50 with variations possible depending on the nature of the small business. The decrease over the three years indicates that TLDC has increased its total assets at a faster rate than its total liabilities. Examining the dollar amounts on the balance sheet, it can be concluded that TLDC has increased the amounts of accounts receivable, inventory, and property, plant, and equipment at a faster rate than its increase in accounts payable and long-term debt, indicating possible operational weaknesses.

Performance Ratios

These ratios measure how well the small business has performed in terms of resource management and profits. Such performance ratios combine aspects of a financial ratio together with those of an operating ratio.

Activity Ratios   These ratios, also referred to as *asset management or turnover ratios*, measure the small business's use of assets to generate revenue and income. Generally, the higher the turnover, the more efficiently the business is managing its assets—although too high a turnover may indicate problems in meeting the operating needs of the business.

- **Accounts receivable collection ratio.** This ratio consists of two related ratios:

    1. **Accounts receivable turnover.** This ratio measures the number of times accounts receivable are collected in the year. Turnover is calculated by dividing total sales by the average accounts receivable (beginning balance plus ending balance divided by two). The higher the accounts receivable turnover, the better the small business is in collecting quickly from its customers. The funds are thus available for use in the business's operations. However, if the turnover is too high, it can be a signal that the business is overly strict in its credit policies and may possibly be losing business to its competitors. In many instances, customers drift toward suppliers who give them the most flexibility regarding payments. Small business owners must keep in mind that they are trying to get out of the accounts receivable business and focus on being in the cash conversion business through such techniques as cash in advance (especially for small

purchases), electronic funds transfers for quicker payment with pricing negotiated accordingly, desired prices net of payment discounts, and so forth. In effect, this creates another operating consideration as to the reduction of accounts receivable.

	xxx1	xxx2	xxx3
Total sales	6,250	4,680	3,240
Average accounts receivable	1,470	840	670
= Accounts receivable turnover	4.25	5.57	4.84

The accounts receivable turnover is too low and most likely unacceptable for TLDC. Over the past three years, the company is increasing its accounts receivable to make sales that not only may be quality sales to quality customers, but also may result in poor profitability due to payment concessions and slow/no payments. In addition, TLDC is moving in the reverse direction from reducing accounts receivable and increasing the cash conversion cycle.

2. **Accounts receivable collection period.** This ratio measures the number of days it takes the business to collect its receivables. The collection period is calculated by dividing the average daily sales (sales divided by 365 days) into the accounts receivable balance.

	xxx1	xxx2	xxx3
Accounts receivable	1,860	1,080	600
Average daily sales	17.12	12.82	8.88
= Days collection	108.6 days	84.2 days	67.6 days

This means that it is taking approximately 109 days on the average for a sale to be converted to cash by the business. This has increased over the last three years from 67.6 days, and 84.2 days—all unacceptable collection periods, with the situation worsening. This raises the possibility that the business's collection efforts are not being pursued vigorously or that the sales and credit policies are too loose, with too many sales made to marginal or undesirable customers.

- **Inventory turnover ratio.** This ratio measures how efficiently the business is using its inventory resources. It is usually calculated by dividing the cost of goods sold for the year by the inventory balance.

In turn, the average age of the inventory can be calculated by dividing the inventory turnover rate into 365 days in the year.

	xxx1	xxx2	xxx3
Cost of goods sold	3,800	2,890	2,090
Inventory balance	2,680	1,200	800
= Inventory turnover	1.42	2.41	2.61

The ratios shown here indicate extremely slow-moving inventory. When examining the change of turnover or age of inventory, management may conclude that TLDC is stocking more inventories or the inventory is becoming less saleable. It is also possible that slow-moving or obsolete inventory is building up. Under these circumstances, the small business owners might consider a product mix analysis or more effective inventory control procedures—keeping in mind that the goal is to get out of the inventory business, not to increase it.

The longer inventory is held the more costly it is for the business, considering such factors as carrying costs, risk of loss or deterioration, obsolescence, and the anxiety of selling off the inventory at a markdown and possible loss resulting in sacrificing future sales. While management should work with the small business owner to push inventories to zero, management should also be aware to maintain a minimum level of inventory to maintain effective customer service. It is this minimum level of inventory that becomes the yardstick to set for inventory levels.

Profitability Ratios   These ratios measure the small business's ability to earn a satisfactory profit and return on investment. These ratios are extremely important as investors and lenders tend to avoid businesses with poor earnings potential and creditors are wary of insufficient profitability because of the increased risk of loss.

- **Net profit margin.** This is probably the most commonly used measure of performance, though it may not be the most useful. This ratio measures how much of each sales dollar is retained as profit.

	xxx1	xxx2	xxx3
Net income	1,150	850	620
Net sales	6,250	4,680	3,240
= Net profit margin	18.4 percent	18.2 percent	19.1 percent

The ratios shown here for TLDC indicate that while net income and sales are increasing over the three-year period, the net profit margin has actually decreased.

- **Gross profit margin.** This measure is a related profitability measure that calculates gross profit as a percentage of sales to determine the profitability of the small business's basic operations.

	xxx1	xxx2	xxx3
$\dfrac{\text{Gross profit}}{\text{Net sales}}$	$\dfrac{2,450}{6,250}$	$\dfrac{1,790}{4,680}$	$\dfrac{1,150}{3,240}$
= Gross profit margin	39.2 percent	38.2 percent	35.5 percent

The increase in gross profit margin, even though small, indicates that TLDC is able to maintain the profitability of its operations. However, management must ascertain whether the calculated gross profit margin is a desired one and, if so, whether it can be increased even further.

- **Return on investment.** Return on investment (ROI) is an exceedingly important measure because it shows how effectively the business is using its invested funds in total. ROI is a generic term in that there are numerous ways in which it can be calculated. Management should be fully aware of the specific ROI calculation being used in each situation before setting it up as a financial/operational control. The following two basic ROI formulas are commonly used.

  1. *Return on assets* measures the profit-generating efficiency of the total assets of the business.

	xxx1	xxx2	xxx3
$\dfrac{\text{Operating profit}}{\text{Total assets}}$	$\dfrac{1,150}{7,700}$	$\dfrac{850}{4,930}$	$\dfrac{620}{3,670}$
= Return on assets	14.9 percent	17.2 percent	16.9 percent

  2. *Return on equity* measures the effectiveness of the investment made by the owners in the business. It is a measure of the overall return to the owners.

	xxx1	xxx2	xxx3
$\dfrac{\text{Net income}}{\text{Total equity}}$	$\dfrac{1,150}{2,080}$	$\dfrac{850}{1,250}$	$\dfrac{620}{640}$
= Return on equity	55.3 percent	68 percent	96.9 percent

Considering present alternative safe rates of return with minimal risk, both of the ratios given here seem attractive. The subjective factor that needs to be taken into account is the element of risk and how much extra return is appropriate to compensate for that risk. There is no single answer to that question since risk is a factor that must be evaluated by each business. Needless to say, a higher return would be appropriate for such a small business as opposed to an investment in a Treasury bill.

An effective method to review these ratios in full context is to summarize the ratios selected for each small business client in a summary report that is presented along with the financial statements. The software used by the small business should provide the capability for calculating these ratios automatically at the time of producing the small business's financial statements. An example of such a report for the Lucky Dog Company is shown in Exhibit 9.5.

EXHIBIT 9.5   The Lucky Dog Company: Financial/Operational Ratio Analysis

	XXX1	XXX2	XXX3
1. Survival ratios			
a. Liquidity ratios			
i. Working capital	2,790	1,400	870
ii. Current ratio	2.57	2.30	2.05
iii. Quick ratio	1.06	1.19	1.08
b. Leverage/solvency ratios			
i. Debt to equity	2.70	2.94	4.73
ii. Debt to assets	.73	.75	.83
2. Performance ratios			
a. Activity ratios			
i. Accounts receivable — turnover —	4.25	5.57	4.84
Collection period	108.6 days	84.2 days	67.6 days
ii. Inventory — turnover — Age	1.42	2.41	2.61
b. Profitability ratios	257 days	151 days	140 days
i. Net profit margin	18.4%	18.2%	19.1%
ii. Gross profit margin	39.2%	38.2%	35.5%
iii. Return on investment			
Return on assets	14.9%	17.2%	16.9%
Return on equity	55.3%	68.0%	96.9%

From the review and analysis of the basic ratios shown above, you should get some clear indications that TLDC is losing control over its investments in assets. For instance:

- Accounts receivable collections are extending significantly, with indications of overextended credit, less-than-quality sales, selling rather than servicing the customers, and poor collection procedures.

- Inventory investment is expanding rapidly, with a decrease in turnover leading toward older inventory, obsolescence, risk of inventory evaporation, excessive storeroom costs and procedures, and anxiety to sell out of inventory at any price, even at a loss.

- Overall investment in assets is rising faster than sales activity, forcing the owners to use these assets (property, plant, and equipment) to produce sales to justify their long-term investment.

- There is heavy debt and interest burden relative to the amount invested and reinvested through profits by the owners, resulting in a high financial risk.

- The ratios make ROI results (return on assets and return on equity) look attractive, but at what risk to the overall financial and operational health of the business?

The analysis of TLDC's financial and operational results as discussed earlier disclosed a number of successes along with several problems that the owners probably were not aware of, which include:

- Reported profitability has improved but balance sheet assets (e.g., cash, receivables, and inventory) have been compromised, resulting in cash conversion and operational concerns.

- Sales have improved but controls over credit limits, payment terms, collections, and quality sales have deteriorated.

- Cash flow problems have resulted in the present cash position being beneath a safe buffer level, with accounts receivable going uncollected for too long a time and accounts payable being used dangerously for short-term financing.

- Accounts receivable increases that have resulted in the booking of sales but not necessarily profits has used up a significant amount of funds.

- Inventory has gotten out of control due to the need to use property, plant, and equipment far past the point of making sales, but rather to add to inventory.

- Substantial funds have been invested in plant and equipment, deemed necessary by the owners to justify their need for increased capacity.

- Borrowing has increased, which in turn has increased the business's interest expense as well as placed a burdensome emphasis on producing quality profitable sales.

- Accounts payable have increased due to the inability to pay vendor bills, with a strain on cash, and using vendors as a means of short-term financing, creating concerns about vendor relations—especially the business's critical vendors. Such practices will result in increased vendor prices and a further drain on an already-receding cash position.

KEY OPERATING STATISTICS

In addition to looking at financial and related operational data, small business management must also look at key operating data related to such operational areas as customer order backlog, sales statistics, accounts receivable, inventory, and personnel. From the information reviewed thus far it is apparent that sales, accounts receivable, and inventory have all increased. However, other operational areas, such as customer order backlog and personnel statistics, cannot be readily analyzed through financial data only. These increases might be signs of a healthy, growing company or they might not be. For example, such increases can be interpreted as:

- New sales emanating from less-reputable customers might create possible collectibility problems.

- Backlog (customer orders waiting order fulfillment) might mean unsatisfied customers who will take their business elsewhere.

- Accounts receivable booked at the time the sale is recorded may become uncollected accounts.

- Inventory buildup is really unshipped (and unordered) product that might not be ordered or might be sold at a large markdown, resulting in cash but not profits.

Is it a healthy business, or is its weakness being hidden?

The correct interpretation of what is happening to a small business like TLDC makes it possible to distinguish between the healthy business that is desired or the sick business that has lost the agility and quickness needed to survive. It is the responsibility of management to develop effective reporting controls for its business segments and functions.

To demonstrate the use of effective reporting controls, the case study shown in Exhibit 9.6 for The Lucky Dog Company provides an analysis of the reports and related controls presented in this chapter.

EXHIBIT 9.6   **Action Reporting Controls: The Lucky Dog Company**

Having reviewed and analyzed the reporting controls relative to The Lucky Dog Company (TLDC) financial and operational reporting, you should now be in a position to recommend specific reporting controls to the owners as well as specific actions to take at this time. If you need refreshing or reinforcement you might go back and review:

- Comparative balance sheets
- Comparative income statements
- Uses and sources of funds
- Financial and operational ratio analysis

Based on your review, what would you suggest to the owners of TLDC as to reporting controls and actions to take?

Suggested Response

Balance Sheet Comments

- Cash has decreased to almost nothing—well below a minimum buffer safety position. The uses and sources of funds need to be strictly controlled, with the owners and management reviewing each sale as to its quality and quick collectibility, and each expense as to its value-added necessity.

Cash is king—maximize inflow, minimize outflow.

- Accounts receivable have greatly increased over the three years—by over three times with the collection period exceeding 108 days. Each sale that results in a receivable should be reviewed and approved as to its legitimacy related to quality customer, credit limit, acceptable terms, and ability and timeliness to pay. The owners may also want to review their cost and pricing policies so that they are not selling their product for less than actual costs.

This area is out of control—as a result TLDC has found itself in the accounts receivable business. The major reason for this situation is the owners' push to get more sales, many times to undesirable customers, which has created production crises, relaxed credit terms, and increased customer complaints due to unmet delivery schedules and product quality problems. Minimal collection follow-up is being done and customers are withholding payments pending resolution of their problems.

Get out of the accounts receivable business; get into the cash conversion business.

- Inventory levels have greatly increased—by over three and a third times with decreases in inventory turnover to less than two times a year and inventory age of over 180 days. Each item in inventory needs to be analyzed for disposition such as:
  - Ability to be sold at a profitable selling price without sacrificing future sales.
  - Selling at a markdown for those items that can be converted quickly to cash without jeopardizing TLDC's current sales goals. Hopefully, the markdown price will still contribute something to real cash profits.
  - Obtaining as much cash as possible for those items that are deemed old and/or obsolescent to stop the costs of carrying inventory for unsaleable items.
  - Selling the remainder for scrap, getting as much as possible in cash.
  - Stopping producing for inventory, even if it means idle capacity—and producing for customer orders to the extent possible.

- There appears to be a philosophy that if TLDC uses its increased plant capacity to create inventory it will be sold, but this is not happening. As a result, TLDC finds itself in the inventory business. This situation not only contributes to the cash flow problem, but also clogs the plant facility and reduces efficiency.

Produce for customer needs, not for inventory.

- Accounts payable have greatly increased—by almost four times, resulting in some loss of critical vendors (or paying cash on order or delivery), increases in material and product costs, accompanied by a decrease in quality and timely deliveries.

Do not pay until you have to, but do not overstrain vendor relations.

- Borrowing has increased—by almost 175 percent over the three years, resulting in increased payment and interest expense, which places a greater risk on the business and causes anxiety to make sales so as to pay off the loans.
- Retained earnings have increased—by over three times, indicating profitability. However, it is known that the extent of uncollectible bad sales in receivables and the amount of unsaleable inventory sold for cash produces a loss.

Income Statement Comments

- Sales have increased by almost two times. However, it is not known what the extent of good collectible sales is, versus the extent of nonquality sales. Emphasis appears to be on making sales and not on the good customer service to quality customers that may result in additional sales and quality referrals of other customers.

Make the right sale to the right customer at the right time.

- Net income has almost doubled, but one must keep in mind that this is accrual accounting and not cash accounting. In other words, net income is on the books but the cash related to these sales may go uncollected.

Net income is not profit until the cash is collected and it exceeds total cost.

- Material costs have increased by over two times, with some of this increase due to increased sales and inventory as well as the increased cost of materials due to changing vendor payment relationships.
- Labor costs have increased over one and a half times, with some of this increase attributable to increased sales and inventory. However, if the additional property, plant, and equipment were justified by large decreases in labor costs, further analysis may be required to determine whether TLDC is achieving the expected economies.
- Other product costs have also increased, over one and a half times. Each element of these costs needs to be controlled as to which ones are necessary, which ones can be reduced, and which ones can be eliminated.
- Selling expenses have increased greatly, by more than twice, with some of the increase attributed to increased sales; other causes may be selling pressures by the owners at the same time that sales have become harder to obtain. The entire selling activity needs to be better controlled so that the sales force is guided by an effective business selling plan as to what to sell, to whom, in what quantity, and at what time—as well as an acceptable definition of customer service. The sales force must provide that level of customer service while simultaneously making desired sales. This may necessitate controlling sales activities and methods of compensation as well as cost-to-price relationships.

- General and administrative expenses have also increased, by almost 275 percent. Each element of these expenses must be individually controlled and analyzed as to their necessity and whether they provide value-added activities. Some such expenses are fair game to reduce and eliminate without adversely affecting operations. Is TLDC in the employment and management and administration business? Personnel costs need to be decreased so that any such costs are those that add true value to the business.

Eliminating unnecessary non-value-added costs adds to the bottom line.

Other Comments

- Backlog is a growing percentage of sales volume, indicating that TLDC is having increasing problems in getting customer orders into and out of production and shipped to the customer in a timely manner. The increase in backlog also points to deterioration in customer service, with some customers canceling their orders and going elsewhere and others reducing future business with TLDC. This is an area for high controls working toward the eventual elimination of backlog. Backlog is entirely too high, particularly in light of TLDC's tenuous cash position.

Backlog needs to be converted into sales before it defaults to the competition.

- Customer sales by product line (particularly for products A and B) show that sales to several of the top customers (the 20% that provides 80% of sales) have remained flat or declined. Questions that need to be answered include:
  - Does this represent general customer dissatisfaction for these customers as well as others?
  - Are there quality problems, such as product quality, service quality, and timeliness?

- Has the desired level of customer service been neglected?
- Has the quest for sales, *any* sales, decreased the emphasis on customer service and cash conversion?
- Are sales trends for top customers, by product line and item, on an increasing arc, or is sales growth coming mainly from new, more questionable customers?

It is easier to build a business through repeat sales to quality customers than through continually finding new customers.

- Sales prices have come down in each of the three years. This can be a result of the owners' desire to sell as much as possible (to justify the investment in property, plant, and equipment?), or the result of increased competition, and/or customers' push to lower their costs and prices. Both sales prices and related costs need to be more fully controlled in an effort to reduce costs to the extent possible as well as control profitable pricing to meet competition.

Reducing product costs may increase profits or reduce sales prices.

- TLDC is in the property, plant, and equipment business with its heavy investment in fixed assets. Such assets need to be reviewed and analyzed to determine whether they are truly necessary. An excess of fixed assets represents not only an investment cost, but also operating costs for such things as maintenance, depreciation, electricity, and operating personnel. Possible solutions to free up some cash and make operations more economical and efficient might be selling off some equipment, using excess plant capacity (over the need for real customer orders) more efficiently through renting the space, using it for finished-goods work for others, becoming an outsourcer for specific operations for others, and/or expanding the business with increased quality sales.

> Minimize finite capacity and use it effectively.

- TLDC, like most small businesses, is dependent on a limited number of customers—20 percent of all customers providing 80 percent of total sales. While this situation creates an advantage in assisting these customers in defining their needs, forecasting their purchases from TLDC, and providing more effective customer service, it also creates the disadvantage of a substantial loss of sales and profits if one or more of these customers stop dealing with TLDC. This is quite possible due to TLDC's present operations, so this area needs to be closely controlled and monitored.

> Service existing quality customers to build your business.

Operational Statements

The information uncovered through the preceding financial reporting and analysis assists management and operations personnel in identifying the impact of financial policies and conditions on the business's cash and profitability positions. However, effective operational analysis should go beyond financial analysis to include a more in-depth review and analysis of specific areas of the business's operations as well.

Most companies are in more than one business; that is, they offer their customers a number of different product lines. For instance, the business may offer a low-end, a medium, and a high-end line; or a basic, standard, and custom or specialty line; or it may provide a basic piece of equipment (e.g., copy machine), replacement parts, and supplies. An analysis of the business's records can be used to develop individual income statements for each of its product lines or business segments.

In many cases, such an analysis, employing existing records, may be extremely difficult or costly. Therefore, it is best to establish what

EXHIBIT 9.7   Income Statement by Product Line

	Total	Product A	Product B	Product C
Net Sales	$12,500	$ 5,900	$ 4,300	$ 2,300
Cost of goods sold				
Material	2,260	760	740	760
Labor	3,260	1,600	1,300	360
Manufacturing expenses	2,080	1,040	720	320
Total cost of goods sold	7,600	3,400	2,760	1,440
Gross profit	4,900	2,500	1,540	860
Selling expenses	1,120	348	58	186
General and administrative expenses	1,480	816	246	418
Total operating expenses	2,600	1,164	832	604
Net profit	2,300	1,336	708	256
Sales — % of total	100.0%	58.1%	30.8%	11.1%
Gross profit — % of sales	39.2%	42.3%	35.8%	37.4%
Net profit — % of sales	18.4%	22.6%	16.5%	11.1%

information will be needed in setting up the business's reporting system. Data collection and computer processing procedures should automatically provide the desired operating data and statistics.

An example of an income statement by product line is shown in Exhibit 9.7.

Note that each product line in Exhibit 9.7 can be considered a separate business or profit center. In addition, the business can consider each product within a product line as a separate profit center, as well as each production job, customer order, or each individual customer. Each of these analyses helps to determine exactly what is happening currently, trends in previous periods, and what remedial action may be necessary.

Such product line reporting should be integrated with the original sales forecast and modifications, which should be part of the business's planning process. Such reporting allows management to determine whether they are progressing toward the right goals and whether any action must be taken. Such action could result in product modifications, sales and marketing changes, or changes in customer philosophy, work plan, or sales methodologies. It is the ability to determine specifically what information is significant to report that makes the reporting most valuable to the individual users and to small business management.

Other Operating Indicators

In addition to financial data, ratios, and trends, the business should look at other key operating indicators such as backlog, real customer sales, accounts receivable and collections, inventory changes, personnel levels and use, and so on. Based on the operational analysis, it is apparent that sales, accounts payable, accounts receivable, and the number of employees have all increased. Is this the sign of a healthy, growing company? Growing, yes; healthy, not necessarily. Such increases can be interpreted completely differently—for example:

- Increased sales may be the result of sales to existing customers exceeding safe credit limits or to less-desirable customers, creating possible collectibility or nonpayment problems.

- Increased accounts payable may mean increases in returned merchandise to vendors, indicating poor vendor quality, production stoppages, and unacceptable vendors.

- Increased accounts receivable may mean recorded sales without corresponding collected accounts, and customer returns, indicating poor internal quality and customer dissatisfaction, resulting in loss of future sales.

- Increased number of employees may mean more management and increased expenses, without corresponding increases in value-added productivity.

- Increased work volumes may be more a function of building personnel empires and keeping those employees busy, rather than of real volume increases.

- Increased backlogs of work may be more an indication of inadequate systems and procedures, poor work practices, improperly trained staff, and so on, rather than of actual increases in volume.

The correct interpretation of what is really happening in the business makes it possible to distinguish the healthy company with best practices from the sick organization with many operating deficiencies. It is better to identify such problem areas before and as they happen—and take quick remedial action—rather than wait until it is too late.

Examples of such operating reports are shown in Exhibits 9.8, 9.9, and 9.10.

EXHIBIT 9.8	Operating Information by Product Line		
	Product A	**Product B**	**Product C**
1. Sales prices and units sold			
Total sales in dollars	$ 5,900	$ 4,300	$ 2,300
Units sold in 000s	62.0	55.4	65.6
Average unit price	$ 95.16	$ 77.62	$ 35.06
2. Backlog statistics			
Total backlog in dollars	$ 1,980	$ 1,360	$1,060
Percent of sales	33.6%	31.6%	46.1%
3. Accounts receivable			
Total accounts receivable in dollars	$ 1,680	$1,240	$ 800
Collection days	103.9	106.1	127.0
Turnover times	3.5	3.4	2.9
4. Inventory			
Total inventory in dollars	$ 2,400	$ 1,760	$ 1,200
Turnover times	1.4	1.6	1.2
Average inventory age in days	258	230	304

Conclusion

Effective operational analysis procedures allow a small business to identify its critical problem areas and opportunities for positive improvement—maximizing positive aspects of existing procedures and focusing on the most critical areas. Through coordinating activities of various areas, the analysis process achieves positive changes in these areas simultaneously. The process also allows such areas to work together in the analysis of present practices and the implementation of new systems and procedures. In this manner, all areas learn with less reinventing and change within the same time period.

Such analysis can be a standalone project to identify critical problem areas and provide standardized improvements. It can also minimize the need for reinventing good practices that already exist in another part of the organization or repeating those that have so far been unsuccessful. Comparisons can also be made between the ways in which different people perform the same task in the same area, or among performance across different work units within the business. It can also provide detailed knowledge of operations and its effect on real profits and cash flow.

In the review of operational reporting concerns, a number of areas of potential improvement were identified to make the business operate more

EXHIBIT 9.9   Payroll and Employee Analysis

	Current Year		Previous Year	
	Number of Employees	Annual Dollars	Number of Employees	Annual Dollars
Type of Payroll				
Manufacturing:				
Manufacturing operations	102	$2,285	90	$1,624
Manufacturing supervision	26	975	17	841
General and administrative:				
Accounting functions	38	787	31	634
All others	34	693	26	522
Sales department—salespeople	12	620	10	465
Management	8	512	6	348
Total—all payrolls	250	$5,872	180	$4,434

	Current Year		Previous Year	
	Sales to Employees	% of Sales	Sales to Employees	% of Sales
Payroll Costs To Sales				
Manufacturing operations	$122,549	18.3%	$104,000	17.4%
Manufacturing supervision	480,769	7.8%	550,588	8.9%
Accounting functions	328,947	6.3%	301,935	6.8%
Other general and administration	367,647	5.5%	360,000	5.6%
Sales staff	1,041,667	5.0%	936,000	5.0%
Sales management	1,562,500	4.1%	1,560,000	3.7%
Total employees	50,000	47.0%	52,000	47.4%

	Current Year	Previous Year
Average Cost per Employee		
Manufacturing operations	$22,400	$18,044
Manufacturing supervision	37,500	49,470
Accounting functions	20,700	20,452
Other general and administration	20,380	20,077
Sales staff	51,700	46,500
Sales management	64,000	58,000
Total employees	23,488	24,633

EXHIBIT 9.10   Customers by Product Line

	Current Year		Previous Year	
Customer Name	Sales Dollars	Percent	Sales Dollars	Percent
Product A				
Paul Brothers Company	$1,978	33.5%	$1,440	29.4%
Apex Industries	1,706	28.9%	1,230	25.1%
Kontrol Manufacturing	566	9.6%	453	9.2%
Sandstone, Inc.	346	5.9%	578	11.8%
Textite Industries	270	4.6%	434	8.9%
Ace, Inc.	442	7.5%	259	5.3%
Total	5,308	90.0%	$4,394	89.7%
Other customers	592	10.0%	501	10.3%
Total — all customers	$ 5,900	100.0%	$4,895	100.0%
Product B				
Paul Brothers Company	$ 335	7.8%	$ 460	15.0%
Apex Industries	475	11.0%	640	20.8%
Kontrol Manufacturing	678	15.7%	368	12.0%
Sandstone, Inc.	252	5.9%	84	2.7%
Textite Industries	173	4.0%	36	1.2%
Ace, Inc.	858	20.0%	637	20.7%
Total	2,771	64.4%	$2,225	72.4%
Other customers	1,529	35.6%	845	27.6%
Total — all customers	$ 4,300	100.0%	$3,070	100.0%
Product C				
Paul Brothers Company	$ 100	4.3%	$ 220	15.8%
Apex Industries	144	6.3%	212	15.2%
Kontrol Manufacturing	319	13.9%	69	4.9%
Sandstone, Inc.	477	20.7%	187	13.4%
Textite Industries	520	22.6%	368	26.4%
Ace, Inc.	---	---	142	10.2%
Total	1,560	67.8%	$1,198	85.9%
Other customers	740	32.2%	197	14.1%
Total—all customers	$ 2,300	100.0%	$1,395	100.0%

economically, efficiently, and effectively. The implementation of such improvements places the business in a better position for future growth and profitability and will enable the business to compete more effectively in the marketplace. Although there are many other aspects of the business's operating practices that can be addressed for productivity, cash flow, or profit improvements, these materials contain effective examples of the types of conclusions and recommendations that can result from such an operational analysis. Because each business is different and each analysis is different, the resulting findings, conclusions, and recommendations will also be unique to each specific business.

In this present business atmosphere, with emphasis on customer service, quality, economies and efficiencies, profit maximization, and cash management, such an analysis becomes not a one-time, standalone project, but an ongoing process of searching for best practices in a business program of continuous improvements. The application of operational analysis and reporting procedures is everyone's responsibility.

CHAPTER 10

Internal Controls for the Small Business

A s the small business owner knows, establishing, implementing, and utilizing internal controls seems to be a costly venture that gets in the way of getting things done—and seems to compromise the flexibility of the owners in making their own decisions. Some of the reasons that can be used to convince the small business owner to implement effective internal controls include:

- More efficient and effective operations, increasing the possibilities of greater real profits

- Increased ability to provide accurate operating and financial data for effective decision making in all aspects of the company's operations

- Increased employee, customer, and vendor confidence in the business, resulting in greater possibilities for growth and prosperity

- Assurance that operations are working in a controlled environment, allowing the owners and management to release their need to overcontrol

Standing still often results in losing ground.

What Is Business Risk?

Business risk is the likelihood that material damage can be done to a business due to the lack of ongoing risk assessment and related control activity implementation—that is, threat reduction.

- *Inherent risk* is the lack of internal controls coupled with the likelihood of material misstatement—for example, retail inventory without periodic counts or reconciliations.

- *Control risk* is the likelihood that the design of the internal control system will not prevent or detect material misstatements on a timely basis—for example, retail inventory with counts performed once every five years or bank reconciliation lapses.

- *Detection risk* is the likelihood that review procedures will not detect material misstatements—for example, vouching paper documents only in a computer-processing environment.

> Assessing risk is like planning for success in that fantasy exceeds the reality.

Possible Areas for Controls

As part of identifying critical operational areas for control, small business owners should work together with management and operations personnel to identify:

- Opportunities for improvement (to be the best that the business can be)

- Gaps in performance (where the business is compared to where owners want it to be)

- Best practices—both internal and external (where the business can gain sustainable competitive advantage)

In determining areas where internal controls would be appropriate, the following criteria can be used:

- **Large numbers in relationship to other functions.** Functions to be investigated could include revenues, costs, percentage of total assets, number of sales, units of production, and personnel. For example, in a small manufacturing business, the most critical areas might be the inventory or production control functions; in a service-oriented business, control concerns might be large payroll expenditures with payroll and personnel costs being critical.

- **Controls are weak.** That is, there is a lack of an effective manufacturing control or reporting system, weak storeroom procedures, and lack of proper inventory controls. For example, there are products lying around the shipping area in a disorganized manner. Or, upon observing manufacturing operations you realize that there are no effective controls as to what customer order goes into production next (other than the owner's whims) and no daily productivity reports as to production activity. These are examples of inefficiencies and waste concerning the business's daily operations where controls should be tightened or utilized.

- **Areas of abuse or laxity.** That is, there may be inventory and production controls that allow transactions to go unreported and undetected, uncontrollable time and cost reporting, and ineffective personnel evaluation procedures. For example, take a typical small business where inventory storeroom procedures and records do not exist, and which relies on the factory employees to obtain what they need with no controls as to what was used and what remains. In the same operation, reliance may be placed on each employee as to when the job is started, which job is worked on, and when the job is completed—ignoring the needs of the customer or the business.

- **Areas difficult to control.** For example, there may be ineffective storeroom, shipping, or time recording procedures. Effective storeroom operations ensure proper controls (both physical and record keeping) over materials received from vendors and then disbursed out for a job or to a customer—and possibly excessive materials returned back to the storeroom. Without such controls that ensure adequate materials being on hand, customer orders cannot be properly entered into production. In addition, inadequate controls increase the probability for materials to disappear through improper handling or outright pilferage. Once the customer's order is complete, there also needs to be adequate controls to ensure that it is shipped on time—because until it is shipped and the customer receives the merchandise, the customer will not process the receipt for payment. Time recording procedures ensure that all employees are productively working and that such time recordings result in proper cost recordings as well as plant scheduling.

- **Functions are not performed efficiently or economically.** There may be ineffective procedures, duplication of efforts, unnecessary work steps, inefficient use of resources such as computer processing equipment, overstaffing, and excess purchases. For example, take the small business that has no records as to what is on hand. If the material or product cannot be found ("I know it's here somewhere . . .") it will be reordered or reproduced. This results in excessive purchases, duplication of manufacturing efforts, and unnecessary work steps. You must be keen to identify such weaknesses in operations and be able to communicate the effects on operations of such lack of controls.

- **Areas indicated by ratio, change, or trend analysis.** Areas can be characterized by wide up or down swings when compared over a number of periods. Examples include sales changes by product line, costs by major category, number of personnel, and inventory levels. For example you may compare sales and inventory levels for the business's major products, noticing that the products that show increasing sales over a period of time also show decreasing levels of inventory. Conversely, those products showing a decline in sales demonstrate an ongoing increase in inventory. In this instance you must be able to recognize what is happening. Typically such a situation results by controlling inventory based on past demand rather than on present customer orders.

- **Owner-/management-/stakeholder-identified weaknesses or needs/expectations.** The owner may express a concern as to inventory shrinkage, that is, more inventory being utilized than required in producing a stated product mix. This could be due to poor receiving operations allowing materials to be pilfered before entering the system, materials never received in the storeroom, materials being taken from the storeroom unauthorized, excess materials being disbursed to a job with the excess never being returned to the storeroom, or poor manufacturing and quality control procedures that result in more material being used than is necessary. It is incumbent on the business to identify the specific weaknesses and related controls in such instances.

> Controls are there to help manage operations, not to get in the way of efficiency.

INTERNAL CONTROLS AS BEST PRACTICES

Effective internal controls for the small business must be designed and implemented to meet the specific needs of the owners, the manner in which the business is operated, and the reasons for which it is in existence. Within this framework, the internal control implementation process is performed as follows:

- Review operations to determine the present methods of operations, what controls are in place (if any), and the identification of desired controls to enhance operations.

- Identify internal control best practices that ensure the efficiency of operations without sacrificing operating effectiveness or incurring unnecessary costs, wasted efforts, or unwieldy work practices.

- Owners, management, and operations personnel work together to implement effective internal controls in a program of continuous improvements.

- Leave the residual capability with each operational area so that operational personnel can apply such internal control procedures on an ongoing basis.

- Convert the findings and implementation of internal control recommendations to efficiency of operations and increased profitability to the small business.

> The process of internal controls for the small business cannot be accomplished with criticism of owners, managers, and operations personnel. It needs to be sold as a program directed toward economies and efficiencies that produce increased operational results.

Small Business Stakeholders

A stakeholder is anyone who establishes performance expectations for the small business, can evaluate and judge the quality of operations, and has a stake in ongoing operations' surviving, growing, and prospering:

- Owners/family members/investors: internal/external
- Management/supervision: internal
- Employees/subcontractors: internal/external
- Customers/end users: external
- Suppliers/vendors: external

Internal control results provide the stakeholders:

- Data necessary for effective resource allocation
- Strategic focus for the business
- Objective measures for review, evaluation, and improvement
- Detail plans for improving operations
- Internal and external competitive performance measures
- Evaluation tools to compare the business's performance and results against stakeholder expectations

> If you run your business only for yourself, you will most likely wind up by yourself.

INTERNAL CONTROL CONCEPTS

Internal control is an ongoing process implemented by the people in an organization, sometimes with the assistance of an outside business advisor. It is a process, a means to an end, and not an end in itself. It is affected by people, and is not merely policies, procedures, employee manuals, and forms. Internal control can be expected to provide reasonable assurance, but not absolute assurance, to the small business owners and management that operations are moving in the desired direction toward the achievement of the small business's goals and objectives. Such internal controls, even the best that the outside advisor can imagine, cannot ensure the small business's success or even survival. Good controls cannot make up for inadequate management and inefficient operations. Internal controls and effective operations must go together.

Internal controls and effective operations go together.

The best controls possible should be developed and implemented, but there must be some dollar or operational benefit to the control. For instance, to control the theft of office supplies at an estimated $1,000 per year does not justify a control costing $10,000.

The cost of the control does not exceed the benefit.

An example of the cost of control exceeding the cost of the lack of the control, related to the control over travel expenses, is shown in the case study in Exhibit 10.1.

Accepting the status quo can result in slipping in place.

EXHIBIT 10.1   Checking Up

ACE Consulting has a staff of eight consultants, who spend most of their time out of the office. The head of the firm, Jack Jones, requires each consultant to submit his or her travel expense report every two weeks. Jack expects all expense reports to be on his desk the Monday following the end of the previous week. Jack spends at least two days verifying the correctness of each expense report. He checks the charges as appropriate to each client, the amount of travel bills (air and auto), meal expenses (there is a $40-per-day maximum), nonclient charges, as well as footing and crossfooting each report. As part of his verification procedures he may spend time by calling the consultant, the client, airlines, rental car companies, and so forth. Jack is extremely conscientious not to bill his clients any more than necessary or have any of his consultants cheating on an expense report. He rarely finds anything significant, but believes the cost of these procedures is worth the element of prevention. What would you suggest to Jack?

Suggested Response

- Footing and crossfooting of expense reports is not a managerial function. Initially, the consultant responsible for the expense report should ensure that the report foots and crossfoots. Where available, the preparation and submission of such expense reports should be computerized whereby the computer program can foot and crossfoot as well as check for other exception conditions such as exceeding the daily meal allowance, correct client and job coding, and excessive nonclient charges. As each consultant has a laptop computer, this procedure should be achievable.
- Verifying charges such as the amount of travel bills, meal expenses, client charges and so forth should be the responsibility of each consultant. Jack needs to release his control and emphasize self-motivated, disciplined behavior on the part of his professional staff.

The present system builds mistrust in the minds of the staff as related to Jack. In addition, Jack's time is much too valuable to be spent on such policing-and-control clerical-type activities. The amounts found incorrect, if any, are insignificant compared with the cost of Jack's time and the negative atmosphere it creates for the staff.

Effective internal controls must start at the top with the small business owners and top management. If the owners ignore the internal controls, it usually provides the opportunity for the employees to follow suit. Such a situation is depicted in Exhibit 10.2.

A good model is like a good dinner: the more you have the more you want.

EXHIBIT 10.2   Owners Have to Eat

Herb and Mindy own a small specialty supermarket in an upscale section of their town. The business has been able to provide them with a very good living. In addition, they look at the store as the source of their own food and household goods. The employees, who are relatively low paid, turn their backs on the practice, although they know it is not right. Some of the employees believe in the old adage, "What's good for the goose, is good for the gander." This allows them to take their own weekly shopping out of the store without paying or preying on their guilt. They rationalize it as part of their pay.

What would you suggest to correct this situation? How would you deal with Herb and Mindy to convince them to change their habits?

Suggested Response

Herb and Mindy understand the advantage of owning their own small business and having the business provide their personal shopping as a business expense. However, the business is providing them with a good living and they do not need to do this. Due to their practice, some of the other employees feel that they have the same right for the business to provide their weekly shopping. As adequate controls do not exist, the cost of such activities cannot be determined. Good business practice dictates that these transactions be recorded properly and that effective controls exist to ensure that these transactions are handled correctly. To convince Herb and Mindy to stop this practice, you would have to convince them not only that proper controls would stop the employees from following their lead but also that by recording all proper business expenses and sales they would be provided with more accurate information on which to evaluate and build their business.

Effective internal controls can be developed and initiated by the small business owner with the help of management and operations personnel, but unless the controls are monitored as to compliance they may provide false assurance as to controlled operations. The case study shown in Exhibit 10.3 describes a situation where the owners believe that with internal controls in place there is no need for them to be there or for such controls to be monitored.

Systems prevail; people come and go.

EXHIBIT 1O.3   Out of Store, Out of Mind

Penny and Henny own a men's and women's apparel store. As both of them have lost interest in operating a retail-clothing store, they have hired a store manager, who has hired five part-time high school student employees. Penny and Henny rarely visit the store. They rely on the store manager to manage things properly. A computerized point-of-sale system was implemented at the time of hiring the store manager. Penny and Henny felt confident that the controls embedded in the computer system were sufficient to prevent any shenanigans. However, over the past year, the business's CPA has noticed a relatively large decrease in recorded sales accompanied by a large increase in inventory purchases.

A computer system can interrogate only those transactions that are properly entered into the system. A retail point-of-sale system processes transactions, usually using bar-code recognition from the item tag, as they are entered at the time of the customer payment and are subsequently reconciled with daily cash register details and totals by operator settlement procedure. Theoretically, all items entered into the system are controlled and properly recorded. However, if items are improperly bar coded or a tag from another item is substituted or the computer system has not been updated as to current prices, the computer system will record the transaction as all right but it will be an incorrect entry—which will probably go undetected. Another flaw in expecting the computer system to exercise full control over operations is that only items entered are exposed to the controls embedded into the software. Those transactions that bypass being processed or are rung out through a cash register not connected to the computer system never become part of the business's transactions.

What would you suggest to correct this situation?

Suggested Response

- *Inventory control:* There needs to be proper operating controls over inventory received, on-hand, and sold with periodic reconcilement by item as to sales and remaining on-hand.
- *Disciplined behavior:* The store manager and the part-time employees must be properly trained to ensure that every item that leaves the store with a customer is properly processed and payment received. Penny and Henny had invested in an electronic system that sent out a siren if an item left the store with its sensor still attached to the item. Each employee was trained to detach the sensor before processing the item. However, the manager and employees tend to ignore the siren if it goes off. The manager holds her ears until the siren stops.
- *Development of operational control reports* for Penny and Henny's review showing each day's activity as to sales, returns, over-and under-cash positions, and so on. In addition, Penny and Henny should initiate a practice of unannounced store visits to physically monitor operations.

There is a suspicion on the part of the outside CPA that merchandise is leaving the store without being recorded by the store manager and/or the employees. Adequate controls over all inventories should make it more difficult for this to continue. Should an individual, manager or employee, be identified as taking merchandise, the individual should of course be fired. Should such merchandise shrinkage continue, the responsibility should be placed on the store manager, possibly developing a bonus system for sales and profit increase that would include a bonus reduction for inventory shrinkage.

Internal Control Objectives

Internal control is a process within an organization designed to provide reasonable assurance regarding the achievement of the following primary objectives:

Safeguarding of Assets

- Door locks
- Insurance coverage
- Security guards
- File security: manual and data files
- Legal assurance
- Instruction and operating manuals
- Emergency procedures
- Secure facilities
- Proprietary measures (i.e., patents, royalties)
- Warehouses and proper inventory storage and control procedures
- Computer security: equipment, programs, and data files
- Offline control and reconciliation procedures for computer systems

Compliance with Policies, Plans, Procedures, Laws, Regulations, Contracts

- Do we have the right policies and procedures? (Example: inventory counts and reconciliations)
- Do we monitor the regulatory environment for impact on our business?
  - Regulatory changes: federal, state, and local
  - Tax and IRS considerations
  - Economic changes (i.e., interest rates, commodity supply, general business conditions)

Accomplishment of Established Goals and Objectives for Operations or Programs

- Profit, market share
- Sales statistics: by product line and product

- Customer statistics: by sales volume and profitability
- Cost containment
- Maximum results at the least costs
- Social and community needs
- What problems are we trying to solve?

Reliability and Integrity of Information

- Information needs are defined.
- Competent personnel are in place.
- Information provided is accurate, timely, and useful.
- Information identifies exceptions and indication of cause of the problem.
- Effective feedback system is in place to ensure information used correctly.

Economical and Efficient Use of Resources

- Standards of economy and efficiency are defined.
- Best practices for the business are in place.
- Operations are conducted in the most economical manner, using the most efficient procedures, resulting in maximizing results.

The small business success formula in Exhibit 10.4 summarizes the flow of controls within the small business.

CONSIDERATION OF FRAUD

Although internal controls are implemented to prevent fraudulent activities, they may not totally prevent fraud—especially if the owners are involved in or condone the fraudulent activity. In addition, it is not possible to determine how much was actually saved, including the survival of the business, by implementing a particular control procedure. For instance, can the extent and cost of preventing fraudulent expense reporting be determined by the use and cost of the preventive control? In addition, when dealing with other areas, such as sales, manufacturing, and personnel, the staff's interest in

EXHIBIT 10.4   Small Business Success Formula 6

$$OC + F/AC = TC$$

$$OC = Operating\ controls$$

$$F/AC = Financial\ and\ accounting\ controls$$

$$TC = Total\ controls$$

The concept here is that if operating controls are implemented adequately to ensure that all legitimate small business transactions are handled properly, there is a good chance that they will also be recorded accurately through the accounting systems. The responsibility for establishing proper operating controls starts at the top of the business with the owners and pervades the organization down to the lowest level of employee responsibility. Without top-level support and discipline and assurance that all employees follow through on such controls, these controls become unworkable. Top management must also exercise control behavior that serves as a model for the rest of the organization. While adequate operating controls may ensure the accurate flow of business transactions to accounting personnel, it doesn't ensure that all such transactions are properly recorded into the accounting system. This requires the existence of adequate financial and accounting controls offline over the control of input and output as well as adequate processing controls embedded within the computer software. In working with a small business to help it become successful, grow, and prosper, you must identify both operating and financial/accounting controls, ensure that they are implemented and followed, as well as ascertain that they are maintained effectively.

controls may be less than their concern for performing their own functions with minimal inhibitors.

Asset misappropriation usually affects two major asset types for fraud—cash and inventory, with cash being the favorite. Being in a cash-type business (i.e., laundromat, vending machines, casino operations, food service) makes it easy to misappropriate cash funds—for the owners as well as employees. Dealing strictly in cash also increases the difficulty in implementing effective controls and makes control monitoring more significant. Three major ways to embezzle cash are as follows:

1. *Skimming* is the taking of cash before its entry into the accounting system, such as from cash sales and accounts receivable payments.

2. *Larceny* is the removal of cash after it is entered into the accounting system, such as taking cash on hand or cash from a bank deposit.

3. *Fraudulent disbursement* is the payment of cash to an unauthorized person. This may take the form of check tampering, false register

disbursements, billing schemes, payroll schemes, and expense reimbursement schemes.

Detection of Cash Misappropriation

The following indicators should be considered to determine the small business's risk of cash misappropriation. These indicators should be established in the small business's control structure and control reporting:

Skimming

- Decreasing cash on hand and in bank
- Decreasing cash by using credit card sales
- Sales declines with increase in cost of sales
- Accounts receivable increase compared with cash
- Delay in posting of accounts receivable payments
- Unrecorded or understated sales
- Write-off of receivables
- Receivable lapping schemes: paying off receivables with other customers' receipts
- Unauthorized customer refunds to a third party in collusion
- Larceny
- Unexplained cash discrepancies
- Altered or forged deposit slips
- Customer billing and payment complaints
- "In-transit" deposits at time of bank reconciliation
- Pocketing cash sales
- Taking cash from the bank deposit
- Misuse of inventory (i.e., taking home the remainder of a product)
- Unauthorized asset requisitions and transfers
- Taking home product and equipment and not returning it (i.e., laptop computer)
- Fraudulent sale and shipping to colluded location
- Fraudulent purchase and receipt at colluded location

Fraudulent Disbursements

- Soft expense increases, such as consulting, advertising, professional services
- Address matches: employee to vendor
- Vendor address post office box or mail drop
- Vendor name consisting of initials or suspect name
- Voided, missing, or destroyed checks
- Billing schemes: setting up a shell company, vendor collusion, personal purchases
- Payroll schemes: phantom or ghost employees, overpayment of commissions, falsified time or salary recordings and payments
- Expense reimbursement schemes: nonexistent expenses, overstated expenses, fictitious expenses, multiple requests for reimbursements
- Check tampering: forged signature, forged endorsement, altered or colluded payee
- Cash register tampering: not recording, improper voids, colluded refunds, taking cash overages

Take the money from your employer—why look for strangers?

Checklist of Fraud Indicators

In establishing operating controls to assist in detecting fraudulent activities, you should consider the following items to include in the small business's control system:

- Accounts with illogical balances (debits where credits should be, credits where debits should be, direct posting instead of journalizing)
- Lack of explicit policies and procedures
- Lack of vacations by key employees and others in sensitive positions
- Lack of segregation of duties within the constraints of the small business

- Employee dealings with the business (i.e., employee sales and purchases)
- Lack of sequential records (checks, purchase orders, invoices)
- Missing fields in databases (customers or vendors)
- Cash flow reporting and problems: cash sources and uses
- Unreasonable expectations/difficult to control functions, markets, and so forth
- Infrequent or lack of effective monitoring
- Cost saving strategies as to effective implementation and use
- Inexperience in markets and startup considerations
- Unmanaged growth/decline causing undetected bad practices
- Unusual business practices such as discounts for cash, customer pickup procedures, employee borrowings of equipment and supplies
- Autonomous/isolated business units or individuals with inadequate monitoring
- Results that are illogical in the current context such as increased sales or no change in operations, resulting in decreased profits
- Manual adjustments or management overrides of a questionable nature
- Slow reaction to findings, problems, issues
- Perfect documentation where imperfection is more the rule
- Lack of budgetary control of a formal or informal nature (comparing what is to what was expected)

Many small businesses cannot afford the luxury of employing a large number of employees so that there can be an effective segregation of duties—a golden internal control principle. In fact, the typical small business may employ one individual, full time or part time, to handle the entire accounting function. Exhibit 10.5 discusses such a situation.

Internal Control Considerations

In developing and implementing an effective internal control system for the small business client, you need to be aware of all financial and

EXHIBIT 10.5   The Bookkeeper Did It

Julia has been the bookkeeper for a small family-owned furniture store for over 20 years. As it was a small business, a CPA firm prepared the tax return based on the figures on the books but never audited the business. In effect, Julia *was* the company's accounting department. She maintained the books, posted all of the entries, prepared and made bank deposits, signed all the checks, and reconciled the bank account. When the family decided to sell the business, the prospective buyer demanded an audit of the business's operations by his own CPA firm. The following was uncovered in the audit:

Julia had made checks out to herself over the years. These were deposited in her own personal checking account. The check was entered as void in the books, with the amount of the check added to a payment for inventory or an expense account. When the checks she had cashed were returned with the bank statement, she would tear them up. The CPA also suspected that Julia was skimming money from customer cash payments, and never recording them on the books. As the company had never performed a physical count of its inventory, the CPA fell onto Julia's scheme as the books showed over $300,000 more than the actual inventory.

Based on the CPA's discovery, the sale was never consummated. As the company had no way of knowing how much Julia had embezzled, they had no recourse for recovery. The store went bankrupt before it could be sold at a much lower price.

If you had been this company's CPA, what controls would you have implemented for this business?

Suggested Response

- Separation of duties to the extent possible:

  - Cash receipts: receipt of cash and preparing and making the bank deposit from the recording of cash receipts to customer accounts
  - Independent bank reconciliation—probably by the external CPA
  - Periodic independent physical inventory and reconciliation to financial records

- Operating controls

  - Proper authorization of all vendor purchases—chained to a real customer order or inventory approval by the owner or other authorized individual
  - Reconciliation of all open customer orders as to moneys due and subsequent payments by the owner or sales personnel, which should agree with the books of record
  - Proper inventory control procedures over receipts, on-hand quantities, and issues

operating aspects of the business. In addition, you need to be knowledgeable of internal controls that can be effective in the small business environment, especially in dealing with the specific operational idiosyncrasies of each small business.

Internal Control Breaks

An *internal control break* occurs when an error or irregularity can be traced to a control weakness. It is helpful to identify weaknesses before major control problems occur. Once management is aware of an internal control break, they can take steps to alleviate it.

Examples of control breaks include:

- Unauthorized payments
- Incorrect or unauthorized journal entries
- Unauthorized access to funds
- Unreconciled accounts
- Unauthorized use of assets

Some tools to help identify control breaks include:

- Financial reporting
- Company checks returned for insufficient funds
- Late reports
- Discounts not being taken
- Missing reports
- Operations
  - Customer complaints
  - Materials delivered not to specifications
  - Reduced profit margins
  - Disgruntled employees
  - Increased defects in finished goods
  - Inadequate raw materials
  - Oversupply of finished goods
  - Returns by customers
- Compliance
  - Regulatory penalties
  - Regulatory investigations
  - Unsafe working conditions
  - Potential fire hazards
  - High warranty expenses
  - High legal expenses

Establishing Controls over an Operation: Accounts Payable

In establishing effective internal controls over an operation or activity the following areas must be considered:

- Control environment. How well is the corporate culture communicated?
- Control activities. Are processes and controls documented and understood?
- Risk assessment. Are major risks and opportunities identified?
- Monitoring. Is it ongoing and documented?
- Information and communication. How is it done, with what frequency, and how assessed?
- Safeguarding of assets
- Compliance issues
- Accomplishment of objectives
- Reliability of data
- Economical and efficient operations

An example of internal controls considering the above factors for the accounts payable function includes:

- Match payments to orders
- Code payments to proper accounts
- Purchase orders/requests linked to production and budgets
- Approved supplier lists
- Rotation of buyers
- Purchase order database
- Instant update of inventory and payment records
- Control/subsidiary ledgers
- Check stock and signature plate control
- Bids over threshold require approval
- Reconcile operating account separate from accounts payable
- Avoid partial payments
- Segregate duties: setup from payment

- Escheat unpaid claims
- Sales tax management
- Social Security or federal IDs on file for payees
- Pay on original invoices only
- Credit memos, discounts taken/lost are tracked
- Dedicated time for check runs
- No manual checks
- Stamp receipt date
- Accounts payable errors tracked
- Automated system
- Average day's invoices outstanding
- Complaint tracking (about payment)
- Incorrect invoice tracking

Business Process Components

The small business control system consists of proper and practical establishment of controls that enable the business to operate most efficiently as well as provide an adequate control environment that helps the business to grow and prosper. In developing such a control system, the following business components need to be taken into consideration:

Income/Revenues
- Customer relations and service
- Credit policies
- Billing procedures
- Accounts receivable
- Cash receipts
- Sales forecasts
- Sales order procedures
- Product or service delivery
- Related party transactions: family members, employees

Cost / Expenditures

- Budget system
- Vendor relations and evaluation
- Purchase requisitioning
- Purchasing procedures
- Accounts payable
- Receiving procedures
- Cash disbursements
- Vendor reliability: quality, timeliness, price
- Payroll and labor distribution
- Related party transactions: family members, employees

Product / Service Providing

- Production control
- Inventory control
- Product/service delivery (i.e., shipping, providing of services)
- Quality control
- Fixed assets: level and use of facilities
- Cost accounting systems: product/service, functions, customer
- Pricing policies

Finance / Treasury Functions

- Debt management
- Investment management
- Income distribution
- Risk and insurance
- Collections and bad debts
- Accounting systems
- Financial and operational reporting
- Tax considerations

Information Technology
- Information needs assessment
- Hardware and software considerations
- Computer processing procedures
- Controls: online processing and offline control procedures
- Computer hardware and software security issues
- General and application controls
- Service delivery evaluation

Every activity needs to be controlled to be most effective.

Types of Controls

As related to the previously listed business process components, the following types of controls should be considered in implementing the small business control system:

- **Preventive.** Keep undesired events from happening:
  - Locked doors, cabinets, and equipment (i.e., computers)
  - Preventive maintenance of production and office equipment
  - Computer passwords inclusive of physical computer equipment, processing application, data files, and type of transaction
  - Security guards where applicable
  - Supervisory review of operating activities and subsequent reporting
  - Data controls (i.e., offline versus online, data file backup)
- **Detective.** Identify undesired events:
  - Supervisory review of activities and comparison to expected outcomes
  - Output reports—exception and control listings for corrective action
  - Reconciliations (i.e., cash, inventory)
  - Physical safeguards (i.e., receiving, inspection, shipping, counts)

- **Corrective.** Repair undesirable events:
  - Supervisory review directed to taking corrective action to prevent reoccurrence
  - Data file recovery procedures
  - Equipment maintenance to ensure continuity of proper operations
  - Notification of suspect items to appropriate parties for proper corrective action
  - Corrective action itself (fixing the cause, not the symptom)
- **Discretionary/nondiscretionary.** Manual versus automated:
  - Human (active) interaction versus automated (passive; automated controls cheaper, less time consuming, occur without physical action)
  - Software imbedded (i.e., check digits, PINs, passwords, limit tests, control totals)
  - Supervisory review of transactions
  - Dual control (more than one approval for a transaction)

Representative Control Procedures

A summary of general control procedures that should be considered in the development of a small business internal control system includes:

- Proper authorization of transactions
- Adequate segregation of duties
- Proper design of documents (i.e., pre-numbering where applicable)
- Safeguarding assets and records
- Reconciliations
- Independent verifications (i.e., confirmations)
- Computer controls: general and application
- Management reviews

How to Segregate Duties (at a Work or Activity-Unit Level)

Large organizations have the ability to properly segregate functions from a control standpoint, such as initiating, approving, processing, recording, and reviewing financial transactions. In the typical small business, this ability to segregate functions across separate individuals or departments is rarely available or practical. The best that can be done may be to assign specific control activities to individuals assigned other operating tasks as well. Keeping this in mind, here are some tips to help you in segregating duties for a small business:

- Define tasks that need to be accomplished by initiating, recording, processing, reporting criteria.
- Assign initiating activities to separate individuals.
- Assign recording, processing activities to separate individuals.
- Assign reporting activities to separate individuals.
- Maintain supervisory oversight of individuals (supervisor ideally does not perform initiating, recording, or processing).
- Have self-assessment reporting done by supervisory personnel to upper management.
- Maintain internal monitoring (ideally separate individuals or departments).

PERFORMANCE MEASURES

These measures are included to stimulate your thinking about appropriate measures to monitor as a tool to detect control weaknesses or noncompliance. However, remember that the measures you select should fit the process, products, and goals. Measures should be designed to get at root causes for internal control weaknesses.

Accounting Performance Measurements

- Late reports
- Errors in reports
- Input errors
- Errors reported by outsiders: customers, vendors, employees
- Complaints: customers, vendors, employees
- Amount of time and cost for corrections
- Amount of time spent on accounting activities
- Processing times: receivables, payables, payroll, general ledger
- Policies and procedures:

- Processing frequencies (i.e., payables twice a week)
- Dollar limits: purchasing, receivables, payables
- Credit policies and terms
- Employee advances and expenses
- Labor distribution: time recordings, cost allocations, approvals

Clerical Performance Measurements

- Manual versus automated
- Waste: duplication, forms, scrap, unnecessary activities
- Administration errors (not using the right procedure)
- Activities not done on schedule
- Data input not received on schedule
- Transaction coding errors: timecards, sales orders, payment vouchers
- Period reports not completed on schedule
- Unwieldy activities and lost time
- Inefficient procedures

Product/Service Development Performance Measurements

- Inaccurate cost estimates
- Product/service quality: meeting customer expectations
- Problems not corrected
- Time required to make a change/correct a problem
- Unsuccessful transactions: sales quotes, on-time deliveries
- Quality control: scrap, rejects, rework, customer returns
- Problems encountered in other areas or products
- Time and cost to correct customer problem
- After-sale customer service: incidences, cost

If you don't know what you're shooting for, you'll never hit the target. (*Fire, aim, ready!*)

An Organizational Checklist of Control Best Practices

Although the evaluation of performance measures may provide some insight as to areas of weakness and inadequate controls, it is also valuable to know and identify those pockets of best operating practices. The following checklist can be used to assist you in such identification of best practices. A specific small business may have some of these control best practices present, most of these present, few of these present, or none of these present. It is up to you to determine which of these controls will provide operational benefits far outweighing the cost of the control for the specific small business.

- Organizational mission, goals, and objectives are established and documented.

- Processes to measure and report achievement of goal and objectives are in place.

- Segregation of duties is in place for financial activities such as payroll, purchasing, accounts receivable, and cash handling.

- Expenditures are tracked and compared to budgets on a timely basis. Budget status reports are prepared and provided to the manager on a regular basis.

- The cost to process a transaction (e.g., purchases, payables, receivables) does not exceed the amount of the transaction or a factor thereof (i.e., 400%).

- Departmental records ("shadow" financial systems) are reconciled to general ledger.

- Cash receipts are promptly recorded, safeguarded, deposited, and reconciled.

- Individual accountability for cash is maintained at all times.

- Accounts payable payments are supported by purchase orders, vendor blanket agreement, or personal services agreements.

- Payments for personal services, which constitute an employer/ employee relationship, are properly approved and paid through the payroll system.

- Vendor invoices, including rapid-pay invoices, are approved prior to payment.

- Purchases and sales of materials or services with employees or a near relative are properly controlled.

- Equipment is properly maintained and controlled through preventive and necessary maintenance.

- Overhead and shift differential charges by employees are reviewed for validity and correctness.

- Complete documentation and approval supporting travel and entertainment expenditures is on file.

- Employee-time-worked records are properly reviewed and approved.

- Employees are properly hired, oriented, trained, evaluated, and fired.

- Employee performance evaluations are prepared and reviewed with the employee on a timely basis. Corrective action is properly followed up.

- Employees are cross-trained to provide flexibility in workloads and to keep the number of employees to a minimum.

- Processes for measuring and assessing quality of customer service are in place.

INTERNAL CONTROL REVIEW: THE 12-STEP PROGRAM

Once you are ready to begin implementing an effective internal control program, it is good to know how to go about it. The following 12-step program may provide some guidance in ensuring the success of such implementation efforts.

1. Use subjective understanding of the small business environment together with objective measurement of best practices. Consider the reality of the small business and knowledge of the organization to determine areas of concentration.

2. Assess the ability of management to achieve its stated goals. Does management exercise proper control over operations or is the business operated more on a day-to-day crisis basis?

3. Review of internal controls should be structured to examine controls from the top to the bottom and vice versa. Sometimes the control itself

needs to be questioned as to its necessity and its cost to operational value. Questions should be developed at both the transactional and the process levels.

4. Assess the limitations that specify the range of acceptable business activity. Understand the process of establishing those limits. Is there budgetary control? Have units of activity been related to actual or budgeted dollars?

5. Review risk management by function—accounting control, sales department, service-delivery activities, cost accounting, and so forth. Determine the extent of internal control knowledge at the middle-manager and supervisor level. Determine that controls are related to risk mitigation.

6. Evaluate the strategic planning process. How does management plan and then assess where the organization as a whole is going? Does management assess how functions within the organization promote the mission of the entity as a whole?

7. Evaluate the initiatives associated with the strategic planning process. Are strategies congruent with the mission of the organization and achievable? Is it formal or informal or is it nonexistent?

8. Understand activities and functions:
   a. There should be enterprise-wide understanding of the organization.
   b. Use employees from operational areas to enhance expertise.
   c. Understand all functions and activities and their purpose.
   d. Findings and deficiencies must turn into implementable recommendations.
   e. Monitor business activities and key operating and performance indicators.

9. Direct the review process to high-risk exposures and evaluate compensating controls. Develop the review plan based on risk priorities rather than set schedules. Identify the organizational exposures and focus the review process on them. Determine how management makes up for shortfalls in internal control or whether none exists.

10. Provide consultative service to management that is *value added*—help the small business implement controls that provide benefits that

exceed their cost. Assist management in achieving organizational-mission-related objectives.

11. Evaluate the ethical culture of the organization. How is ethical awareness communicated? Are laws and regulations complied with? Is ethics part of the internal control structure? Are business activities at all levels conducted with an eye to ethical behavior?

12. Evaluate the risk management program of the entity as a whole. Determine the extent of internal control knowledge at the senior manager level. Determine whether management considers risk mitigation in their planning.

Operational Model

The model should be: Doing the right things the right way at the right time. *Remember the mission of the organization.* Determine the basic principles on which it conducts its operations. These principles then become the foundation on which the organization bases its desirable control practices. Examples of such business principles include the following:

Effective Operation

- Mission—the customer service and cash conversion businesses.

- Customer focus—public service or commercial enterprise; best product for least cost. It is easier to build your business with satisfied active customers who continue to purchase your product and refer you to others, than to continue to look for new customers.

- Set selling prices realistically to sell all of the product that can be produced within the constraints of the production facilities.

Processes

- Efficient—identify customers; develop marketing and sales plans with the customers in mind.

- Produce for the company's customers, not for inventory. Serve the customers; do not sell them.

- Cost conscious—do not spend what does not need to be spent; a dollar not spent is a dollar to the bottom line. There is more to be done here than increasing sales.

- "Quality in everything we do"; strive for perfection; settle for excellence and best practices.
- Maintain the competitive advantage.

Workforce

- Empowered, accountable, interdisciplinary, teamwork—hire needed employees only when they multiply effectiveness—the company makes more from them than if the owners did it themselves. Motivate employee self-disciplined behavior.

Work Environment

- Safety and security—develop contingency plans for the positive or negative unexpected.
- Facilities and infrastructure—keep property, plant, and equipment to the minimum necessary to maintain customer demand.

Basics

- Ethics/integrity/legal/compliance.
- Trust—build trusting relationships with critical vendors; keeping them in business keeps the company in business.

Internal Controls for Operations

This is a summary of critical internal control aspects of operating a successful small business where the controls enhance rather than curtail chances for success.

Definition

Internal control refers to the methods and procedures used to provide reasonable assurance regarding the achievement of objectives in the following categories:

- Safeguarding assets
- Ensuring validity of financial records
- Promoting adherence to policies, procedures, regulations, and laws
- Promoting effectiveness and efficiency of operations

In general terms, internal controls are simply good business practices. They include anything that serves to safeguard assets or to improve the effectiveness and efficiency of operations.

Responsibilities

- Management is responsible for establishing specific internal control policies and procedures. Every employee is responsible for ensuring that established internal controls are followed and applied.

- Internal auditors (or others outside of operations) evaluate the effectiveness of control systems, monitor control systems, and contribute to ongoing effectiveness of control systems. External auditors, if applicable, review control systems for impact they have on financial reporting and compliance with requirements of external agencies.

Control Principles

- **Separation of duties.** Duties are divided so that no one person has complete control over a key function or activity.

- **Authorization and approval.** Proposed transactions are authorized when they are consistent with policy and funds are available.

- **Custodial and security arrangements.** Responsibility for custody of assets is separated from the related record keeping.

- **Review and reconciliation records.** These are examined and reconciled to determine that transactions were properly processed and approved.

- **Physical controls.** Equipment, inventories, cash, and other assets are secured physically, counted periodically, and compared with amounts shown on control records.

- **Training and supervision.** Well-trained and supervised employees help ensure that control processes function properly.

- **Documentation.** Documented policies and procedures promote employee understanding of job duties and help ensure continuity during employee absences or turnover.

- **Cost/benefit.** Costs associated with control processes should not exceed expected benefits.

Recommended Internal Control Practices

Payroll: Separation of Duties

- To properly control payroll activities, different employees should be responsible for updating the payroll/personnel system (online or paper), reviewing personnel actions, and reviewing the monthly distribution of payroll expense reports.

- An employee not involved in updating the payroll/personnel system or in preparing or approving payroll timesheets should distribute payroll checks and pay statements.

- Authorization and approval—forms should be approved only by persons with delegated authority.

- Current signature authorization forms should be on file in the Accounting Office. Employees should not approve actions affecting their own pay. Supervisors should approve employee attendance records. Supervisors should approve any time recording or reporting alterations.

- Custodial and security arrangements—payroll records should be filed in a secure location with access limited to authorized personnel. Payroll checks should be kept in a locked, secure area pending distribution. Presentation of identification should be required when releasing checks to employees not known to the person distributing checks.

- Review and reconciliation—payroll expense reports should be reviewed and approved. Any questionable or irregular entries should be immediately investigated and resolved. The person performing the review should sign and date reports to signify that the review has been satisfactorily completed and any discrepancies resolved.

Procurement of Materials and Services

Separation of Duties. Separation of purchasing-related duties should be established so no single person has total control over any purchase transaction. To the extent practical, different individuals should be assigned responsibility for:

- Approving purchase requisitions and orders

- Receiving ordered materials
- Approving invoices for payment
- Reviewing and reconciling the monthly general ledger

Authorization and Approval. Purchases, invoices, and check requests should be approved only by persons with delegated authority. Signature authorization forms should be up-to-date and on file in the Accounting Office. The receipt of goods and services should be verified prior to approving invoices for payment. Verification should be made that invoiced amounts are correct, accounts charged are correct, object coding is correct, and payment has not already been made. Low-value purchasing policy requirements should be observed.

Supply and Equipment Inventories. To ensure separation of duties, employees assigned to perform physical inventories to confirm that materials and equipment listed on inventory records are actually on hand should be persons other than those responsible for maintaining custody of the items or subordinates of the custodian.

Equipment Inventory Modification Request Forms. Equipment inventory modification request forms should be approved by someone not directly responsible for custody or disposal of equipment.

Authorization and Approval. Purchase requisitions should be approved by a person delegated with approval authority. Inventory adjustments for returned, missed, damaged, and stolen items should be approved by department management.

Custodial and Security Arrangements. Security arrangements for safeguarding inventory should be proportional to its value and portability. Off-business use of equipment should be allowed for valid business purposes only, should be approved by the department head, and a record maintained. Equipment should not be used for personal purposes. The number of employees having access to inventories should be held to a minimum. Locks should be re-keyed or changed whenever significant personnel turnover occurs. Keys should be obtained from all terminated employees.

Review and Reconciliation. Items should be inspected for condition prior to their inclusion in the inventory. Obsolete, inactive, or damaged items should be removed from inventory. Physical counts of large supply inventories should be taken annually. Equipment should be counted biennially.

Cash Receipts

Separation of Duties. Separation of duties should be established so that different employees are responsible for:

- Receiving and recording cash collections
- Balancing daily cash receipts to related cash recordings
- Verifying that the deposit amounts reflected in the general ledger are in agreement with departmental records

Cash Accountability. Individual accountability for cash should be maintained at all times. Transfers of cash between two people should be jointly verified and documented. Supervisors should verify cash deposits, voided transactions, and cash overages and shortages.

Recording and Depositing. All cash receipts should be recorded on a cash receipt form, cash register, or a properly controlled computer database at the time of receipt. Checks should be made payable to the entity and promptly endorsed for deposit upon receipt.

Review and Reconciliation. Cash receipts should be balanced to receipt records on the day received. Deposit receipts should be verified to ensure the recording of the proper amount. Deposit entries in the general ledger should be reviewed and verified.

Petty Cash Fund. Establishment and review of petty cash funds should be properly authorized, maintained in a secure location accessible only by the fund custodian of record, and used only for appropriate business purposes. A supervisory employee with signature authorization and not responsible for custody of the fund should review expenditure documentation, verify that the total fund amount is accounted for, and approve requests for fund replenishment.

Custodial and Security Arrangements. Cash and checks should be stored in a locked receptacle located in a secure area. Custodial responsibility for a fund should be assigned to only one employee, with a designated alternate.

Review and Reconciliation. All petty cash disbursements should be supported by a receipt documenting the expenditure. The fund should be counted and balanced at least monthly or when replenished by a supervisor not responsible for maintaining the fund.

Billing and Accounts Receivable   The use of an accounts receivable system is recommended for billings to external parties.

Separation of Duties. Different persons should be responsible for:

- Billing and maintaining accounts receivable records
- Receiving or handling incoming payments
- Reconciling receivable records to the general ledger

Custodial and Security Arrangements. Invoices should be prepared for all charges and issued on a timely basis. Invoices should be issued in numerical sequence. Blank invoices, credit memos, and cancellation forms should be controlled to prevent misuse.

Review and Reconciliation. Receivable reports should include aged listings of all amounts due, should be reviewed at least monthly, and should be balanced to the related general ledger account. Delinquent account balances should be examined and follow-up with customers should be initiated on a timely basis to facilitate payment.

Budgetary Control   Budgets should be prepared at least annually and should be based on realistic expectations of revenues and expenses. General ledgers should be reviewed monthly to verify charges to expenditure accounts and should be reconciled to the department's financial records. Actual expenditures should be compared to budgeted amounts, and variances should be identified monthly. Financial and budgetary status reports should be regularly provided to responsible, accountable managers.

Information Systems   New systems should be developed or acquired using a structured system development approach and should be completely tested prior to implementation. Systems should be fully documented, including operations and program and user documentation. All changes to computer programs should be properly authorized and documented. Audit trails and edit routines should be built into systems to ensure effective processing. Logical and physical access security should be in place for programs, databases, and data files. Equipment should be properly safeguarded against theft, power fluctuations, and electronic viruses. Backup and recovery processes should be in place to ensure continuity of operations. Backup media should be stored offsite, remote from the production files. Employees should be properly trained and cross-trained to prevent an unduly high degree of reliance on one knowledgeable employee. Employees should receive appropriate information on managing and protecting confidentiality of passwords. Use of copyrighted software and unauthorized software should be controlled.

Conflict of Interest   Staff should be kept informed of policies regarding conflict of interest. Staff should disqualify themselves from participating in any business decisions in which they may have a personal financial interest.

Materials and Services   Materials and services should not be sold to or purchased from employees or near relatives of employees unless management has determined that the materials or services sales or purchases are not available from other sources.

Documentation   Departments should prepare a written mission statement and communicate it to employees. The department should document its internal policies and procedures, its business practices, and its goals and objectives. Employees should have ready access to departmental and company-wide policies and procedures (hardcopy, computer-based, or web-based). Documentation supporting all business and financial decisions and activity should be prepared, approved at the appropriate level, and retained.

If things are going well, you must have overlooked something.

EFFECTIVE CONTROLS BY TYPE OF BUSINESS

There are some internal controls, such as effective reporting systems, that apply to most small businesses, while there are other controls that pertain primarily to the specific type of business, such as manufacturing, retailing, or professional services. Following are six suggestions each for effective controls for selected types of small businesses. The list of businesses and controls is not meant to be all-inclusive nor are the suggested controls meant to be the most critical ones. This checklist is meant only to be a starting point to provide some initial guidance in dealing with one or another type of business. As you review the checklist, see whether you can add other controls for each type of business based on your own experiences.

There are many types of small businesses other than the ones mentioned in the following. However, each of them has some of the same general concerns in common. A good rule in establishing proper controls within the small business environment is the application of good business practices, which may require educating the owners and others as to the merits of operating their business in the most economical, efficient, and effective manner possible—and as to the fact that internal controls provide benefits greater than their costs.

1. Owners and management establish a disciplined control environment for others to follow, using themselves as role models.

2. Established controls communicated to all employees with expectations that they be followed.

3. Effective reporting system developed and in place that allows management to take immediate action to correct the cause of the present control weakness and prevent the same from happening in the future.

4. Input, processing, and output reconciliation procedures in effect for all offline systems, including point-of-sale systems, and online computer systems.

5. Business consistently operated based on communicated basic business principles and best practice considerations in all areas of the business's operations.

6. Delegation of authority and commensurate responsibilities to the lowest level possible within the business so that each worker is responsible for controlling his or her own operations in a self-motivated, disciplined manner, which releases top management from unnecessary policing and control of all employees.

Know the business you're in and establish a competitive advantage.

Manufacturing

Small manufacturers typically need to compete with larger manufacturers who can take better advantage of the economies of scale. Thus, the small manufacturer must be quicker and more flexible than its larger competitors to achieve a competitive advantage (unless it is one of those lucky small businesses that have a proven niche market).

1. Inventory levels are kept to a minimum, always pushing toward zero. Raw materials are ordered from vendors to be delivered just-in-time for entry into production. Finished goods are produced for shipment to customers based on entering real customer orders into production to meet customer-requested delivery dates. The emphasis then becomes work-in-process inventory, where it is to be kept to a minimum and at least 80 percent related to real customer orders at any one time. A customer order should be in work in process the least time possible, ensuring all customer orders being completed and shipped on time.

2. Finite manufacturing facilities should be used expeditiously, taking into account over- and undercapacity situations, with plans as to what to do. Manufacturing plant and equipment should be kept to the minimum necessary to meet customer demands.

3. Direct manufacturing costs, material and labor, should be strictly controlled. Material costs should be kept to the lowest level possible through effective vendor negotiations that establish long-term commitments as to price, quality, and timeliness. Material usage should be strictly controlled so that only necessary material needed to produce the product is entered into production—moving toward an absolute one-to-one relationship as to quantity of material per quantity ordered. Other controls over material relate to the reduction or elimination of scrap, rejects, and rework. Labor costs need to be controlled to maximize productivity as to cost per item as well as the

reduction or elimination of setups and increases in productivity without sacrificing quality.

4. Control over all non–direct manufacturing activities in an effort at reduction and elimination in costs of such things as receiving, incoming inspection, storeroom operations, quality control, floor supervision, repairs and maintenance, packing, shipping, and material handling.

5. Production control and scheduling system that allows for real-time tracking of all customer orders to enable the business to ship at the right time with the desired level of quality.

6. Manufacturing only those products desired by the business's customers so that items produced are shipped directly to the customer and not placed into inventory.

Keeping your customers (and vendors) in business is your business.

Retailing

There are many different types of retail establishments, from the small newsstand to the large clothing store. However, all of them share some attributes in common, such as the buying and reselling of merchandise. If the merchandise purchased (i.e., the buying function, often controlled by the owners) sells quickly at the desired price, the retail operation will probably be successful. However, if the merchandise doesn't sell, not only is there a buying control problem but also an inventory problem as to what to do with the unsaleable merchandise.

1. Utilizing limited store capacity most effectively so that every item placed for sale turns over within an expected standard period of time. Avoid getting into the markdown business—sell your merchandise at desired prices.

2. Operating the retail establishment in a pleasant manner so that customers are attracted to enter the store and become regular

customers. It is easier to build your business by selling more to regular customers than by trying to persuade new customers to buy.

3. Building the business based on selling more product to quality customers rather than continually trying to attract new customers. Control customer service and develop customer loyalty.

4. Building effective controls over the behavior and performance of in-store employees so that each one provides consistent and desired customer service. As such employees working in retail tend to be lower paid than in other businesses and may be more transient, this is a particular trouble spot. Make each employee a part of the business.

5. Implementing effective point-of-sale systems that ensure that all sales are recorded (especially cash sales) and that each register terminal is effectively settled on a daily or shift basis.

6. As inventory shrinkage is a major loss item for most retailers, develop effective security checks (electronic and otherwise) on both the front door as well as the back door. It is not only questionable customers that may borrow merchandise (with no intention to return it) but also employees who believe such a benefit is coming to them. Keep inventory to a minimum, especially in the back room.

Make your customers' shopping trip a real *buying experience*. Create the *wow* for your customers.

Services

Some small businesses sell a product; others provide a service such as plumbing, electrical, roofing, auto repairs, home improvements and the like. It is usually more difficult to fully satisfy a customer as to a service rendered than with a product purchased. As someone other than the seller normally produces the product, there is a third party to blame should the customer be dissatisfied. However, with the providing of a service, the small business and its employees (including the owners) are directly responsible should the customer not be completely satisfied.

1. As these small businesses are providing a type of personal service, each individual providing such services must be controlled as to behavior, providing of service, efficiency, and customer rapport.

2. Establishment of basic business principles as to how to treat the customer. The customer should see positive consistency regardless of the individual providing the service.

3. Effective pricing methodologies that ensure not losing the sale due to excessive pricing. As many of these services are subjective, there is a tendency to charge for each activity as well as an override for materials. Where possible, it is best to give the customer a fixed price that includes all of your costs.

4. Controlling the add-on. Many service-type businesses may quote a fixed price and then attempt to change it based on an add-on situation that could have been seen on the front end. Building contractors many times depend on the add-ons to produce a profit on the job.

5. Reducing or eliminating the nonservice charges from the billing process. These include activities such as obtaining the materials, travel time, breaks, going to get a part they should have had with them, and attempting to recover the cost of the estimate (even when advertised as free). These should be included in the hourly rates and as part of an estimate or fixed price.

6. Establishing standards for each service activity on which the customer is billed. The customer should not be penalized for the work efficiency differences between your service employees.

If your business is service, then service is what you deliver.

Professional Practices

There are many small businesses that provide a product to the customer, which is paid for at the time of sale or billed for later collection. However, there are other small businesses that provide a professional service, such as lawyers, insurance agencies, travel agencies, title and mortgage companies, and CPA firms. These businesses typically provide the service with a subsequent bill based on the services provided. Some of these businesses base their billings on time expended while others bill based on the service rendered.

1. Since these businesses are providing a personal professional service, the most critical factor is the personnel providing such services. Each individual must be controlled to ensure a consistent quality of providing such services. Remember, each employee represents the business to the public.

2. Controlling client billings so that they represent the related services provided. The business may focus on the bill; the client focuses on the service.

3. As the service delivery is only as good as the individual providing the service, the control over such service delivery must be monitored to ensure the proper level of service is being delivered.

4. The greatest amount of cost attributable to providing the client service is the cost of employee compensation. Control must be exercised to maximize the level of service delivered by each employee—and the client must be satisfied.

5. Do the services rendered provide more value to the client than the amount of the bill? Implement controls to ensure that the client receives and perceives such value. A satisfied client will request additional work to be done as well as refer your firm to others. Build your business with satisfied clients.

6. Treat each client and the specific engagement as a profit center. Control the amount of your billings to fit the situation and control costs to ensure a desired profit margin. Make sure that your employees' time recordings are accurate as to including all time, not recording some time (for them to look good), or recording time not spent. You need accurate data to control your business.

As proprietor of a professional practice, always act professionally.

Boutique Shop

While some small businesses believe that the best way to compete with the big guys is through competitive pricing, there are other small business philosophies that have also proved successful. One of these approaches is the *boutique*, where it is not price but service and uniqueness that appeal to a customer base that is willing to pay more for such individual service and attention.

1. These are specialty shops such as jewelry, lingerie, women's clothing and accessories, leather, linens, household accessories, and so forth. For a specialty shop, the first control is to define your business and the customers you seek and then to monitor that you are attracting such customers.

2. With a boutique shop there is expectancy that the merchandise is unique and different and probably more costly than that of a large chain store. Typically such stores attract a higher-end clientele than a so-called national-brand-type store. Controls must be established to service such customers from the time they enter the store until they leave (hopefully, with their purchases).

3. A retail boutique shop requires a different level of personnel than an ordinary retail store. Control must be exercised over all personnel so that they deliver the level of service required to satisfy such a customer base.

4. As the items being sold in a boutique shop tend to have a larger ticket price than those of other stores, physical controls must be in place to ensure that only purchased items leave the store, and controls must exist over the inventory in the store.

5. For such special customers the environment in the store must be controlled to be commensurate with the pricey merchandise. For instance, there should be a comfortable corner for nonshoppers to wait in, artistically arranged display cases and merchandise, very attentive sales personnel, attractive presentation and wrapping, and easy exit upon paying.

6. Control over all merchandise: As the items tend to be pricier, there must be more care taken as to what is purchased and placed in the store. While turnover may be expected to be longer than for a less expensive store, there still must be controls as to how long merchandise should sit in the store awaiting a buyer. Use your

regular customers and reach out to them to help move slow-moving merchandise—avoid getting into the markdown business.

> If a boutique, be unique.

Restaurant/Food Service

A restaurant/food-service-type business is dependent on attracting sufficient customers to maximize its capacity for serving based on the type of meal—that is, breakfast, lunch, dinner, or snack. Controls need to be established to ensure efficient use of the finite capacity of the facility, abilities of the serving staff, and building of a loyal, repetitive customer base.

1. Control your customer base. Develop methods to attract an ongoing customer base so that you are less dependent on one-time or transient customers.

2. Establish controls as to your operating procedures, such as seating customers, table setup, nibbles while waiting to order (coffee, water, bread, etc.), efficient bus and wait staff, order taking, kitchen operations, table clearing, and bill paying.

3. Control the customer and traffic flow. Establish controls as to expected table turnover for each type of meal—breakfast, lunch, and dinner—and monitor results. Remember, the greater the turnover the greater your profits and tips for your wait staff.

4. As most restaurants pay their bus and wait staff very little, expecting customer tips to be the major portion of their compensation, there need to be controls and expectations over these personnel so that they are working for the business and not for themselves.

5. One of the major costs for a restaurant is the food cost. There must be proper portion control for each meal served so that food costs are balanced with the customer's perception of value. A satiated customer will return; others will not. In addition, the food itself must be controlled, as it is not only perishable but also susceptible to inventory shrinkage (usually by employees).

6. Control over payments that bear some relationship to the meals served. The payment process should be speedy and efficient to ensure getting the customers out when they are ready. There are too many businesses that work hard on getting the customer into the business but not so hard on getting the customer out.

It is not just a meal; it is a *dining experience*.

Accounts Receivable Business

There are many small businesses that primarily sell their products and services on a cash or credit card basis at the point of sale. However, there are still those small businesses that maintain the business tradition of selling on credit—that is, submitting a bill, setting up an account receivable, and then waiting to collect their payment. These businesses could include small manufacturers, food brokers, and linen and uniform suppliers.

1. As it is desirable to get out of the accounts receivable business, controls should be established to determine whether the business is moving in that direction. A specific control might be establishing a dollar limit, such as $500, where the sale must be paid for in cash or by credit card, thus eliminating the cost of billing and collections for such small purchases.

2. As most businesses have a limited number of customers that make up a large proportion of their sales (usually, 20% of total customers result in 80% of total sales), an acceptable control would be to negotiate prices that would include paying the bill at the time of delivery or receipt—hopefully through electronic funds transfer.

3. Establishment of effective credit controls so that the business doesn't sell more to its customers than prudent business principles dictate that the customer can pay for comfortably. Remember, a sale is not cash or a real profit unless it can be collected profitably.

4. When a new customer demonstrates its willingness to buy additional products or services and shows an ability to pay in a timely manner,

the small business must control its respective credit policies to enable the customer to purchase more while monitoring the controls placed on each customer.

5. For those customers where the business must bill, set up a receivable, and then collect, the business needs to control the billing on a timely basis (at the time of delivery or prior) to ensure that the customer receives the bill prior to or at the time of receipt of the products or services. For professional services, payments should be received in advance on a retainer system for repetitive services or at the time the service is provided, leaving billing only on an exception basis.

6. Once the bill is entered as an account receivable, it must be strictly monitored and controlled to ensure timely payment within the business's stated credit terms. If a discount is offered for early payment (i.e., 2%, ten days), make the after-discount amount result in the desired sale price, resulting in a penalty for those that don't pay on time. Effective collection procedures must be instituted so that outstanding amounts are timely collected, credit policies are strictly enforced, and delinquent customers are not sold additional products or services.

Inventory Business

Although it has been mentioned previously that the small business should do what it can to reduce or eliminate inventory (that is, get out of the inventory business), there are some small businesses where inventory *is* their business. Such businesses might include lumberyards, hardware stores, wholesalers and distributors, and supply houses.

1. Establish controls that monitor which inventory items sell repetitively and to what extent based on customer demand so that inventory items and levels on-hand reflect such customer demand.

2. Determine which products should be kept on hand (i.e., reasonably priced, highly repetitive items), which ones should be supplied on a timely basis by other vendors (i.e., easily accessible items where the cost of carrying the item does not justify maintaining it on-site), and which products should be ordered for the customer as needed (i.e., large-ticket items not normally ordered).

3. Control all inventory on hand to ensure correct recording and storing of incoming items (with reconciliation of updated balance), proper maintenance of items on-hand (i.e., cyclical inventory counts reconciled to computer records), and accurate storeroom issues settled to some form of customer sale.

4. Maintain ongoing sales records and customer demands that integrate with the inventory control system to determine amounts to maintain on-hand so that on-hand inventory is kept to a minimum while still meeting all customer demands.

5. Control physical inventory so that no item moves into or out of inventory without the proper recording of a receipt from a vendor delivery and bill or an inventory issue supported by a customer bill. Establish effective controls that segregate the functions of inventory receipts and issues from the reconciliation of inventory records.

6. Control storeroom operations so that direct responsibility over all storeroom operations is clearly assigned, which eliminates the possibility of others being involved with receipts and issues of inventory—this includes the small business owner and other unrelated management.

For an inventory business, inventory controls the business.

Cash Business

As previously mentioned, it is desirable for many small business owners to be in the cash business. Dealing strictly with direct payments in cash allows the business owner to reduce the cash conversion time period from sale to collection to zero—a desirable business practice for any business. However, dealing directly with cash presents numerous control problems as uncontrolled cash can be easily subject to employee misappropriation and theft. Examples of cash businesses include laundromats, vending machines, amusement arcades, casinos, pay telephones (although a dying breed), and parking meters.

1. Control cash payments with a backup system such as a recording meter, cash register record, or printed and/or electronic record that can be reconciled independently from the counting of cash.

2. Segregate the functions of cash pickup, cash counting, and settlement procedures. Ensure that an independent party from the cash operation reconciles the cash to the backup record.

3. Ensure that any employee who handles cash is properly bonded, trustworthy, and responsible. In many small businesses, the owners don't trust anyone other than themselves with the actual cash, creating an operational bottleneck at times that could bring operations to a standstill.

4. Establish controls for each cash terminal that produces a range of expected business volume that can be compared to actual receipts. Also control the incidences of over- and under-cash conditions by outlet that may indicate some control flaw at the site or with the reconciliation and settlement procedures.

5. Impress upon the owners the value of recording all cash receipts rather than diverting cash directly into their pockets. Besides the ethical and legal issues, such cash diversion results in inaccurate recording of sales, which makes it difficult to accurately provide advice and direction for the business.

6. As all small businesses are in the cash conversion business and it is desirable to receive cash at the time of providing the product or service, the business should factor such direct cash conversion into its cost and pricing strategies. Cost and pricing controls should assist the small business owner in accurately determining correct prices to stay competitive.

Be in the cash business, but *control* the cash.

Conclusion

Internal control refers to the methods and procedures used to provide reasonable assurance regarding the achievement of objectives in the following categories:

- Safeguarding assets
- Ensuring validity of financial records
- Promoting adherence to policies, procedures, regulations, and laws
- Promoting economy, efficiency, and effectiveness of operations

In general terms, internal controls are simply good business practices. They include anything that serves to safeguard assets or to improve the effectiveness and efficiency of operations. Management is responsible for establishing specific internal control policies and procedures. Every employee is responsible for ensuring that established internal controls are followed and applied.

Duties are divided (separation of duties) so that no one person has complete control over a key function or activity such as authorization and approval and transaction processing. The review is done of transaction processing, and records produced are examined and reconciled to determine that transactions were properly processed and approved. Note that well-oriented, trained, and supervised employees help ensure that control processes function properly. In addition, documented policies and procedures (formal or informal) promote employee understanding of job duties and expectations. Keep in mind that costs associated with control processes should not exceed expected benefits.

If you can effectively control operations, then you can effectively control financial results.

CHAPTER 11

Information Technology Control Considerations

O nce upon a time, in the early 1960s, most small businesses maintained their accounting books of record on a manual basis. These books of record consisted of various ledgers such as accounts payable, sales and accounts receivable, payroll journal, and the general ledger—usually each one controlled by a separate individual, and sometimes under lock and key or kept securely in an impregnable safe. All of these ledgers were posted and calculations verified by hand. Vendor and payroll checks were drawn manually with review and approval and signature performed by an authorized individual. At this time, larger organizations were installing mainframe computers with random access memories, allowing them to computerize their accounting functions. In the 1970s, the concept of the *minicomputer* (a mini-mainframe at much less cost and size) came into existence, enabling some small businesses to be able to afford to computerize. However, it was not until the *microcomputer* (also known as a *personal computer* [PC]) was introduced by IBM in August 1981 as a business processor that computerization was recognized as a possible tool for the small business and became a possibility and a reality for almost all small businesses, as we see today.

Most small businesses presently process their financial and accounting transactions in a microcomputer environment. These small businesses, of all sizes, are processing those financial transactions and maintaining account balances upon which the business and the external CPA rely in the preparation of financial statements. Continual decreases in the price of this equipment, together with increases in processing capability, have made the purchase and use of these computer systems quite attractive. In addition, there are many software packages on the market for financial and accounting applications at relatively low costs for small business processing.

In addition to decreasing prices and increasing capabilities, the use of microcomputers has become much easier with purchased application software designed to be used in an interactive mode ("user friendly"), which allows the user to have limited knowledge of computer processing and control procedures. Due to this sometimes-uncontrolled operating environment, you should be aware of the control considerations discussed in this chapter when relying on computer-processed financial and accounting data.

"User friendly" is not user accuracy.

The advent of the PC for business purposes has made computerization available to almost all organizations. Due to publicized security and control problems with using PCs, the small business owner is concerned about related controls and operating in such a computer environment. In addition, as small businesses are processing their accounting and financial data using such computer systems, there is also a concern as to the accuracy and reliability of such data. The purpose of this chapter is to present the basic principles involved in identifying and assisting the small business client to be aware of computer controls that ensure effective, secure, and accurate computer operations.

Although you do not need to be an information technology (IT) professional or a computer programmer to effectively operate a microcomputer, you should have sufficient knowledge as to how the system works (both hardware and software), what control measures need to be in place to ensure the integrity of accounting and operational data, and what steps are necessary to achieve the most productive use. As almost all small businesses have moved from manual record keeping to the use of computer processing (some quite a while ago, others only recently), you must be aware of the special considerations of a computer environment, such as general and application controls and the ability to process accounting transactions in a controlled operating atmosphere that ensures the integrity of the data.

OVERVIEW OF COMPUTER OPERATIONS

Someone (internal and/or external) should possess a working knowledge of how small business computer systems operate, hardware and software, and the control environment in which they should operate. One of the major considerations in designing the operating environment in which the microcomputer is to be used is whether it is to be a single-user or multiuser operation. A single-user system is where one CPU (central processing unit, that is, the motherboard with its microprocessor chips) is used with various peripheral components allowing one user to use the system at a time. A multiuser system is where a single CPU is used by more than one data terminal with a different user at each terminal, running different programs simultaneously.

Normally, it is recommended that the small business use a single-user system for processing accounting transactions so as to minimize the possibility of other users encroaching on the data files. Another alternative is to remove the accounting data files from the system when not used and to restrict access to the accounting files to only authorized users with specifically assigned processing functions (i.e., inquiry only and specific transaction updating). Multiuser systems usually are necessary when various users have to access the same files at the same time and cannot wait for the single-user system to become available. A local area network (LAN), which is used for data transmission within the same building or location, requiring some sort of cable connection and special LAN communications software, serves a purpose similar to a multiuser system.

The small business in today's electronic environment may have a need for its computer system to communicate with other small and large organizations' computer systems. As such communication (especially using the Internet) is becoming more prevalent, you should be aware of the methods of communication and the controls involved.

A small business PC processing system has two basic parts: hardware and software. Hardware constitutes the physical components of the computer system such as CPU, keyboard, monitor display, data storage devices, and printer. Software, however, constitutes the part of the computer system that you cannot see or touch, that is, the computer programs (such as accounting applications) that instruct the computer as to what specific functions to perform. You do not need to be a computer programmer or even understand how to program the computer to use computer software effectively. However, it is helpful to understand what computer software is and how it works to get the best use of it and have it operate in a controlled environment.

The computer is always right—or is it?

Such microcomputer systems can be used as standalone systems, internal LANs, part of a wide area communications network (WAN) via modem or wireless technology using laptops, or as a front-end processor to an umbrella system (i.e., workstations electronically tied into an organization-wide computer network), or in some combination.

Control Objectives for IT

It is helpful to understand what the control objectives for IT processing are so that you can assist the small business owner in implementing those controls that are most pertinent to the level and methods of computer processing. Areas to be considered include:

- Critical success factors
- Key goal indicators
- Key performance indicators

Critical Success Factors

IT control and security issues start at the top of the organization with the owners and management personnel. Those at the top need to be committed to the concept of operating the business's PCs in a controlled environment and understand its importance. Such commitment establishes the concept of overall IT governance, which is communicated and delegated downward throughout the business. Critical success factors under this concept include:

- IT governance activities are integrated into the enterprise governance process and leadership behavior.

- IT governance focuses on the enterprise goals, strategic initiatives, the use of technology to enhance the business, and on the availability of sufficient resources and capabilities to keep up with the business demands.

- IT governance activities are defined with a clear purpose, documented, and implemented, based on enterprise needs and with unambiguous accountability.

- Management practices are implemented to increase efficient and optimal use of resources and increase the effectiveness of IT processes.

- Organizational practices are established to enable: sound oversight; a control environment/culture; risk assessment as standard practice; degree of adherence to established standards; monitoring and follow-up of control deficiencies and risks.

- Control practices are defined to avoid breakdowns in internal control and oversight.

- There is integration and smooth interoperability of the more complex IT processes, change and configuration management.

- An independent reviewer focuses on IT and evaluates IT controls.

Key Goal Indicators

There are many reasons to process the small business's financial, accounting, and operating transactions using PCs. Small business management must be aware of not only the possibility of reducing costs through computerization but also the many byproducts that computer processing can bring to the business, such as:

- Enhanced performance and cost management

- Improved return on major IT investment

- Improved time to market

- Increased quality, innovation, and risk management

- Appropriately integrated and standardized business processes

- Reaching new and satisfying existing customers

- Availability of appropriate bandwidth, computing power, and IT delivery mechanisms

- Meeting requirements and expectations of the customer of the process on budget and on time
- Adherence to laws, regulations, industry standards, and contractual commitments
- Transparency on risk taking and adherence to the agreed organizational risk profile
- Benchmarking comparisons of IT governance maturity
- Creation of new service delivery channels

Key Performance Indicators

The ease and use of computer processing for the small business has opened up many of the avenues and advantages that the large organization has enjoyed for many years—closing the competitive gap in this area for the small business. Some of these key performance indicators include:

- Improved cost-efficiency of IT processes (costs versus deliverables)
- Increased number of IT action plans for process improvement initiatives
- Increased utilization of IT infrastructure
- Increased satisfaction of stakeholders (survey and number of complaints)
- Improved staff productivity (number of deliverables) and morale (survey)
- Increased availability of knowledge and information for managing the enterprise
- Increased linkage between IT and enterprise governance
- Improved performance as measured by IT balanced scorecards

IT controls enhance IT performance.

IT Controls

IT general controls encompass the environment in which applications (financial, accounting, and programmatic) are processed. Effective general controls provide the proper environment for effective internal accounting and program controls. General controls increase in significance as more and more critical applications are processed through the computer system. Their purpose is not normally directed to any one computer application, but to all applications processed by the computer system. When general controls are weak or missing, it must be ascertained whether application controls exercised in user areas satisfy internal control requirements. A computer installation in a small business, by the nature of its relatively small size, predominant use of purchased software packages, and its ability to be fully operable by one computer operator, carries intrinsic IT general control concerns.

IT application controls are those internal controls that relate to the specific processing requirements of an individual application, such as accounts payable, accounts receivable, and general ledger. During the review of application controls, any weaknesses identified during the review of general controls should be tested as to the availability of compensating controls within the software application.

Application controls are intended to ensure that there are no errors in:

- **Input.** The recording, classifying, and summarizing of authorized accounting and financial transactions
- **Processing.** The maintenance/update of master file information
- **Output.** The results of computer processing

In the review and evaluation of IT controls, you should be aware of the following control considerations:

- Lack of segregation of functions
- Location of computer(s)
- Limited knowledge of IT
- IT controls:
  - Input controls
  - Data entry controls
  - Processing controls

- • Output reconcilement procedures
- • Data file library procedures
- • Master file maintenance
- Disk storage/backup
- Software packages
- Physical/logical security
- Passwords
- General controls
- Application controls

Lack of Segregation of Functions

- Between IT and users
- Within the IT department

Typically the computer system is controlled and operated by the user department (i.e., accounts payable, accounts receivable) that in many small businesses becomes the IT department. These user personnel (often, only one person) may initiate input transactions, perform data entry and control operations, make system inquiries, and process accounting/financially related reports. In addition, data terminals (computers or dumb terminals) may be located elsewhere within the business for data input and updating by other user departments—resulting in these personnel being computer operators for their applications.

To remedy this situation, you should consider:

- Independent initiation and authorization of input transactions by someone other than the computer operator
- Input controls, processing controls, and output settlement procedures to be handled by a person(s) independent of the computer operation
- Assigning of distinct staff personnel (other than computer operators) the functions of data preparation, data control, and data file/program librarian as part of their overall responsibilities
- Having personnel assigned computer-operating responsibility only to enter and process data through the computer as related to computer operations.

It is the separation of *functions*, not the separation of individuals.

Location of the Computer

- In the user's area

- In a nonsecure, non-temperature/humidity-controlled environment

The PC, due to its relatively small size and user orientation, is normally located within the user's area in an accessible location requiring user and application software security to control misuse of the system. Proper controls in such an environment to limit access to computer systems and related software and data files only to authorized individuals might include:

- Physical key-and-lock systems
- User passwords
- Application program and data file security passwords
- Functional passwords, such as inquiry only, transaction update, and master file maintenance

Limited Knowledge of IT

- By management personnel
- By user personnel
- By computer operators

Microcomputer hardware and software is designed for ease of learning and use; this allows for personnel with limited IT knowledge to purchase and operate them effectively. Such personnel do not need to know how the computer system works or how to program for it. Such a computer operations atmosphere can result in a lack of understanding of the need for data and processing controls, resulting in an undisciplined control environment.

As the owners, small business management, and the external CPA place reliance on the accuracy of financial transactions and the integrity of account balances, they must ensure themselves that proper controls are implemented and in effect, such as:

- Input controls
- Data entry controls
- Processing controls
- Output reconcilement procedures
- Data file library procedures
- Master file maintenance

Knowledge is power; computers are power—*control* the power.

Disk Storage/Backup

Hard-disk storage devices for application programs and large databases are susceptible to damage and destruction, such as disk read errors, corrupted cylinders and tracks, poorly controlled backup (usually using a backup tape/disk/CD-ROM device) and recovery procedures, and operating failures.

Data storage and backup on small diskettes or tape or CD-ROMs is susceptible to damage, loss, misplacement, misappropriation, and use of the wrong diskettes or CD-ROMs. In addition, these data media are sensitive to data destruction such as magnetic or electrostatics, humidity, extreme temperatures, fingerprints, pen/pencil impressions, and so on.

Some procedures to consider relative to the control of disk storage include:

- Disk data file and program library procedures, ensuring the correct data files are being used, backed up, and recovered, with no unnecessary data files being available to the computer operator
- Use of properly controlled hard disk operating and backup procedures
- Replacement of backup media (diskette, CD-ROM, or tape) after a period of time (i.e., six months) or a number of uses (i.e., 100 uses)
- Adequate backup copy library procedures, including in-house and offsite storage
- Periodic checkup and maintenance for hard disk drives and cleaning of disk drive read/write heads

You do not need to do backup until you need the backup and then it is too late.

Software Packages

Most small business computer users utilize application software packages for their major accounting systems that make it relatively easy for the non-IT-knowledgeable user to perform necessary computer processing. These accounting packages operate in an interactive processing mode that is designed to edit out bad data, but not necessarily wrong or duplicate data. However, this "user- friendly" approach does not usually allow the user to incorporate necessary internal accounting controls into the system; the user must accept those controls that have been provided by the software vendor (who may not be too knowledgeable about internal accounting controls). The system documentation for the accounting software package is also dependent on the software vendor and it may not be adequate to fully describe the system and accounting controls, and it may not relate to the reality of the computer processing. In this situation, it is the responsibility of the user to review and evaluate the software package before purchasing and implementing to ensure required accounting controls, such as:

- Input editing and validation procedures
- Data entry input controls
- Processing controls
- Error condition identifications
- Error correction controls
- File update procedures
- File maintenance procedures
- File control procedures

The user defines the controls; the software provides the controls.

Physical/Logical Security

Microcomputer systems—used as a standalone system or a data terminal as part of a LAN or a larger processing system—can be housed in a relatively small area, often on a desktop within the user area. In addition, when operating within a LAN environment, the LAN file server housing the system's databases and programs may not be secured properly, many times accessible to any or all users and others. Both of these conditions cause some physical security concerns.

Some controls that should be considered relative to the physical security of computer hardware and software include:

- Access controls to computer hardware; use of physical lock and key, and security user passwords. Stricter controls are dictated for a LAN file server.
- Environmental controls to protect against excess humidity, temperature variations, or other atmospheric conditions.
- Electrical connections, such as separate power line, surge devices, and uninterruptable power supplies (UPSs).
- Fire protection devices for hardware, data files, and programs; fire/smoke detection and extinguishers.
- Protection of data files and programs when not in use; fireproof secure facilities.
- Backup procedures for hardware, data files, and programs. Both onsite and off-premises.
- Off-premises storage for important data files, programs, documentation.
- Insurance coverage, such as equipment cost, reconstruction of data files, business interruption, loss of records, and so on.

If there is no access, there is no attempt.

Passwords

Most software developers of applications who provide for a password structure allow a degree of flexibility in designing your password structure.

Passwords should be long enough so that random or systematic attempts to access accounting records by searching for a valid password are time consuming or lead to detection. A password that is too long may result in employees posting their password (for instance, on the monitor screen), increasing detection. Normally, a password of five or six characters (with no meaning) is sufficient security.

Rules for the assigning of passwords include:

- The password gatekeeper (the one responsible at the site for controlling passwords) only assigns individual passwords.
- The gatekeeper assigns passwords only to those who have authorized data entry or inquiry responsibilities.
- Password allows only for specific transactions or data access in individual's area of responsibility.
- An original password is communicated orally and not in writing.
- Users are trained to keep passwords confidential.
- Passwords are assigned on an individual basis (not globally).

The use of passwords includes the following functions:

- Users commit passwords to memory with no written record.
- Password procedures inhibit printing or displaying the password; passwords are not printed out on reports.
- Users have a limited number of attempts to enter a password (i.e., three), and if unsuccessful, further entries from that terminal are prohibited until supervisory action is taken.
- Users are required to change their password frequently (i.e., after 60 days). Some systems hang up if this is not done.
- Users sign off each time they leave the terminal. Some systems have automatic signoff if inactive for a time (e.g., three minutes).
- Users keep passwords confidential.
- Users (or gatekeeper) design passwords that are random and do not contain employee's/child's names, birthdates, and so on.
- Users leaving the company or whose responsibilities have changed are deleted immediately from the password file. The gatekeeper flags inactive passwords for review.

The gatekeeper has the ultimate responsibility to assign original passwords and maintain the password file. The password file should be encrypted, protected by its own password, and protected from access by all users except the gatekeeper. Only the gatekeeper, who periodically scans the file to ensure only authorized users are present and that access rights are appropriate, updates the password file. The gatekeeper reviews all reports of terminal activities and invalid access attempts. All invalid access attempts are followed up as they happen.

The password file indicates (via a password matrix) the functions and resources that each password can have access to. Upon entry of the user's password, the user can carry out only the functions that have been preauthorized in the password file.

Limiting functions by the use of passwords can also be achieved as follows:

- Restrict the terminal, such as inquiry or cash receipts only.
- Use of menus, on sign-on providing a menu of authorized items.
- Resource restrictions, such as read only.

If you don't know the password, you don't get the access.

General Controls

In the review and evaluation of IT general controls for a microcomputer installation, one should be aware of the following:

- Organization and operation controls
- Systems development

Organization and Operation Controls
Segregation of Functions between IT and Users   In many small business computer installations, the personnel who operate the equipment are within the user department. These personnel (often, one person who may not be full time) may initiate transactions, perform data entry operations, make system inquiries, and process financial-related reports. The owner, when

confronted with this type of situation, should make sure that compensating controls such as input/processing/output settlement procedures are handled effectively by a person(s) independent of the computer operation.

Prohibiting IT from Initiating or Authorizing Transactions Where computer operators are found to be initiating or authorizing transactions, the owner must make sure that offline controls are adequate to ensure that unauthorized transactions are not entering the system. Personnel independent of the computer operations should perform the function of transaction initiation and authorization.

Segregation of Functions within the Computer Operation Typically, one or two individuals who are also the computer operators handle all of the necessary control functions such as data preparation, data entry, data control, and data file librarian. Although economics do not dictate the use of separate individuals for each of these control functions, distinct personnel can be assigned these functions as part of their overall responsibilities. This results in only the computer operator entering and processing data through the computer system, with the control functions segregated.

Systems Development Systems design, including the acquisition of software packages, should have participation by owners, users, accounting personnel, and external CPAs. Although most small business microcomputer installations use purchased software packages (with documentation dependent on the vendor), the users should define their systems requirements prior to purchase so as to ensure their processing and control requirements exist and are operational in the software purchased. In addition, the system must be fully tested (as to internal controls and processing results) and approved prior to implementation to ensure that it operates according to user-defined system specifications.

Other areas to consider relative to systems development include:

- Written specifications and documentation as to adequacy and accuracy
- Systems testing prior to implementation
- Final approval by management, users, and IT personnel
- Master file and transaction file conversion controlled
- Program change controls
- Acceptable level of documentation (online and offline)

Hardware and Systems Software Controls   Control features inherent in computer hardware, operating systems, and other supporting software should be utilized to the maximum possible extent. Many of the control features included with larger computer systems such as data file internal label checking may not be available in a microcomputer with data files on hard disk, CD-ROM, and diskettes. Microcomputer operations are more dependent on operator handling and external labeling procedures. However, operators should be aware of hardware error detection procedures (boot-up diagnostics), necessary preventive maintenance, recovery procedures from hardware and software errors, and file control procedures. Systems software should be subjected to the same control procedures as those applied to application programs.

Access Controls to Hardware, Software, and Data Files   Microcomputer systems, due to their relatively small size and user orientation, many times are physically located in the middle of a user area, accessible to anyone. In addition, with the increased use of local area networks (LANs) connected to a central file server (with a large hard drive containing the shared data files), hardware security of the file server becomes even more critical. Proper controls in such an environment to limit access to the computer system only to authorized individuals might include:

- Physical key-and-lock system (room and hardware)
- User passwords (by data terminal, application, and function)
- Programs and data files (encrypted, hidden files, library function, backup procedures, storage)

Data Control Functions   A control function that is independent of the computer operation should exist that is responsible for:

- Receiving all data to be processed
- Ensuring that all data are recorded
- Following up on errors detected during processing to see that the transactions are corrected and resubmitted by the proper party
- Verifying the proper distribution of output

The computer operator, who may also be user personnel, often performs this control function. The owner should ensure that such a data control function exists and that it properly coordinates user and computer activities.

Physical Security   Microcomputer systems can be physically housed on a desktop within the user area, or relatively anywhere. Although most systems today use large hard-disk data storage for ongoing data file and program storage, they also may use relatively small diskettes, CD-ROMs, or magnetic tape cartridges for backup storage purposes, which creates physical security concerns. Some controls that should be reviewed relative to such physical security include the following:

- Physical access to hardware, storage media, and backup data files
- Environmental controls to protect against excess humidity, temperature variations, or other atmospheric conditions
- Electrical connections, such as separate power line, surge protectors, and UPSs
- Fire protection devices for computer hardware, data files, and programs
- Backup procedures for hardware, data files, and programs
- Protection of data files and programs when not in use
- Off-premises storage of important data files, programs, and documentation

General controls control the processing environment

Application Controls

IT application controls are those internal controls that relate to the specific processing requirements of an individual application such as accounts payable, accounts receivable, and general ledger. During the review of application controls, any weaknesses identified during the review of general controls should be tested as to the availability of compensating controls within the software application.

Application controls are intended to ensure that there are no errors in:

- Input—the recording, classifying, and summarizing of authorized accounting and financial transactions
- Processing—the maintenance/update of master file information

- Output—the results of computer processing
- Accounting controls and audit trail

Microcomputer applications are predominantly purchased software packages from either a software house selling directly to the end user (or through a third party that may offer authorized modifications) or a retail outlet selling on an "off-the-shelf" basis. Even though this is the most likely scenario for small business computer users, the burden is still on the users to:

- Define their specific systems specifications.
- Analyze existing software packages to determine which package most closely meets their needs and provides necessary controls.
- Test out the chosen software package.
- Ensure that the package is compatible with the entity's operating systems and procedures.

There may be some instances where the business has had a software development firm customize (sometimes using database or spreadsheet software) or modify existing software to meet its specific needs. While this is not the normal occurrence, where this exists, these procedures must be reviewed as well.

In the review and evaluation of application controls in a microcomputer environment where purchased software packages is the norm, the business owner would be most concerned about:

Input Controls   There are four basic categories of input that need to be controlled.

1. Transaction entries; largest volume, biggest number of errors
2. File maintenance; limited volume, continuing impact
3. Inquiry transactions; no change, triggers decisions
4. Error corrections; more complex than original entry, offers a greater opportunity for additional errors

Input controls over these types of transactions are designed to ensure that:

- Data received for processing is properly authorized.
- No errors occurred in keying the data through the keyboard into machine readable form.

- Input data is complete: no data has been lost, suppressed, added, duplicated, or otherwise improperly changed.

- Errors or other rejected data are properly reentered into the system.

In a well-controlled system with adequate input controls, the user departments establish control totals prior to submitting data for processing using some of the following techniques:

- Footing totals (i.e., dollar or quantity fields)

- Hash totals of various numeric fields (i.e., account numbers)

- Self-checking digits (i.e., customer numbers, vendor numbers)

- Record counts (i.e., number of purchase orders, invoices, checks)

- Zero balancing (i.e., subtracting each entry from an initial total entered so that the last item brings the balance to zero)

The computer system accumulates these same control totals during processing so that they can be compared to the offline totals and differences resolved before processing continues. These input control totals are used to ensure that all transactions initiated and authorized are processed and are free of missing or erroneous data. Typically, such input controlling does not exist in a microcomputer system as most software packages rely on interactive processing and online editing procedures that ensure no "bad data" entering the system. However, such processing controls do not ensure no "wrong data" (duplicate entries, missing transactions, or unauthorized entries) entering the system. Thus, there needs to be some form of input transaction controlling and reconciliation to computer-produced totals.

Other input controls that should be considered include:

- Only properly authorized and approved input should be accepted for processing.

- The system should verify all significant codes used to record data.

- Proper edit, validation, and limit and reasonableness tests should be used during data input.

- Correction of all errors detected by the application system and the resubmission of corrected transactions should be reviewed and controlled.

Some computerized procedures that should be considered include:

- Reconciliation to input control totals
- Zero-balancing procedures
- Batch-control reconciliation and error listings
- Input editing and verification
- Data validation
- Limit and reasonableness tests
- Error detection and resubmission

Processing Controls   These controls provide reasonable assurance that the application system is performing as intended, to ensure that all authorized transactions are:

- Processed as authorized
- Included in the processing
- The only transactions processed (no unauthorized transactions being added)

Such processing controls included in the application programs are designed to prevent or detect the following types of errors:

- Not processing all authorized input transactions
- Erroneous processing of the same input more than once
- Processing and updating of the wrong data file(s)
- Processing of illogical or unreasonable input or output
- Loss of data during processing

Processing control weaknesses may greatly affect the data records, resulting in lost or duplicated data records and errors in balance-forward amounts. In addition, program logic and processing errors may go undetected for a long time, adversely affecting the results of computer processing.

Some of the processing control procedures that should be considered include:

- Processing control totals should be produced and reconciled to input control totals.

- Data file totals are produced that can be reconciled to the previously run program. These are called *run-to-run* controls. The formula for ascertaining the correctness of such run-to-run totals is: Beginning data file total, plus total transactions, equals ending data file total.

- Controls should prevent processing the wrong data file. PC processing may not use effective internal label checking procedures, but a greater dependency on manual external label checking. Operating procedures should include such techniques as checking file dates, size in bytes, control totals, record counts, and so forth.

- Limit and reasonableness checks should be incorporated within programs (i.e., net pay cannot exceed $1,000).

- Run-to-run controls should be verified at appropriate points in the processing cycle, basically from one computer run to another where the number of records or file control totals have changed.

Other processing controls to be considered include:

- Data file identification
- Data file control (record counts, etc.)
- Master file update procedures
- Master file maintenance
- Internal processing tests
- Specific amount or account tests
- Limit and reasonableness tests
- Comparison of different fields within a data record
- Validating input data against a master data file or table
- Validation of self-checking numbers
- Logic checks
- Comparison to a range of values

Output Controls   In a microcomputer processing system, output controls are designed to ensure that:

- Output data representing the results of computer processing, such as computer reports, data files, screen displays, checks, invoices, and so on, are accurate, complete, and reasonable.

- Output reports (hardcopy and screen displays) are distributed or accessible only to authorized personnel.
- Data file output is properly controlled and identified.

Specific output controls that should be considered include:

- Output control totals should be reconciled with input and processing controls (output reconcilement procedures).
- Output should be scanned and tested by comparison to original source documents, for transactions that cannot be controlled by the establishment and balancing of control totals (for example, changes to master files of nonnumeric data such as employee name and/or address, item descriptions, and numeric data such as pay rates, selling prices, and item numbers). The system must provide adequate output data for this purpose.
- Systems output should be distributed or made accessible only to authorized users—output reports and screen displays.
- Data file output is properly controlled and identified, through such techniques as record counts and control totals, run-to-run control procedures, external labels, backup library procedures, and so on.

Accounting Controls and Audit Trail   The accounting software package should produce printed evidence of computer activity that makes up an inclusive accounting control/audit trail package that would include printing such reports as:

- Data input list (of valid accepted items), which can be reconciled to offline maintained input controls.
- Input error list, showing all error transactions for correction. This listing could include all input errors, even those corrected immediately through the keyboard, or only those not corrected at the time of keyboard input.
- Error correction list, showing disposition of corrected items. If the software maintains an internal computer suspense file of all errors (which is the preferred system of control), then the printout should show the original error condition and the result of the correction.

- Master file update listing, showing the results of processing, and providing update control totals that can be reconciled to offline-maintained control totals.

- Master file maintenance listing, showing the master file record contents prior to the maintenance, the maintenance transaction itself, and the master file record contents as a result of the file maintenance update. This listing should be produced every time a master file maintenance is performed, so that its results can be verified for accuracy back to the original file maintenance source, prior to any further master file updates.

Application controls control the processing.

Common Small Business IT Control Weaknesses

In working with the small business you need not know technically how the hardware and software works electronically, but you should be able to assess whether the business is processing its transactions, especially accounting and financial transactions, in a controlled environment. Some of the more common control weaknesses and suggested remedies that you should be aware of when reviewing the small business's computer processing procedures include:

- **Unauthorized access, theft, or vandalism of computer hardware.** All computer equipment should be physically secured in work areas where computer hardware exists. Access to these work areas should be inhibited and/or locked barring entry to the computer and all peripherals. If operating in a LAN environment, there should be increased security over the PC file server. If the small business operates in a complex environment, you might also consider contracting for an alternate site arrangement.

- **Unauthorized access, theft, or vandalism to magnetic media.** Limit physical access to the computer and these data files by using restraint key locks. To prevent access by unauthorized users, use password controls by PC, user, application, and job function or task. Encrypt passwords and files of sensitive applications. Consider the use of hardware cards that provide double protection when used with passwords. Back up all sensitive software and data files and control access to the backup (separate data file library function where possible). Keep copies of backup files onsite and offsite in fireproof, lockable storage facilities under the user's control. You might also consider removing accounting and financially sensitive data files when not using or updating (e.g., general ledger).

- **Processing errors or omissions by computer operators— intentional or unintentional.** At minimum, use password control at the PC system level to control processing only by authorized users. If possible, use password controls at all levels—application, function (i.e., inquiry only, file/record update, and master file maintenance), and activity level (i.e., dollar update or changes, non-dollar changes only, and identifier such as name and address changes). Also you should make sure individuals monitor unauthorized PC access using a system access log with effective follow-up on attempts by unauthorized individuals. If operating in a LAN environment, restrict applications and data files accessible to users based on authorized activities.

- **Lack of proper and accurate documentation.** Hardware documentation including how to use the PC and its operating system provided by the PC vendor at the time of sale rarely exists today. Accurate PC operating instructions, including both online and offline control procedures, should be developed by the actual computer operator (and reviewed for accuracy) to ensure proper processing procedures as well provide for continuity of operations should another operator be required.

- **The software vendor provides whatever level of documentation is in existence.** This is one of the weakest areas of control in the PC environment. Documentation for some of the more popular (usually lower-end) software packages can be enhanced through the purchase of third-party documentation books such as the *For Dummies* series. You should review software documentation to ensure that it meets a minimal level of standards. If the software was custom developed or modified by a third-party vendor, the documentation should be fully reviewed as to completeness prior to having the system turned over to the user. Such documentation must be updated as changes are made to the software.

- **Loss of data due to system problems.** Maintain periodic backup of programs and data files—from daily to monthly, especially on sensitive data files—both onsite and offsite. Assign a separate individual data librarian duties to ensure accuracy of backup storage.

- **Introduction of viruses to software and data files.** Maintain effective policy restricting the data that can be placed on the system and by what source. Use antiviral software to check new and existing software and data for viruses. Maintain strict control over sensitive data files.

- **Software vendor, third-party modifier, or custom system developer goes out of business.** Maintain arrangements with other technical and software firms as backup to enable the business to easily convert or bridge their data to another software processing system in a timely manner so that operations do not need to be curtailed. You should have a number of such firms that can be relied on in your network to properly service the business from a technical standpoint.

Identify the control weakness, control the cause.

To assist in obtaining a working knowledge of the small business's computer operations, a control questionnaire such as the one shown in Exhibit 11.1 can be used. With such a questionnaire you can use professional judgment as to what is pertinent to the specific small business, as not all IT controls would be appropriate.

IT Control Examples

As previously mentioned, you need not be a computer expert or a technical genius to provide technical assistance to small businesses operating in a computer environment. However, someone at the small business should

EXHIBIT II.I   **Computer Control Questionnaire**

IT Planning

1. Is there an overall IT plan for the entity? Does it cover all needs including financial and accounting systems, as well as operating requirements?
2. Is a hardware feasibility study part of the IT plan?
3. Does the IT plan make the best possible use of microcomputers and the use of LANs and wide area communications?
4. Have adequate organization and departmental problem statements together with systems specifications been prepared?
5. Are the necessary personnel resources available to implement and operate the elements of the IT plan?
6. Has a preliminary survey been performed that clearly documents the requirements of the new system?
7. Has a cost/benefit analysis been performed for the new system with realistic estimates?
8. Has software been identified in the IT plan? How was it selected? Does it cover all essential features?

Purchased Software Packages

1. Have arrangements been made for appropriate user participation in detail design specifications?
2. Has the software package been adequately evaluated and tested?
3. Does the software contain the necessary procedures to provide for proper internal controls when implemented?

   - Passwords (terminal access controls)
   - Edit and validation routines
   - Control totals or transaction lists
   - Exception reports
   - Management trails

4. Is the software and user documentation adequate?
5. Has the conversion of existing information to the new system been adequately controlled?
6. Will the addition of the new software application cause overall systems performance to suffer? Has the need for additional or new hardware been considered?

Organizational Controls

1. Has a proper segregation of duties been achieved within the IT department (if one exists)?
2. If a separate IT department exists, does it not:

   - Initiate and authorize transactions
   - Record transactions

3. Within user departments, are the following activities segregated from each other wherever possible?

- Initiation of transactions
- Authorization of transactions
- Recording of transactions
- Input, processing, and output control activities

If not segregated, has the best possible segregation been achieved? Wherever possible, are automated controls used to help ensure the completeness, accuracy, and authorization of data?

Application Systems Maintenance and Documentation

1. Where software packages have been purchased off the shelf:

   - Is data on new versions of the package regularly reviewed to see if such updates are desirable?
   - If an updated version is acquired, is it adequately reviewed and tested prior to being put into use?

2. Is there a users group for the software package? Does the entity participate in the users group?

3. Are changes to the software by employees limited to those that can be made through routines (i.e., data base manipulators or report generators) available in the package?

4. Have any outside contractors made changes to the software? Are the contractors authorized by the software developer? Document changes.

5. Are all such outside changes properly reviewed and tested by the contractor and the user before they are accepted?

6. Are all program changes tested before the updated software is used to process the company's transactions?

Prevention of Record and Equipment Loss

1. Are there written procedures for computer operators to follow that require the regular copying of data files for backup?

2. Are all copies of transactions (on magnetic media) since the last backup stored properly so as to facilitate reentry?

3. Has a disaster plan been prepared that includes what to do onsite and hardware and software recovery procedures? Have arrangements been made and tested as to hardware backup?

4. Are copies of the following stored off-premises?

   - Operating systems
   - Application support software and utilities
   - Application programs
   - Systems, program, and user documentation
   - Copies of data files: master and transaction files

5. Have insurance arrangements to offset losses due to business interruption and to defray the cost of data reconstruction been considered?

(Continued)

EXHIBIT II.I **(Continued)**

Input Controls

1. Are input transactions properly authorized by operations personnel?
2. Are standardized input forms used and are they prenumbered with the numerical sequence being accounted for?
3. Are input forms checked for completeness and accuracy before they are submitted for data entry?
4. Are source documents canceled by data entry to prevent duplicate data entry?
5. Is the maximum possible use made of magnetic media data to reduce the amount of data to be entered?
6. When transactions are rejected, is the input document corrected by the initiator and reentered on a timely basis?
7. Are transaction or file totals used to control the correct and complete entry of all transactions?
8. Are transaction totals balanced or verified by someone other than data entry personnel?
9. At a minimum, do different individuals perform the following activities?

   • Authorizing transactions
   • Initiating and recording transactions on the terminal
   • Input controls: reconciling input transactions to processing

Output Controls

1. Have output controls been designed to help offset weaknesses that may exist in controls over the use of operating systems and utilities?
2. Is all computer output subjected to one or both of the following controls before being used?

   • The output data file subjected to file balance controls
   • Output reviewed by user management, with a periodic check of results and calculations made

3. Are all significant data files subjected to balance control procedures?
4. Is master file data periodically printed out for review by an appropriate employee?
5. Is material output reviewed by an employee with sufficient knowledge of the business so as to spot obvious errors or suspect items?

Computer Viruses

1. Are all diskettes (particularly program diskettes) and CD-ROMs received from third parties scanned for viruses before being used?
2. Are program media purchased only from reputable sources and received in secure packaging?
3. Is there a policy to prohibit the use of pirated software or software procured through irregular channels?
4. Are new programs added to a PC or the LAN done only by one authorized person?
5. Is some form of virus detection software in use?
6. Have arrangements (including outside professional help) to recover from a virus infection been determined and documented?

Transaction Control Procedures

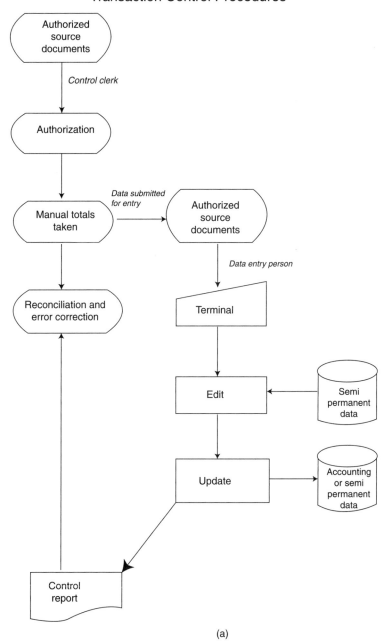

(a)

(Continued)

EXHIBIT II.2 **(Continued)**

Transaction Control Procedures Data Terminal Input Control Procedures

Terminal Operators	PC System Response	Data File Accessed
1. Enter customer.	1. Search stored data for customer number. 2. If match found, display customer name and address on terminal screen.	Customer data
2. Reconcile name to sales order. 3. Enter ship date.	1. Error message—if date is "impossible" or in incorrect format.	
4. Enter product code.	1. Search stored data for product code. 2. If match is found, display product description.	Product data
5. Reconcile product code and description to sales order. 6. Enter quantity.	1. Format check. 2. Reasonableness check. 3. Inventory availability— message displayed as required.	Product data
7. After all products are entered, enter total quantity for order.	1. Computes total quantity and compares to total entered. 2. Reports and requires any imbalance to be corrected before entry can be further processed.	

(b)

provide coordination between such technical individuals and firms to ensure that the business is provided adequate software to address its operations and control requirements. This person should have a working knowledge of how computer hardware and software operates and the necessary controls—both online within the application software and offline within the client's operations. Exhibits 11.2 and 11.3 depict graphic flowcharts and documentation of controls for:

- Transaction control procedures for customer sales order entry: data terminal input control procedures (Exhibit 11.2)
- Sales order entry processing computer control procedures (Exhibit 11.3)

Flowchart of Sales Order Entry in a Computerized Environment

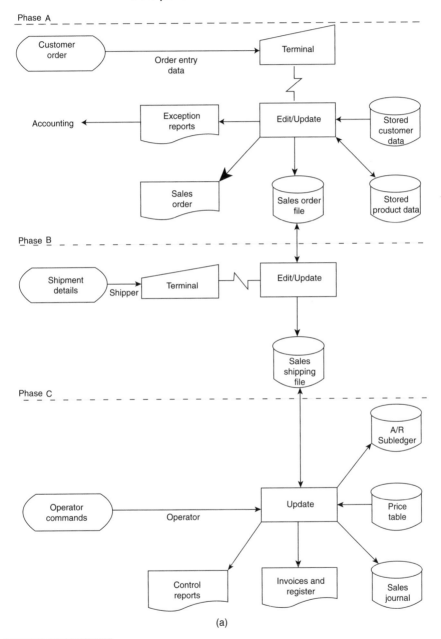

(a)

EXHIBIT 11.3   **(a) Sales Order Entry Flowchart and (b) Computer Control Procedures**

(Continued)

EXHIBIT 11.3 (Continued)

Computer Control Procedures

Purpose	Input	Program Logic	Output
1. Enter a sales order.	Document sales order Customer data file Product data file	1. Edit sales order. 2. Update—add order to sales order file.	Updated sales order file Sales orders Exception reports
2. Record a shipment.	Document sales order signed by shipper	1. Update—to change status to "shipped." 2. Create shipping file.	Updated sales order file Sales/shipping file
3. To send invoice to customer for payment.	Sales shipping file Price table Accounts receivable file	1. Update—to change status to "invoiced" 2. Update—sales journal file. 3. Compose invoice. 4. Setup print for: • Invoice register • Control reports on shipments and invoices	Updated sales Journal file and sales/shipping file Invoices Invoice register Control reports
4. Record sales in accounting records.	Updated sales journal file A/R data file	1. Update A/R ledger. 2. Update status to posted on sales journal file.	Updated A/R and sales journal files

(b)

Review these examples so that you obtain an idea as to how such controls might work in a PC-processed application for a small business. Such controls, of course, would need to be modified to match the specific application software being used.

DEVELOPING A WEB SITE

Many small businesses have or are contemplating setting up a web site for their business—to promote, increase customer service, offer and take orders for products or services, and provide online services. Although you would not typically engage yourself as a web designer, implementer, and maintainer of web sites, you should possess adequate knowledge to advise the small business as to using web sites to its advantage for business growth. Some areas to consider in working with a small business include:

Some Myths about Web Sites

- Developing a good web site only takes a few hours of anyone's time.
- It is easy and inexpensive to set up your web site.
- Once implemented, you can expect hits (and orders) from your web site almost immediately.
- It is easy to generate business and sales from your web site.
- You do not need a web consultant—anyone can do it.
- Do not worry about advertising and marketing; with a good web site your customers will find you easily.

Purposes of a Web Site

- Build the business's image.
- Provide better customer support.
- Make technical information more easily available to your customers.
- Help the business develop a prospective client list.
- Conduct customer (present and prospective) surveys.
- Offer products and take orders (and money).
- Provide online services.

Reasons for a Web Site

- Capability brochure only—easy and inexpensive (with off-the-shelf or free Internet software). Consider whether to maintain a static or flexible web site.

- Transactional web site—lengthy process (e.g., up to six months) and costly (e.g., $10,000+). Create transactions such as order inquiries, online training, and so on.

- Full e-commerce—more complicated with need to consider taking orders, tracking inventory, fulfilling orders, billing and collecting from clients and so on—and keeping it up.

What to Put on the Web Site

- About the business—who you are and what makes you unique
- Personnel capabilities—who each one is and what they can do and have done
- Services and products—what and how you provide your services, and products available for sale (or for free)
- How to contact the business, departments, and individuals
- The business's qualifications—what you do, what you have done, and whom you have worked for (your customers)
- How to order—if the site contains items for sale or on request
- Linkages to other web sites
- Other items: animation, quotes, quips, anecdotes, departments, and columns
- Guestbook to record visitors to your site for follow-up marketing
- Linkages within your web site such as homepage, departmental pages, back, forward, and links to move freely from one page or section to another

Other Concerns to Consider

- Accuracy and up-to-dateness of information; integrating your web site with back-end systems such as inventory and shipping systems
- Systems support needs—software and support staff

- Need for outsiders such as web technical personnel and marketing/public relations firms
- Advertising and promotion—to get clients to your web site
- Selecting an appropriate domain name (a URL)—one that is obvious or draws attention
- Banner ads—where to place elsewhere and whether the business sells them for its web site
- Analytical tools to learn about your customers and prospects (those who visit your site)
- Targeted e-mail marketing programs—to spread the word about your web site, products, and services
- Offline advertising—promoting your web site
- Web site linkages—from other sites to yours, and from yours to others
- Update items, such as services and products, departments and columns, professional tips, anecdotes, changes in personnel, and so on
- Support items, such as software, personnel, and hardware
- Search engines—which ones to be on and how to keep current

While you need not be technically proficient and put under undue pressure to stay current with the daily changes in the PC processing world, you must stay current on the ever-changing trends and terminology in the field. Some of the more common terms at the present time related to the PC world, hardware and software, and its control environment are defined in Exhibit 11.4.

Understanding IT basics such as hardware and software concepts and related controls together with knowledge of offline control procedures is usually adequate for the small business as to operating its computer systems in an effective control environment. However, what is important is to be aware not only of IT controls but of how to implement such controls (and which ones) so that the small business's efficiency of operations is not brought down by unwieldy and unnecessary controls. A case study example of identifying and implementing financial/accounting and operational controls for a small business is shown in Exhibit 11.5.

EXHIBIT 11.4   Pc Glossary of Common Terms
(Continually Subject to Change and Update)

1. **Application software** Software programs (or packages) specifically designed to solve a particular business/accounting problem, such as payroll, accounts payable, accounts receivable, general ledger.

2. **Audit trail** An internal control system incorporated into accounting applications that allows the user to trace source data input to computer produced output reports and to trace the computer produced output reports back to the original source data.

3. **Authentication** The process of determining whether the user trying to enter a particular system, program, or other device is authorized to do so—minimally, a secure password system.

4. **Backup procedures** Duplicate copies of data files and programs stored on magnetic media in secure, locked, fireproof facilities onsite and offsite.

5. **Backup system** PC hardware and software that is available for compatible use in the event of a failure to the user's computer system.

6. **Balance controls** Controls, usually established offline, to provide an independent check over the completeness and integrity of computerized accounting records.

7. **Batch control** A procedure whereby all transactions are added up prior to computer processing. That total is then compared with a control total produced by the computer system after processing.

8. **Batch processing** The control procedure by which data input items are controlled by a batch (usually no more than 50 items) with predetermined control totals that can be reconciled to computer-produced batch control listing totals.

9. **Boot** Process of starting or initializing the PC, which includes clearing the memory, checking internal devices, and loading the operating system (e.g., Windows).

10. **Bug** An error in the programming logic of a processing routine on the computer that causes the program to process incorrectly or not at all.

11. **Call-back approach** An authentication procedure used in telecommunications that calls back the user once a request to use a system is made. This ensures that the user is working on an authorized hardware device or is in an authorized physical location.

12. **Central processing unit (CPU)** The computer processor responsible for processing, storing, and receiving data—a highly sophisticated microprocessor chip resident on the PC motherboard.

13. **Check digit** A digit formed by a calculation on the digits of a number according to a specified formula and then appended to that number, which is used to provide protection against transposition, transcription, and random errors (e.g., last digit of a checking account).

14. **Control total** A manually calculated total(s) from a batch of source documents, which is also calculated and printed during computer processing. An individual independent of computer operations matches the manually produced, predetermined total to the computer produced total and reconciles any differences.

15. **Database** A structured collection of logically related data organized to facilitate information access and retrieval—such as inventory records, customer information, and so forth.

16. **Data drives** Devices that store information on a removable medium such as floppy drives (floppy disks hold 100,000 characters), CD/DVD drives (CD 70 million characters, DVD up to 900 million characters), and thumb drives (excess of 100 million characters).

17. **Dumb terminal** Computer terminal with little or no memory, capable of performing only basic functions such as entering, displaying, or transmitting data.

18. **Encryption** The use of special algorithms to secure data (programs, data files, passwords) through scrambling the data. Encryption replaces readable data with a series of characters that only the intended recipient can convert back to readable form.

19. **Firewalls** A personal firewall operates on a single PC and can be part of the operating system or a separate program that runs as an application. The purpose of the firewall is to prevent hackers and others from gaining access to the PC or sending messages that might compromise the PC or stored data. It blocks communication from other PCs not on your network or on the Internet. A network firewall protects a group of PCs.

20. **Hard drive** A data-recording system using solid disks or magnetic material turning at high speed that stores large amounts of information. The data is retained even if power isn't provided to the hard drive.

21. **Hardware** Computer system equipment including the CPU and peripheral equipment (e.g., monitor and printer).

22. **Hash total** A control total of a specified field of a batch of input records used as a batch control total (e.g., customer number or item number).

23. **Integrated system** An information system in which data entered for one application is made available for a number of applications without having to reenter the data for each application.

24. **Local area network (LAN)** An interoffice (or facility) network of a group of electronically linked PCs capable of sharing data and peripherals.

25. **Mass storage** A device for storing programs and data outside the computer's memory, such as external hard disk drives.

26. **Memory** That portion of a computer system where the programs and the data those programs use are stored when being processed (e.g., RAM).

27. **Microprocessor chip** Thin piece of silicon or other semiconductor material, containing the microscopic electronic circuitry that enables the computer to perform complex tasks extremely rapidly.

28. **Modem (MOdulator/DEModulator)** A device to convert computer data into audible tones and back again for transmission over phone lines.

29. **Motherboard** A plastic board that holds the CPU and other integrated circuits to enable the PC to function.

30. **Network** A group of computers that communicate data between them—may be local area network or wide area network.

31. **Password** A key word or number code, known only to the authorized user permitting access to programs and files. Each user has a unique way of identification so that the system can verify the user's identity such as:

    - Something the user knows (password)
    - Something a user has (magnetic stripe card)
    - Something a user is (fingerprint)

32. **Program** A set of instructions for a computer to follow.

33. **Random access memory (RAM)** The most common computer memory, the contents of which can be altered at any time.

34. **Read only memory (ROM)** A type of memory whose contents does not change and cannot normally be altered.

(Continued)

EXHIBIT 11.4   **(Continued)**

35. **Record count** A control used to establish accuracy of processing whereby a count is made of the number of records in a file or in the number of records processed by a program.
36. **Restart and recovery controls** Computerized routines to help ensure that, after a minor interruption of computer resources, processing can be resumed without transactions or data being lost or recorded twice.
37. **Servers** Devices that store information, programs, or printers that are shared among users.
38. **Surge protector** Device to regulate the computer's power source; protects the hardware and the data against damage or loss due to power supply fluctuations.
39. **Switches** Devices used to connect devices in a local area network. They have little intelligence and just pass the message from one device to another.
40. **Telecommunications** The process of transmitting information among separate facilities by electrical, optical, acoustical, and wireless means.
41. **Terminal** A computer peripheral consisting of a keyboard for operator input and a monitor to display computer data.
42. **Transaction data** Information relating to individual transactions flowing from day-to-day activities such as accounts payable and accounts receivable.
43. **Uninterruptible power supply (UPS)** A device that maintains electrical current for a predetermined period of time. It allows continuing operations or sufficient time for the user to power down until normal electrical supplies are restored.
44. **User friendly (user oriented)** Software that is designed to be easily understood by the user.
45. **Virus** An unauthorized program that enters a computer system and damages operating or application systems.
46. **Virus detection software** Specialized software designed to determine whether computer memory, programs, or files contain computer viruses.
47. **Wide area network (WAN)** A network resulting from connecting two or more of any combination of local area networks, laptops, minicomputers, and mainframes so that users may have access to or be able to communicate with others in the system—usually geographically dispersed.
48. **Workstations** Usually thought of as the users' PCs, but can also be thought of as any device that provides information to a user—such as PDAs (personal digital assistants), smart telephones, and even iPods.

EXHIBIT 11.5   **Looking for Controls in the Right Places**

Marty Robbins is the owner of Robbins Specialty Vehicle Products (known as RSVP), a machine shop specializing in the production of replacement parts for the urban transit industry. The company's logo was a bright-red-breasted robin riding on wheels on a railroad track. Over the years, Marty had built up an estimable reputation for high-quality precision-built replacement parts always delivered on time (even in emergency situations) at very competitive prices. RSVP had a repetitive customer base that consisted of 24 major metropolitan area transit systems as well as others on an as-needed basis. Customers used RSVP for small quantities (under 1,000 parts, many times under 100 parts) that they needed on an ASAP basis. Marty's main thrust for RSVP production systems was to meet every customer's delivery needs within the constraints of production capacity.

RSVP at one time had over 20 manually operated metal lathes and support equipment, but a few years ago had replaced this equipment with five fully automated lathes and other equipment. While the new automated equipment ran at extremely high speeds, were fully programmable (which eliminated machining and precision concerns), and required less personnel to operate, they caused a scheduling problem as there were now 5 machines rather than 20. Marty was most concerned with daily shop floor control to ensure that all customer orders were being processed and finished to meet customer commitments.

Marty attended a specialized machine shop manufacturers' conference where he saw manufacturing control software that appeared to solve his shop floor control problem. The software consisted of many modules, including production control, inventory control, cost accounting, shop floor control, purchasing, sales order processing, and integration and interface with a full accounting module. Even though the software included these other modules, Marty did not believe he could use these modules with each customer using their own specs and part numbering system—the software vendor told him that the software accommodated only one number per part for processing efficiencies. Marty was interested only in the shop floor control module. He bought the software and implemented the shop floor control module, which worked quite well in alleviating his daily production scheduling concerns. He installed a computer terminal at each machine location so that the machine operator could key in the results of machine processing—number and operation completed.

Each customer order was handled individually by Marty as each customer had their own part specs and numbering system. Marty reviewed the specs and developed the programming for the automated equipment for each order—setting up each piece of equipment for each specific process. This made him indispensable to the production operation. Many of the customer orders were for parts previously ordered, and most of the customers used interchangeable parts but RSVP viewed each customer's part as distinct. Materials were purchased for each customer order allowing for production overages. However, with RSVP's commitment to quality they usually produced more parts than were ordered by the customer. Any excessive material or parts produced were placed in a storage area in the hopes that they could be used on a succeeding order. In reality, there was no inventory control procedures and this excess inventory continued to build.

As Marty had minimal interest in the business's accounting functions, he left this to the external CPA; a low end reasonable cost software package was purchased for accounting purposes. The CPA told him that the software was user friendly and anyone could operate it effectively. Marty brought his sister-in-law, Lila, in two evenings a week to process whatever accounting transactions had accumulated. Vendor bills for payment were placed in one in-box, customer-billing data in another in-box, and customer checks received in another in-box. All other transactions, such as vendor and customer returns, were handled directly by Marty. All transactions inputted by Lila automatically updated the computerized general ledger. Payroll, for the 18 employees, was processed by an outside computer

(Continued)

EXHIBIT 11.5   (Continued)

service. The payroll processor provided the data for Lila to input into the accounting software. Lila used one of the computers in the shop, as Marty saw no reason to purchase another computer just for accounting.

The outside CPA came in once a month to review the transactions and make any adjustments necessary and then printed a final set of financial statements for Marty — who looked at it briefly, assumed everything was okay, and then walked away to deal with production concerns.

What operational and accounting controls should be recommended to Marty?

Suggested response:

Operating controls
- Maximize the use of the manufacturing control software and all of its modules. Since Marty has already purchased the software package it is probably too late to customize it to fit Marty's business. However, there may be possibilities to modify the software and its processing capabilities to make it more effective. For instance, looking at the issue of each customer and RSVP using a different spec and part numbering system. Upon investigation it was found that the software accommodated up to an eight-character numeric only field for part numbers—Marty and most of his customers used an alpha/numeric field of 12 to 46 characters. Bringing in a local PC software development firm revealed the possibility of developing a front-end processing module that would convert any RSVP or customer part number to an eight-digit number. This allowed the software to combine like customer parts and control production by part number and not customer order.
- With a standardized part number system, RSVP could now achieve economies and efficiencies in purchasing, production, and inventory control. This allowed for RSVP to implement these modules and control a customer order from initiation to completion.
- Control the production order from customer receipt by automatic entry into the sales order and production control system. The computer could then mechanically control the customer order through production, ensuring 100 percent on-time deliveries, reporting only those orders that required management attention.
- Initiate the cost accounting module to accurately pick up material and labor costs as the production order moves toward completion. In addition, other operating controls such as rejects (material and poor quality), rework, excess inventory and production, scrap, and jobs falling behind schedule could be established and reported for action.
- As many of the parts ordered by customers are repetitive orders, that is, the part has been ordered previously, for the specific customer or among all customers, the machine programming does not need to be done each time a part is ordered. In fact, the software allowed for the storage of automated machine programs so that each program could be called from memory rather than redoing the program each time. The front-end part numbering processor made this an easy task to do.
- Integrate the production operation from customer order to customer delivery—when to purchase necessary materials, when to enter the order into production to meet all delivery commitments, monitoring the order through production, shipping the order on time, and timely billing.

- Establish a reporting control system to accommodate the following operating controls:
  - Sales orders received (integrated with sales and customer statistics)
  - Sales orders entered into production on time

Accounting controls

- Integrate the manufacturing control software with the accounting software. Either implement the accounting module within the manufacturing software or determine whether a software bridge can be built (back to the software development firm) to the existing accounting package being used.
- Integrate purchasing, receiving, and vendor performance data for accounts payable transactions. Control vendor payments by vendor terms and availability of cash. Control vendor performance as to price, quality (no vendor returns, rework, or rejects), and ability to deliver on time.
- Bill customer automatically (electronically if possible) at the time of shipment.
- Collect customer receipts electronically by direct bank deposit to the extent possible. For other receipts, control as received, deposit daily, and post through a remittance control system. That is, the remittance control is balanced independently to the bank deposit and cash receipts that are computer-processed.
- Integrate payroll processing with the results of outside payroll processing—submit an electronic entry to the in-house computer used for accounting purposes.
- Purchase a separate computer system for accounting processing with its own control environment. Limit access only to the inside computer operator and the outside CPA. Establish effective general and application controls.
- Update the general ledger automatically through the subsidiary accounting modules such as accounts payable, accounts receivable, and payroll. Limit other transactions with a proper computer produced audit trail.
- Use the CPA as a small business advisor and troubleshooter—there is less value to using the CPA merely to review computer-processed transactions, especially in a tightly controlled environment, and then to produce financial statements.
- Fully utilize the features and controls within the accounting software such as record counts, file control totals, and exception conditions such as overdue (or early) vendor payments, overdue customer receipts, excessive overtime and payroll, and cash shortages or overages.

CHAPTER 12

Organization Structure and the Role of Management

Individuals have many reasons or a prime motivation to start a small business, such as avoiding having to work for someone else, wanting to be the boss, doing it their way, having power and control over others, and embracing the fantasy of becoming a millionaire (or in today's world, a billionaire). Many times one of these prime motivators obscures the reality of what it means to own, manage, and operate a small business, as with the numerous issues we have already discussed. The individual may bring some management experience and expertise from his or her previous employer—sometimes a good model but often a not-so-good model. The new owner needs to know not only how to technically own and manage the small business but also how to operatively manage the business, dealing with the business's most important element—its employees and other stakeholders. Most of the time, this ability to manage people and organize the business correctly does not come until it is too late and the business has failed.

This chapter discusses the role of the small business owner in properly organizing the business so that it is most efficient and effective, utilizing the fewest number of employees to maximize the desired results. This means that the owner must be an effective manager so as to get the most out of each employee through proper coaching and mentoring tied to a fair compensation program that is based on results and not on putting the time in.

It is not the time you put in; it is what you put into the time.

A small business cannot afford the personnel overhead that a large corporation can absorb. Each small business employee must pay his or her way; that is, the benefits derived from the employee's efforts must exceed the cost of having the employee on board. The owner must be skillful in using each employee to his or her maximum capability, encouraging each employee to take on more responsibility (and authority) and become an integral part of the business.

Benefits derived from each employee must exceed the cost.

A graph of a startup successful small business is shown in Exhibit 12.1, which depicts the difference between the owner's fantasies of success versus practical reality.

Organizing the Small Business

Theoretically, small businesses are put together so that the business can conduct its operations more efficiently, and so that the owners and/or top management can multiply their effectiveness, that is, maximize desired results. Organizing is intended to be a helping process to enable a small business to conduct its business better. However, for many small businesses it has become a costly, getting-in-the-way process. As part of its cost–reduction analysis, the business ascertains whether the organization is properly organized or whether improper organization is the cause of its problems and a critical factor in excessive costs.

Adequate organizational and management control requires that each employee know clearly what his or her role and function is in the business, and exactly what *responsibilities and authority* have been assigned. It also requires proper separation of duties, an important internal control,

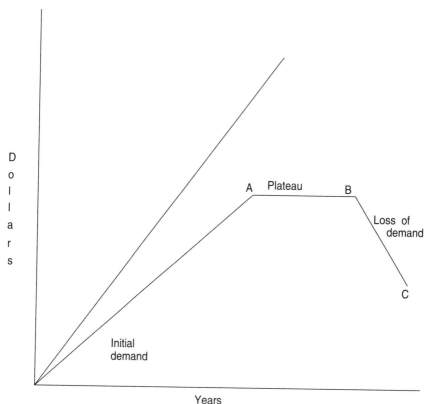

A = First point of innovation:
   Competitors have come in and sales have plateaued
B = Second point of innovation:
   Market has settled and total sales are decreasing
C = Point of retrenchment:
   Get out of business or reinnovate

EXHIBIT 12.1   **Typical Startup**

so that the same individual is not charged with the responsibility for recording as well as reporting on how a particular task or result has been accomplished.

Add employees only to multiply your effectiveness.

The organization of the small business should follow the principles of proper organization, which apply to any size organization and include:

- Clear lines of authority
- Proper division of duties and responsibilities
- Communication between functions and across functions—both upward and downward
- Minimal use of personnel and then only as needed
- Proper delegation of responsibilities and authority
- Management able to effectively control the sphere of their operations and results
- Management and other personnel clearly understanding what is expected of them and the results to be achieved
- Organization established based on the principles of the three *Es*—economy, efficiency, and effectiveness
- The right size organization for what needs to be accomplished—neither under- nor overstaffed—like Goldilocks: *just right*
- Minimum levels of no-value-added employees and management
- Organization no larger than it has to be to accomplish results

Even when the owner understands the above principles of proper organization, normally one of two situations arises:

1. Hiring an individual for each function, just like the big boys, so that the owner can be surrounded with a large staff to order about and control—at quite an unnecessary cost. Sometimes within such an organization, rather than results being accomplished, the employees, including the owner, are getting in each others' way.

More employees do not always produce greater results.

2. Hiring insufficient and incapable personnel (sometimes untrainable) to keep costs to a minimum—resulting in the owner doing more than necessary and running around dealing with one crisis

after another. Such a situation does allow the owner to blame everything on the employees—what could anyone accomplish with these bozos? Another instance of fixing the blame rather than the cause occurs with improper organization with insufficient, *capable* personnel.

> It is not the number of employees; it is having the *right* employees.

It is not easy to know the answer as to how to organize the small business. In the beginning you might be alone as you start your business and follow your dream. Or you might be overly fearful and lonely and bring others, like a partner, into the business too soon or unnecessarily. When starting your business, if you are not sure as to the best way to get started, it is always best to seek advice, paid or not, from those who have been through the process, hopefully successfully. While it is difficult to take advice from others because maybe you believe you know more than they do, *learn to listen*. It is better to start off right than to be sorry and have to blame those providing the advice rather than yourself.

> When I need the experience, I have not had it yet.

An example of starting a small business and seeing it grow with changes in organization is shown in Exhibit 12.2.

WHY ORGANIZE?

The typical structure as shown in Exhibit 12.2 for the Joe Sorry Company would fit most organizations. It is based on a hierarchical pyramid concept in which the ultimate power starts at the top and is delegated down through the pyramid. This model originates from the military, specifically from Napoleon's time. Its purpose was to maintain control within the organization through a chain of command, demanding obedience from each level of the

Joe had been an engineer with a medium-size company that produced specialized printed circuit boards. He had worked with this company since graduating from college as an honors graduate. Joe loved the engineering work and working on projects on his own—dealing with people was a black-death item to him. For a number of years, Joe received sizeable salary increases until one year during his annual evaluation by his manager he was told that he could not continue to receive more money for the same results. His manager told him that the company could afford only a cost-of-living increase (peanuts compared to what Joe was used to receiving). If Joe wanted more money he would have to be promoted into management. Joe, of course, got angry. He knew he was smarter than the rest of the engineers but the last thing he wanted was to manage other people.

Joe decided to leave (taking his retirement fund with him) and start his own business—where the sky was the limit. He started his business in a large garage (which used to be a bicycle repair shop) with low rent. He and his wife Flo were the only employees (who needs employees—they only got in the way). Joe started the business with three small contracts for specialized printed circuit boards with customers of his previous employer that he had developed. He established relationships with four circuit board vendors to provide him with materials as needed. Joe standardized his outside needs and customized his product in-house, making his purchasing and manufacturing simple—just as he had told his previous employer (they would never listen to him as he was not part of management).

Joe and Flo set up the in-house production flow on large second-hand wooden tables that they had bought at a garage sale. When they needed to meet customer delivery commitments, they would have the vendors deliver the boards and at the same time contract with just the number of production personnel to customize the product for the customer. Flo trained the production staff, supervised production, packing, and shipping, and billed the customers. Joe was responsible for engineering, purchasing and vendor relations, and sales and marketing. He worked mainly out of his house and car. As Joe and Flo said in those days, "They were one big, happy family."

JOE SORRY ORIGINAL ORGANIZATION CHART

The original organization chart for the Joe Sorry Company is shown in Exhibit 12.2. The organization structure, while simple, exemplifies many of the principles of proper organization discussed above.

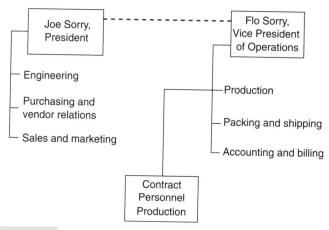

EXHIBIT 12.2   Joe Sorry, Inc. Original Organization Chart

As Joe was able to get more business, the purchase and production cycle continued. The first year Joe worked to build the business, a net profit margin of 20% was reached by sticking with basic business principles—the business realized over $300,000 in sales with a reported net profit of about $60,000 (not bad for any business and more than his previous salary). Joe was working more than he had in his previous job, but now he had ownership and was building appreciation in his own business.

Somewhat quickly the word spread that Joe was providing a proprietary quality product at reasonable prices—better quality and less cost than his previous employer. With his reputation spreading, Joe was now able to bring in more business than his little "garage shop" and he and Flo could handle it by themselves. With Joe's initial success, he now believed that he had the business acumen to run any business successfully (nothing breeds incompetence quicker than success).

Joe reaffirmed his belief that he could successfully run a similar business better than his previous employers. While he did not know everything there was to know about running a business in the beginning, he knew that it was fairly easy to produce a product for less than customers of his previous employer were willing to pay for it. His previous employer made bundles of money in spite of themselves and, in Joe's mind, with gross inefficiencies. With Joe's success, he believed he now knew it all, but what he did not realize was that it is not usually what you know that gets you into trouble, but what you do not know.

Joe, like many new small business owners, had always envisioned having an enormous physical plant and many employees under his control. He wanted to be large just like his previous employer, assuming that larger was better. Joe wanted immediate gratification for being successful as well as being the boss—he wanted what his previous employer had. He did not realize that when he worked for the large corporation he was spending "other people's money (OPM) and now he was spending his own money (OCI or "our children's inheritance).

Joe's business grew rapidly and he and Flo could no longer do everything. The business was expanding in terms of square feet of production and office space needed, total sales, amount of backlog, number of employees, and total payroll. The business was growing too fast and Joe was losing control of those personal hands-on elements that had made the business successful. He was becoming just like his previous employer—eventually we all become like our parents.

Joe's organization chart after three years in business, as shown in Exhibit 12.3, now looked like a camel; that is, a horse created by a committee. The organization had grown based on immediate crises rather than on proper organizational principles. A quick review and analysis of Joe's current organization showed some possible inefficiencies and organizational roadblocks, such as:

PRESENT JOE SORRY ORGANIZATION CHART

- Instead of Joe and Flo handling all of the major functions, they now had 135 employees, and more to be hired.
- Gross payroll was now over $3,000,000 compared to gross sales of $6,250,000. This represents over 48 percent of sales. The company earned a net profit of $830,000 or 13.3 percent of sales. Joe and Flo were making more money but were having less fun.
- The overcrowding of questionable staff personnel such as assistants to the president (Joe) and the vice president (Flo), forepersons and production team leaders, assistant personnel, and receptionists.
- Overabundance of clerical personnel, with 22 such individuals assigned to the various functions.
- A manager assigned to each functional area with undefined responsibilities and expectations.

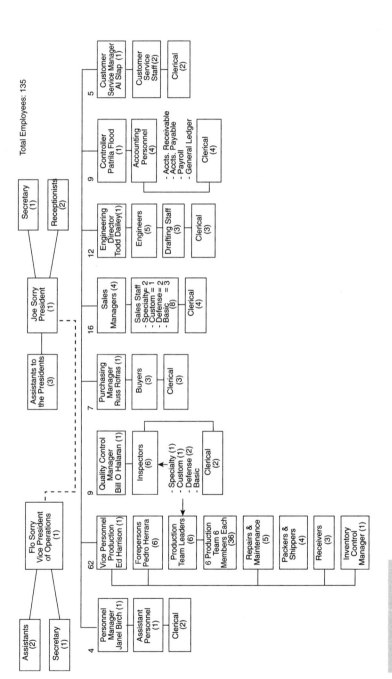

Total Employees: 135

EXHIBIT 12.3 Joe Sorry, Inc. Organization Chart—Present

- Production, quality control, and sales functionally divided by type of product, which may result in improper division of duties and responsibilities and an uneven distribution of work.

- Functions with possible overlapping or duplication, such as both forepersons and production team leaders, purchasing buyers and clerical staff, and sales managers and sales staff.

- Functions that seem superfluous with the presence of a computer system; such as engineers and drafting staff, four accounting staff, and numerous clerical staff.

These were violations of all of the basic principles of proper organization as mentioned previously.

organization that reported to a higher level. To this day, many business organizations still function in this manner, where the purpose for the organizational hierarchy is to police and control those reporting to them to make sure they do their jobs.

Typically, the organization and individual departments or work units spend more time on internal goings-on—who got promoted, who reports to whom, who is more important in the hierarchy, and so on—than on the reasons they exist in the first place. Organizing and reorganizing and implementing the latest organizational panaceas become their goals—as if the structure of the organization were causing the problems. Many times, the type of organization is not the cause of the problem or even the symptom; it is just easier to shuffle people around than to do the right thing.

So why do organizations in the private and public sectors place emphasis on the organizational structure of their operations? The answer, in most cases, is that this is how it has always been. If people were not required to report to other people, they would not know what to do; and how could they be trusted without someone else to watch them? When there is trouble, it is simpler to get rid of an entire department or the troublemaker and avoid facing the real cause of the problem. Many times the real problem is ineffective top management—and rather than admit to that and do what management should have been doing in the first place, it is easier to get rid of other people.

The organizational structure is the tool that is supposed to enable the organization to conduct its business in the desired manner. The purpose of both management and the organizational structure is the same, namely, to use the limited resources entrusted to them to accomplish agreed-on results using the most efficient methods of operation available. If a business used this principle when it put the organization together and made managers and other employees accountable for their results, it would avoid many of the present pitfalls of unwieldy organizational structures.

The small business can avoid the pitfalls of overorganizing.

Those who have ever been managers know that it is usually easier to just do a task themselves rather than spend the time necessary to make sure the person to whom they have assigned the task has done it correctly (i.e., their way). The main reason for having people reporting to a manager is to more effectively accomplish the organization's and the management area's mission, goals, and objectives. However, very rarely is this found to be the case. In many instances, the organization itself, not the accomplishment of results, has become the reason for being in existence.

The organization itself, not the accomplishment of results, becomes the reason for its existence.

The structure is also set up with the intrinsic message that those in a higher position on the chart know more. Hence, much of their time is spent on reviewing the work of those reporting to them and then having them redo it so it looks more like what the manager would do. It is these policing-and-control, review-and-redo processes that make many supervisors and managers superfluous (non-value-added) organizational overhead, and often more hindrance than help. If these non-value-added processes are eliminated, and management is strictly limited to necessities, and the organization creates an atmosphere that encourages the motivation of self-disciplined employee behavior, many of these layers of unnecessary organization and costs can be eliminated.

The small business organizes based on what works.

BUILDING THE SMALL BUSINESS ORGANIZATION STRUCTURE

There seems to be a national trend toward empire building and the power and control that come with it. Even with the present movement toward downsizing, restructuring, reengineering, and so on, with emphasis on getting by with fewer people, those in power are trying to hold onto empires consisting of unnecessarily large numbers of people. Although they are quite agreeable about cutting the other guys' empires, there is considerable resistance when it comes to reducing the size of their own houses. In many instances, even with these quick and short-term remedies for staff reductions, there still remain individuals and layers of organizational hierarchy that are unnecessary (in part, or in total, or in house). It is really important to learn how to build organizations and maintain them properly at all times, using the correct techniques for the various situations.

Making employees responsible for meeting expectations and results, through motivating self-disciplined behavior and an effective monitoring system, eliminates the need for the management and supervisory personnel that exist mainly to police and control individual employees. Use of operating systems that make sense to the employees who use them (who should have had input in developing these systems), within a working-together atmosphere, will increase productivity to the extent that fewer employees overall are needed. The trick is to avoid adding unnecessary personnel as the organization grows, so that it is never in a position to have to cut back drastically. Often individuals are penalized, being laid off for something beyond their control.

Motivating self-disciplined behavior makes the small business more effective.

Many techniques for building an organization structure do not depend on the typical bottom-to-top military model, based on policing and controlling those reporting to each higher level. The small business enjoys the advantages of quickness and flexibility over the larger corporation. The small business need not follow the prevalent model of the large organization; it can be creative and innovative in its organization structure and management models. Some innovative models that could be used in whole or in combination include:

- *Participative management,* where everyone is considered part of the management team, as an individual entrepreneur within the business, and each employee is assigned specific management responsibilities and authority. Each one's input is valued and recognized by the owners, creating a learning organization for improvement and growth.

It is the people in operations who usually know more than the people at the top.

- *Shared management,* where the management of a function such as personnel is shared between two or more employees. One employee may be best at personal relations while another employee may be best at back-office-type administrative activities. By sharing the management responsibilities the business is able to use the best attributes of each individual most effectively. Rather than placing the burden on one individual to possess all of the necessary management skills required in the job, the shared management concept allows each one to contribute effectively and positively to the business using his or her own strengths and capabilities.

- *Team management,* where the responsibility and authority over an operating area is shared between the team members. For instance, rather than have a designated or appointed sales manager (and possibly an assistant sales manager), the entire team is given responsibility for operating the sales function according to the owners'/management's desires. Rather than having a system with each individual competing against the others, such a team management concept usually results in increased cooperation and working together, resulting in the increase of quality sales and business growth—and increased compensation for the sales personnel.

- *Self-motivated, disciplined behavior (no manager),* where each employee is held accountable for his or her own results. Such an approach reduces the need for the owner and other management personnel to police and control each employee—freeing up their time to pay more attention to the business. However, it also means that owners/management must be able to release such control and trust each employee to do the right thing the right way at the right time. It may require increased diligence by management in hiring the right employees (but fewer overall employees) and in proper training and communication. In adapting such an approach it does not mean that each employee goes off on his or her own, but that there are broader and less constraining controls to ensure that results are accomplished. Under this concept, management usually must provide each employee with two permissions:

  1. *Permission to be yourself.* With proper training and an agreed-on understanding by the employees of the results they are being held accountable for, the employees must be allowed to accomplish such results their way using their own individual skills and abilities. Owners and management need to get out of the way as long as the employees accomplish the results, with agreed-on compensation based on the timely achievement of such results.

  2. *Permission to fail.* Under the concept of self-disciplined employee behavior, the employees must be allowed to do things their way (with proper training and guidance). As with all individuals, this opens up the possibility of failure. Under the traditional

policing-and-control model, this would elicit severe criticism from management. Under a self-disciplined concept, the permission to fail is encouraged, as the employees will learn more from what they did wrong than from what they continuously do right. This allows all to learn from their own and others' mistakes in a helpful and learning atmosphere.

> One learns more from what one does wrong than from what one does right.

- *Coaching and mentoring,* where rather than allow the employee to assume a position in the business with minimal training and understanding as to the employee's strengths and weaknesses and then wait for him or her to make mistakes, is a proactive approach to helping the employee learn the job well based on his or her own individual capabilities. The employee is coached as to the most efficient ways in which to do the job to accomplish desired results. As the employee is compensated based on results, this becomes a win-win situation for the entire business. Another concept that may be integrated here is to also compensate the coach/mentor based on overall results—providing an incentive to coach and mentor. Keep in mind that sometimes the best coach is not always the best producer; it is a separate skill, and often an older employee who can no longer perform at his or her old peak level can make an excellent coach.

There is no right answer for all situations—it is important to learn to use a combination of these techniques as they fit the particular small business.

> Emphasize controlling costs and results, not people.

Comparisons between Individuals

Comparing individuals performing similar functions (i.e., production workers, engineers, salespeople, accounting personnel, etc.) is not an exact science, as no two individuals function exactly the same. However, better practices can be identified as to how to use one's expertise and ways of doing the job with others. Such automatic transference of how one performs an activity to another is not usually accomplished easily. Consider the following methods for increasing productivity and transferring best practices between individuals in a small business where flexibility of employees is paramount to effectiveness:

- Making each employee an entrepreneur (i.e., in business for herself) who is responsible for achieving agreed-on results that dictate her own level of compensation.

- Fostering cooperation (and eliminating competition) among employees, as it is now to the benefit of all to increase productivity and resultant profits.

- Creating an atmosphere of self-disciplined behavior, characterized by individual responsibility, working together, and self-learning.

- Elimination of too many so-called management and supervisory personnel with the use of fewer coaches to create a program of continuous improvement and productivity rather than stagnation and unnecessary costs.

- Elimination of costly compensation practices that have an inverse relationship to results achieved.

- Reduction of the number of personnel, as levels of staff are now related to productivity levels and results in direct operating areas as well as management and supervision.

- Use of older, experienced personnel (where former productivity levels can no longer be maintained) as coaches/facilitators so that their experience can be effectively used on a more cost-effective basis.

- Creating effective systems and procedures that allow for the identification and implementation of ongoing best practices in a program of continuous improvements—moving the small business from one of *them-versus-us* to one of working together where each employee has a stake in the business.

- Identification and elimination of nonhelpful systems such as a military model of organizational structure set up for management policing and control of employees, compensation systems that reward seniority rather than results, and budget systems that constrain operations rather than support operational growth and improvements.

What Is Management?

Management can be defined as the entrusting of scarce resources to accomplish desired results through working with others in the most economical and efficient manner—in a healthy climate for growth.

One needs to look at differential systems of management for the small business, such as a coaching model, helpers and facilitators, motivating self-disciplined behavior, and so on that will bring the three *E*s (economy, efficiency, and effectiveness) into the small business and keep them there. Is not the real role of management in the small business to act as a coach, facilitator, or enabler by matching individual needs to the business's needs? Management is responsible for the more effective use of human resources—getting by with fewer people but with greater results—doing the right job, the right way, at the right time.

Fewer people, greater results.

Exhibits 12.4 and 12.5 show in a somewhat facetious way what a good manager is. Although these descriptions are broadly drawn, in many small businesses they are all too true. The small business owner must decide what the role of management is in the business and integrate such understanding back to the purposes of why the business is in existence—that is, customer service, cash conversion, and, of course, to make money and survive.

In a proper manager–employee atmosphere, employees are free to develop and grow. Employees need not spend their time working up strategies of defense or trying to outwit the manager or task giver (and disciplinarian). If managers establish good relationships, they need not shift from role to role, be tough drill sergeants, or pretend to be more than human.

EXHIBIT 12.4   Functions of a Manager

As nearly everyone knows, a manager has practically nothing to do except:

- Decide what is to be done.
- Tell somebody to do it.
- Listen to reasons why it should not be done, why it should be done by someone else, or why it should be done differently.
- Follow up to see if the thing has been done.
- Discover it has not been done.
- Inquire why it has not been done.
- Listen to excuses from the person who should have done it.
- Follow up again to see if the thing has been done, only to discover that it has been done incorrectly.
- Point out how it should have been done.
- Conclude that as long as it has been done, it might as well be left where it is.
- Wonder if it is time to get rid of a person who cannot do a thing right; and reflect that he or she probably has a spouse and a large family and certainly any successor would be just as bad and maybe worse.

Consider how much simpler and better the thing would have been done if one had done it oneself in the first place. Reflect sadly that one could have done it right in 20 minutes and now one has to spend 2 days to find out why it has taken 3 weeks for somebody else to do it wrong.

EXHIBIT 12.5   Myths of Good Managers

- Good managers are calm, unflappable, and always even-tempered. They never lose their cool, never show strong emotions.
- Good managers have no biases or prejudices. Blacks, whites, Hispanics, dumb employees, smart employees, females, males, all look alike to a good manager. Good managers are neither racists nor sexists.
- Good managers can and do hide their real feelings from employees.
- Good managers have the same degree of acceptance for all employees. They never have favorites.
- Good managers provide a learning environment that is exciting, stimulating, and free, yet quiet and orderly at all times.
- Good managers, above all, are consistent. They never vary, show partiality, forget, feel high or low, or make mistakes.
- Good managers know the answers. They have greater wisdom than employees.
- Good managers support each other, present a united front to the employees regardless of personal feelings, values, or convictions.

To those who accept these myths, managing means they must rise above human frailty, exhibit uniform qualities of fairness, consistency, caring, and empathy.

Unless their relationships are good, managers will find that even outstanding managerial techniques are useless.

MANAGEMENT FUNCTIONS

Much has been written and many training programs exist regarding the so-called management functions and how a good manager must master them. It is agreed that these management functions must be understood but only to the extent that they apply to the specific small business and its specific expectations. Not all small business owners and managers are expected to perform all of these functions, nor should they be expected to perform them in the same manner.

Some of the major management functions are summarized below showing some specific subtasks:

- **Planning.** Data collection, forecasting, setting objectives based on desired results, developing strategies, identifying needed resources, specifying constraints, programming, budgeting, setting policies and procedures, considering alternatives, evaluating pros and cons, making decisions, determining schedules, implementing plans, evaluating, and re-planning.

- **Organizing and staffing.** Establishing the desired organizational structure, defining relationships and job responsibilities, creating position expectations, setting job qualifications and expected results, and selecting, training, and developing staff.

- **Directing.** Delegating responsibilities and authority, motivating personnel to achieve results, coordinating interrelated activities, communicating, managing differences, and effecting change.

- **Controlling.** Developing objective performance criteria, establishing a meaningful and helpful reporting system, measuring and objectively evaluating results, taking appropriate corrective action, and rewarding performance based on objective performance criteria.

- **Delegating.** Entrusting responsibility and authority to an employee. Since it is impossible (although this cannot always be clearly seen in the small business) for the owner and other managers to do everything themselves, responsibility for certain tasks must be passed down the line. Delegation becomes a fine balance between owner/

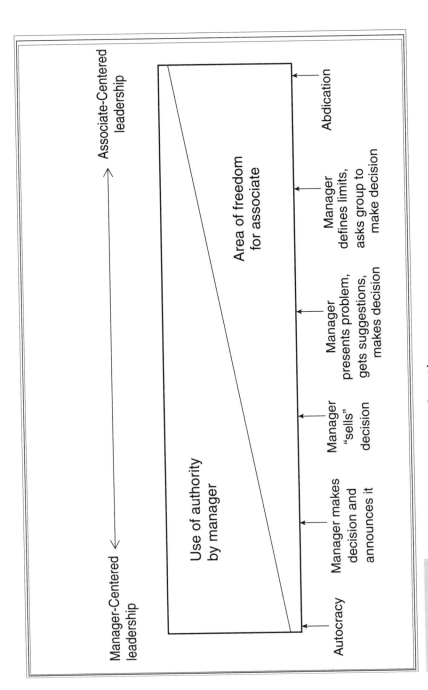

EXHIBIT 12.6 **Range of Manager Delegation**

Manager-Centered leadership ←—————————————→ Associate-Centered leadership

Use of authority by manager

Area of freedom for associate

Autocracy — Manager makes decision and announces it

Manager "sells" decision

Manager presents problem, gets suggestions, makes decision

Manager defines limits, asks group to make decision

Abdication

manager control and associate trust and delegation as shown in Exhibit 12.6.

MANAGEMENT SKILLS

The small business owner can be anyone who has the resources to start a small business. The individual may have come from a larger organization, like Joe Sorry bringing with him the concepts of organization and management learned from their model. Or the small business owner may have no prior experience working for someone else or owning another business. It may be only coincidental that the individual small business owner possesses (or is aware of) the management functions or skills. If the individual has not acquired or does not possess any management skills, as a small business owner the individual must be willing to learn, or his lack of such management skills may doom the success of the business itself.

Some of the skills needed for effectively managing these functions include:

- Keep employees aware of group objectives such as goals of the business and individual objectives.

- Develop a cooperative atmosphere through mutual respect and support and interdependence among the group.

- Establish effective communication through common definitions as to goals, objectives, and expectations and agreement relative to methods of communication.

- Develop standards of performance and behavior through a common understanding of what is expected as well as objective performance criteria and evaluation procedures.

- Exercise control over performance expectations by determining the amount of control necessary, delegating responsibility and authority, establishing degrees of freedom for each employee, and providing guidance and support.

- Distribute rewards fairly and equitably based on agreed-on expectations and objective criteria, making clear what rewards are and what to do to get the rewards, and using agreed-on rewards (money and other kinds that are meaningful to the employee).

Being the small business owner does not mean you own any management skills.

Why Managers Fail

When the small business owner or another individual does not pan out as a manager, only an examination of the particular circumstances will pinpoint the real reason. Some of the reasons why a manager fails can be analyzed only in the specific situation. Sometimes the person is not entirely at fault, as he or she may not have any prior experience in a supervisory or management position; or the owner or previous bosses may never have provided the right kind of training and supervision. In an atmosphere where individuals are promoted to management positions based on their technical expertise or the boss's favoritism, and not on whether they posses any managerial skills, it is no wonder that so many fail as managers—even previously valued, good employees.

To avoid failure as a manager you should keep the following management pitfalls in mind:

- Poor personal relations with workers or with other managers
- Individual shortcomings such as lack of initiative, emotional instability, and so on
- Lack of understanding of the management point of view
- Unwillingness to spend the necessary time and effort to improve
- Lack of skill in planning and organizing work
- Inability to adjust to new and changing conditions
- Lack of confidence in employees reporting to them
- Doubts about delegating to others
- Failure to recognize a role change when promoted
- Lacking basic managerial skills, motivation, and personal attributes to cope with the job of managing

Does the manager fail the business, or does the business fail the manager?

Tools for Self-Appraisal

For most of us it is far easier to see the faults in other small business owners or managers than it is to see them in ourselves. Exhibits 12.7, 12.8, and 12.9 may assist you in appraising your own skills and abilities as a manager.

Conclusion

The small business is in an enviable position in that it can organize and manage its operations in any manner it decides to. The owners and management are not bound by any preconceived concepts or models or regulations, although it is more likely than not that the business will adapt itself to the traditional organization structure and management hierarchical and policing-and-control model borrowed from the large corporations. The purpose of this chapter is to introduce you to other concepts and possibilities. In today's competitive environment, where the big nationals and international corporations strive to eliminate the small businesses as competitors, the small business must learn to be quick and nimble and offer more to its customers in order to survive and grow. Flexibility in organization structure and management concepts can help to make the small business unique and bring back that *wow* factor to its employees and its customers—and other stakeholders.

EXHIBIT 12.7   Assessing Your Management Skills, Abilities, and Attitudes Checklist

The effective manager should have the following management skills and abilities:

Participant Task

Check off those items for which you believe you possess the stated skill or ability. Develop a program for change for those items where you are deficient or do not possess the specific skill or ability.

Develop a system for implementation, feedback, and evaluation so that you can effectively monitor your progress in improving your management skills, abilities, and attitudes.

Skill in listening. Are you:

___ Able to *hear* the problem, the speaker's attitude and feelings, without preevaluating or prejudging them?

(Continued)

EXHIBIT 12.7 (Continued)

___ Capable of listening diagnostically and trying to understand the thinking, the motivations, and the biases of the speaker both in presenting the problem and in working on it?

Skill of empathy. Are you:

___ Able to put yourself in another's place?

___ Able to understand the other person and see the problem from their point of view?

Flexibility and adaptability. Are you:

___ Able to adjust to the environment, conditions, terminology, ways of work, the habits and traditions of the other, so that you can think along the lines of the environment in which you are to provide the help?

___ Able to adjust to the idiosyncrasies of the other without blaming the other, but taking the responsibility for change upon yourself?

Faith and confidence. Do you:

___ Have faith and confidence in the other's capacity to grow and learn from the experience?

___ See, as part of your job, the need to create conditions in which the other not only solves the problem but learns to be a better problem solver during the process of working together?

Realistic analysis. Do you:

___ Have a realistic and accepting picture of the situation?

___ Understand your own motivations, biases, and stereotypes?

___ Know the areas in which you yourself tend to make snap conclusions or prejudgments?

___ Understand your own motivations in entering into the particular relationship?

___ Feel prepared to share those that are appropriate?

Effective communications. Are you:

___ Concerned with developing a real communications system?

___ Looking for points of mutual interest, shared experience, shared values, and standards, as a basis for developing a relationship?

Knowledge of the situation. Are you:

___ As informed as possible on the matter in question?

___ Aware of all the facts related to the situation?

___ Cognizant of all of the factors in the situation such as background, stated and hidden agendas, other's motivations, organizational setups, and so on?

Skills of the other person. Do you:

___ Assess and utilize the skills, knowledge, and experience of the other person?

___ Enter the problem solving as a joint venture?

___ Explore with the other person your mutual contributions and establish a climate of mutual confidence in which these contributions can be utilized without concern as to the source?

Acceptance of the fact that the problem is not your problem. Are you:

___ Prepared to accept the other's solution or method where differences of opinion occur on solutions or methods and where joint exploration has taken place and the difference cannot be resolved?

___ Ready to urge that continuing evaluation of results and actions be built in?

An experimental point of view. Do you:

___ Help the other develop a point of view in which actions that are taken in solving the problem are seen as best judgments?

___ See, as a matter of course, that information is collected on the effectiveness of each action step and further steps are planned based on the results of this information?

EXHIBIT 12.8   **Knowing Your Management Style**

Participant Task

Read each statement, which is followed by four alternatives. For each alternative, put the number 6 for the one that best describes you, 4 for the next best description, 3 for the next, and 1 for the alternative that least describes you.

1. I am likely to impress others as:
   ___ a. Practical and to the point
   ___ b. Emotional and somewhat stimulating
   ___ c. Astute and logical
   ___ d. Intellectually oriented and somewhat complex

2. When dealing with a different point of view, I can usually make progress by:
   ___ a. Getting at least one or two commitments on which to build later
   ___ b. Trying to place myself in the position of others
   ___ c. Keeping my composure and helping others to see things logically
   ___ d. Relying on my basic ability to conceptualize and pull ideas together

3. I feel satisfied with myself when I:
   ___ a. Get more things accomplished than I had planned
   ___ b. Comprehend the underlying feelings of others and react in a helpful way
   ___ c. Solve a problem by using a logical or systematic method
   ___ d. Develop new thoughts or ideas that can be related

4. In the way I work on projects, I generally:
   ___ a. Make sure the results justify spending my time and energy on it
   ___ b. Want it to be stimulating and involve lively interaction with others

(Continued)

EXHIBIT 12.8   (Continued)

___ c. Concentrate to make sure the project is logically developed
___ d. Am most concerned as to whether the project contributes something new

5. In terms of the dimension of time, I concentrate most on:
___ a. My immediate actions and involvements
___ b. Whether what I am doing will become a meaningful memory
___ c. Making sure that any actions I take are consistent
___ d. Significant long-range actions I plan to take

6. I find it easy to be convincing when I am:
___ a. Down to earth and to the point
___ b. In touch with my own feelings and those of others
___ c. Logical, patient, and forbearing
___ d. Intellectually on top of things

When you have completed the above, total the numbers and enter below:

___ Sum of As   ___ Sum of Cs
___ Sum of Bs   ___ Sum of Ds

EVALUATING MANAGEMENT STYLES

Your highest score indicates your primary management style; your second highest score indicates your back-up or secondary style. The As refers to the **Sensor** style, Bs to the **Feeler,** Cs to the **Thinker,** Ds to the **Intuitor.**

a.   Sensor. Emphasizes action, urgency, and bottom line results. Sensors are assertive, quick paced, and confident, favor a "let's do it now" approach, and often are perceived as real doers who make things happen. Like to argue, debate, and haggle—feel they got the edge.
b.   Feeler. Spontaneous, emotional, and people oriented. Emphasizes memories and relationships. Feelers like to personalize their working environment, favor an open, candid, informal approach to both work and personal interaction, and will often make decisions based on gut feelings. They prefer reassurance that you will be back and require empathy.
c.   Thinker. Emphasizes facts, logic, and systematic analysis, tends to be conservative and cautious, prefers to collect all relevant data and then weigh, deliberate, and identify options. Thinkers prefer a logical step-by-step approach to problem solving.
d.   Intuitor. Characterized by imagination, creativity, and innovation. Intuitors emphasize original concepts and daring approaches. They tend to think in long range, global terms, and are often seen as idealistic or philosophical. They usually want respect and agreement.

Some Principles

- Most people have a dominant management style.
- People use a blend of these management styles.
- Management styles are behavioral, and are observable and identifiable.
- People tend to be most responsive to a management style most similar to their own dominant style.
- It is possible to modify your management style to be most effective in communicating with someone with another style.

EXHIBIT 12.9   How Do You Rate as a Manager?

Rate yourself as a manager by inserting in the blanks preceding each question the number corresponding to the rating scale below.

Rating scale: Excellent = 5, Good = 4, Average = 3, Fair = 2, Poor = 1

___ 1. Ability to plan, understanding the mission, function, goals, and objectives of the business.

___ 2. Delegating work (and authority) to the lowest level possible, freeing yourself for more effective managing (coaching and facilitating) and less doing.

___ 3. Placement of the right person for the right assignment and accuracy in estimating time required to complete an assignment.

___ 4. Ability to achieve the desired results through others (motivating employees to achieve results through self-disciplined behavior).

___ 5. Resourcefulness in using workers, materials, and equipment, including provision for peak demands.

___ 6. Ability to use appropriate managerial behavior—being both flexible and adaptable.

___ 7. Proper treatment of employees' ideas and suggestions.

___ 8. Ability to explain work and the *why* of jobs to employees.

___ 9. Being knowledgeable about the situation—as informed as possible.

___ 10. Ability to give constructive criticism and to handle employee discipline.

___ 11. Ability to make necessary decisions, whether right or wrong (giving yourself and employees permission to fail).

___ 12. Ability to give positive feedback and recognition.

___ 13. Understanding of own responsibility and authority.

___ 14. Ability to get employees to do willingly what has to be done.

___ 15. Maintenance of quality work, including getting work out on time.

___ 16. Ability to establish expectations with employees and monitor the results of performance.

___ 17. Skill in handling difficult situations.

___ 18. Ability to objectively evaluate results (impartially toward employees) and reward performance based on objective criteria.

___ 19. Ability to compromise and effect positive changes.

___ 20. Ability to teach and help others grow and develop.

___ 21. Ability to talk the other's language.

___ 22. Ability to cooperate with owners, senior staff, and other managers.

___ 23. Ability to coordinate with interrelated activities.

___ 24. Ability to understand employees' motivational needs.

___ 25. Ability to be comfortable with your authority.

___ 26. Ability to handle grievances correctly.

___ 27. Ability to work under pressure and take appropriate corrective action.

___ 28. Ability to create an effective team (giving yourself and employees permission to be yourselves).

___ 29. Ability to accept criticism and to make personal change.

___ 30. Ability to establish meaningful and helpful systems.

(Continued)

EXHIBIT 12.9   (Continued)

Now, add up your score.

___ Total
___ Average (divide by 30)
___ Rating today
___ Six months from today
___ One year from today

Afterword

One of the major purposes of this book is to dispel the perception that proper business practices and controls—internal, accounting, and operating—are intended to constrain the freedom of the small business at a cost with little benefit to business operations directed toward identifying those instances and individuals where they are:

- Not in compliance with expected standards of behavior and results
- Doing something contrary to the owner's desires
- Performing in a negative manner

Effective business operations enable; they do not constrain.

In other words, the implementation of small business operating practices brings with it a negative atmosphere for the operations of the small business. Since typically most small business employees (and most owners) do not fully understand the need for such practices, there is a great tendency to ignore them, especially as daily crises take over normal operations. This is particularly true when the scope of such practices is limited to establishing controls related primarily to the accounting functions. In this situation, the perception among owners and some employees tends to be that they are doing something that interferes with smooth operations for the benefit of the accounting function and/or the external CPA. Operating employees, including the owners, may find it difficult to understand the need for such practices and controls that seem to impede what needs to be done at the moment.

When we increase the scope of small business practices and controls to include those operations that help the business stay on course and move in the right direction of desired growth, the result is greater communication and understanding within the business as to the need for such practices—especially when the owners and other employees see such growth positively affecting their overall compensation. As the small business grows and prospers, so do the rewards to the owners and all of the workers.

While the larger business is bound by federal regulations as to the existence and effectiveness of stated internal controls, especially those related to the proper processing of accounting transactions and the ultimate development and validity of financial statements, the small business is not bound to such regulations. Although such regulations could be applied to the nonregulated small business just as effectively as to the larger, regulated business, there is no mandate to do so; therefore the small business owner will tend to bypass such controls—particularly as they affect continuing operations. It should be evident that effective operations and controls are a useful tool for any size business—hopefully becoming a profit center rather than a constraining cost center.

If it is not mandated, it will be ignored.

For instance, for the small business owner to implement such typical accounting controls as to ensure that every purchasing transaction is properly approved and that the purchase and payment are accomplished by someone other than the requisitioner or user may be seen merely as an unnecessary and costly procedure. However, if you were to assist the owner to question whether the purchase is necessary in the first place, it would be much easier to convince the owner of the need for such a control as this is money to the bottom line and directly into his or her pockets.

Most often, the small business owner must be convinced as to the need for effective operating practices and controls. While internal management and external business advisors may make some progress in convincing the small business owner as to the need for certain good business practices, normally such attempts fall on deaf ears. However, when you take the approach, as documented in this book, that effective small business practices and controls really encompass all aspects of the business's operations to ensure desired growth, there is a greater likelihood that you will be successful in convincing the owner to implement such practices.

Effective operating practices direct small business operations.

For instance, efforts to implement operating practices to ensure that all sales, cash, and receivables are recorded properly into the accounting records may be unsuccessful if the small business owners see such controls slowing up the sales process or as contrary to their desire not to record all sales. However, if the small business owners and management's attention can be focused on directing the operations of the business by defining their desires for sales and related costs, the chance of acceptance greatly increases. Areas to be considered could include operating considerations such as:

- Which products or services to sell, to whom, and at what amounts
- Which businesses to be in and not to be in
- What customers are desirable (what constitutes a quality customer)
- Determining a pricing structure that provides adequate real profits
- Identifying costs such as direct product or service costs, functional costs, and customer costs, to maintain costs at a minimum and allow for the utmost in pricing flexibility
- Each customer and sale becoming a profit center
- Billing and collection concerns such as collecting in advance or at the time of ordering or at shipment or receipt, as well as use of electronic funds transfer for automatic preapproved payments
- Directing the sales function to properly service the customer to ensure proper growth through increased sales to existing customers together with additional referrals

- Directing the sales effort toward those areas that are most desirable for the growth of the small business

- Maintaining proper customer statistics to control and determine present customer trends and success in acquiring desired new customers

- Product/service analysis to control increasing and decreasing trends by product and customer and to determine present and future customer demands

- Building customer loyalty, which in turn builds the business

As we broaden our concept of best operating practices and related controls for the small business, the whole idea of effectively managing and controlling the business begins to make sense to the small business owner. If successful, the small business should basically conduct its operations through the implementation of effective operating practices and controls together with simple systems that provide real-time reporting so that the owners and management can take immediate action to correct the present situation as well as prevent it from happening in the future.

Fix the cause, not the blame.

Taking an operational approach to running the business helps to adjust the small business owners' focus away from the traditional concept of internal controls, which encompass primarily those accounting-related controls directed toward ensuring that the financial statements fairly present the financial position of the business. It means refocusing efforts toward *all operational activities* of the small business, not only accounting transactions, because operational activities are the building blocks of the accounting transactions. So, while larger, regulated businesses may enjoy the luxury, at some cost, of effectively segregating those duties such as authorizing, processing, and reconciling accounting transactions by the employment of additional personnel, the small, nonregulated business may place a greater emphasis on controlling its operations, such as what products to sell and to whom and at what cost and price, and profit margins.

Focus on business operations and good numbers will follow.

As has been discussed, there are many considerations related to effective operating practices that affect the small business and its growth and success. For instance, the small business owners' purpose for being in business, especially a cash business, may be to maximize the amount of unreported sales going directly into their pockets while at the same time maximizing the amount of business deductions that they can charge against the business— some borderline business expenses, others extremely questionable business expenses. Small business owners must be convinced that it is in their best interest to operate their business in a controlled and disciplined environment and that by including all sales and only legitimate business expenses in their records they will be better able to manage and operate the business for future growth. Such all-inclusive reporting also provides more effective guidance to the small business in its efforts to grow in the right direction.

Small business decisions require knowing *all* the data.
A final thought: *The end* is the place where you got tired of thinking.

Index